Grid
Database
Design

Grid
Database
Design

April J. Wells

Auerbach Publications
Taylor & Francis Group

Boca Raton London New York Singapore

Published in 2005 by
Auerbach Publications
Taylor & Francis Group
6000 Broken Sound Parkway NW, Suite 300
Boca Raton, FL 33487-2742

Library of Congress Cataloging-in-Publication Data

Wells, April J.
  Grid database design / April J. Wells.
    p. cm.
  Includes bibliographical references and index.
  ISBN 0-8493-2800-4 (alk. paper)
  1. Computational grids (Computer systems) 2. Database design. I. Title.

QA76.9C58W45 2005
004'.36--dc22   2005040962

Taylor & Francis Group
is the Academic Division of T&F Informa plc.

Visit the Taylor & Francis Web site at
http://www.taylorandfrancis.com

and the Auerbach Publications Web site at
http://www.auerbach-publications.com

Preface

Computing has come a long way since our earliest beginnings. Many of us have seen complete revisions of computing technology in our lifetimes. I am not that old, and I have seen punch cards and Cray supercomputers, numbered Basic on an Apple IIe, and highly structured C. Nearly all of us can remember when the World Wide Web began its popularity and when there were only a few pictures available in a nearly all textual medium. Look at where we are now. Streaming video, MP3s, games, and chat are a part of many thousands of lives, from the youngest children just learning to mouse and type, to senior citizens staying in touch and staying active and involved regardless of their locations. The Internet and the World Wide Web have become a part of many households' daily lives in one way or another. They are often taken for granted, and highly missed when they are unavailable. There are Internet cafés springing up in towns all over the United States, and even major cruise lines have them available for not only the passengers, but the crew as well.

We are now standing on the edge of yet another paradigm shift, Grid computing. Grid computing, it is suggested, may even be bigger than the Internet and World Wide Web, and for most of us, the adventure is just beginning. For many of us, especially those of us who grew up with mainframes and stand-alone systems getting bigger and bigger, the new model is a big change. But it is also an exciting change — where will we be in the next five years?

Goals of This Book

My main goal in writing this book is to provide you with information on the Grid, its beginning, background, and components, and to give you an idea of how databases will be designed to fit into this new computing model. Many of the ideas and concepts are not new, but will have to be addressed in the context of the new model, with many different considerations to be included.

Many people in academia and research already know about the Grid and the power that it can bring to computing, but many in business are just beginning to hear the rumblings and need to be made aware of ways in which the new concepts could potentially impact them and their ways of computing in the foreseeable future.

Audience

The proposed audience is those who are looking at Grid computing as an option, or those who want to learn more about the emerging technology. When I started out, I wanted to let other database administrators in on what might be coming in the future, and what they could expect that future to look like. However, I believe that the audience is even bigger and should encompass not only database administrators, but systems administrators and programmers and executives — anyone hearing the rumblings and wanting to know more.

The background in Section 1 is designed as just that, background. If you have a grasp on how we got to where we are now, you may want to read it for the entertainment value, the trip down memory lane, so to speak, or you may just want to skip large portions of it as irrelevant to where you are now.

Section 2 starts the meat of the book, introducing the Grid and its components and important concepts and ideas, and Section 3 delves into the part that databases will play in the new paradigm and how those databases need to act to play nicely together.

Structure of the Book

This book is broken down into three sections and twelve chapters, as follows:

Section 1

In Section 1 we lay the groundwork. We cover some background on computing and how we got to where we are. We are, in many places and situations, already taking baby steps toward integration of the new paradigm into the existing framework.

Chapter 1

Chapter 1 will cover computing history, how we got here, the major milestones for computing, and the groundwork for the Grid, where we are launching the future today. It includes information on the beginnings of networking and the Internet, as it is the model on which many people are defining the interaction with the Grid.

Chapter 2

Chapter 2 will provide definitions of where much of the Grid is now, the major players, and many of the components that make up the Grid system.

Chapter 3

Chapter 3 is sort of the proof of the pudding. It provides a partial list of those commercial and academic ventures that have been the early adopters of Grid and have started to realize its potential. We have a long way to go before anyone can hope to realize anything as ubiquitous as commodity computing, but we have come a long way from our beginnings, too.

Section 2

Section 2 goes into what is entailed in building a Grid. There are a variety of ideas and components that are involved in the definition, concepts that you need to have your arms around before stepping off of the precipices and flying into the future.

Chapter 4

Chapter 4 looks at the security concerns and some of the means that can be used to address these concerns. As the Grid continues to emerge, so will the security concerns and the security measures developed to address those concerns.

Chapter 5

Chapter 5 looks at the underlying hardware on which the Grid runs. With the definition of the Grid being that it can run on nearly anything, from PC to Supercomputer, the hardware is hard to define, but there are emerging components being built today specifically with the goal of enabling the new technology.

Chapter 6

Metadata is important in any large system; the Grid is definitely the rule, rather than the exception. Chapter 6 will look at the role that metadata plays and will need to play in the Grid as it continues to evolve.

Chapter 7

What are the business and technology drivers that are pushing the Grid today and will continue to push it into the future? Chapter 7 looks at not only the technological reasons for implementing a Grid environment (and let us face it, the best reason for many technologists is simply because it is really cool), but also the business drivers that will help to allow the new technology to make its inroads into the organization.

Section 3

Section 3 delves into the details of databases in a Grid environment. Databases have evolved on their own over the last several decades, and continue to redefine themselves depending on the organization in which they find themselves. The Grid will add environmental impact to the evolution and will help to steer the direction that that evolution will take.

Chapter 8

Chapter 8 will provide us with an introduction to databases, particularly relational database, which are where some of the greatest gains can be made in the Grid environment. We will look at the terminology, the mathematical background, and some of the differences in different relational models.

Chapter 9

Chapter 9 will look at parallelism in database design and how parallelized databases can be applied in the Grid environment.

Chapter 10

Chapter 10 will take parallelism a step further and look at distributed databases and the ramifications of distributing in a highly distributed Grid environment.

Chapter 11

Finally, Chapter 11 will look at the interaction with the database from the applications and end users. We will look at design issues and issues with interacting with the different ideas of database design in the environment.

Chapter 12

Chapter 12 provides a summary of the previous chapters.

We are standing on the edge of a new era. Let the adventure begin.

Acknowledgments

My heartiest thanks go to everyone who contributed to my ability to bring this book to completion. Thanks especially to John Wyzalek from Auerbach Publications for his support and faith that I could do it. His support has been invaluable.

As always, my deepest gratitude goes to Larry, Adam, and Amandya for being there for me, standing beside me, and putting up with the long hours shut away and the weekends that we did not get to do a lot of fun things because I was writing. Thank you for being there, for understanding, and for rescuing me when I needed rescuing.

Contents

SECTION III: DATABASES IN THE GRID

IN THE
BEGINNING

I

The adventure begins. We will start our adventure with the history of computing (not just computers). Computing in one fashion or another has been around as long as man. This section looks at those beginnings and takes a trip through time to the present. It follows computing as its servers and processors grew bigger and bigger, through the introduction of the Internet, and through the rise of the supercomputer.

We will then take those advances and look at the beginnings of distributed computing, first looking at peer-to-peer processing, then at the beginnings of the Grid as it is becoming defined. We look at the different kinds of Grids and how the different definitions can be combined to play together. Regardless of what you want to accomplish, there is a Grid that is likely to fill the need. There are even Grids that include the most overlooked resource that a company has, its intellectual capital.

Finally, we will look at others who have stood where many stand today, on the edge of deciding if they really want to make the step out of the known and into the future with the implementation of the Grid and its new concepts in computing.

This background section will bring you up to speed to where we find ourselves today. Many will skip or skim the material, others will enjoy the walk down memory lane, and others will find it very educational walking through these pages of the first section.

Enjoy your adventure.

Chapter 1

History

In pioneer days they used oxen for heavy pulling, and when one ox couldn't budge a log, they didn't try to grow a larger ox. We shouldn't be trying for bigger computers, but for more systems of computers.

—Rear Admiral Grace Murray Hopper

Computing

Computing has become synonymous with mechanical computing and the PC, mainframe, midrange, supercomputers, servers, and other modern views on what is computing, but computers and computing have a rich history.

Early Mechanical Devices

The very first counting device was (and still is) the very first one we use when starting to deal with the concept of numbers and calculations, the human hand with its remarkable fingers (and occasionally, for those bigger numbers, the human foot and its toes). Even before the formal concept of numbers was conceived, there was the need to determine amounts and to keep track of time. Keeping track of numbers, before numbers were numbers, was something that people wanted to do. When the volume of things to be counted grew too large to be determined by the amount of personal fingers and toes (or by the additional available fingers and toes of people close by), whatever was readily at hand was used. Pebbles, sticks, and other natural objects were among the first things to extend the countability and calculability of things. This idea can be equally observed in young children today in counting beads, beans, and cereal.

People existing in early civilizations needed ways not only to count things, but also to allow merchants to calculate the amounts to be charged for goods that were traded and sold. This was still before the formal concept of numbers was a defined thing. Counting devices were used then to determine these everyday calculations.

One of the very first mechanical computational aids that man used in history was the counting board, or the early abacus. The abacus (Figure 1.1), a simple counting aid, was probably invented sometime in the fourth century B.C. The counting board, the precursor to what we think of today as the abacus, was simply a piece of wood or a simple piece of stone with carved, etched, or painted lines on the surface between which beads or pebbles would have been moved. The abacus was originally made of wood with a frame that held rods with freely sliding beads mounted on the rods. These would have simply been mechanical aids to counting, not counting devices themselves, and the person operating these aids still had to perform the calculations in his or her head. The device was simply a tool to assist in keeping track of where in the process of calculation the person was, by visually tracking carries and sums.

Arabic numerals (for example, the numbers we recognize today as 1, 2, 3, 4, 5 …) were first introduced to Europe around the eighth century A.D., although Roman numerals (I, II, III, IV, V …) remained in heavy use in some parts of Europe until as late as the late 17th century A.D. and are often still used today in certain areas. Although math classes taught Roman

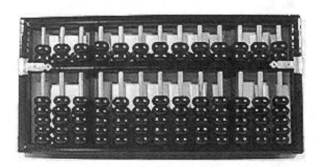

Figure 1.1   The abacus. (From http://www.etedeschi.ndirect.co.uk/sale/picts/ abacus.jpg.)

numerals even as late as the 1970s, many of us probably learned to use our Roman numerals for the primary purpose of creating outlines for reports in school. With the extensive use of PCs in nearly all levels of education today, these outlining exercises may be becoming a lost art. The Arabic number system was likely the first number system to introduce the concepts of zero and the concept of fixed places for tens, hundreds, thousands, etc. Arabic numbers went a long way toward helping in simplifying mathematical calculations.

In 1622, the slide rule, an engineering staple for centuries, was invented by William Oughtred in England, and joined the abacus as one of the mechanical devices used to assist people with arithmetic calculations.

Wilhelm Schickard, a professor at the University of Tubingen in Germany in 1632, could be credited with building one of the very first mechanical calculators. This initial foray into mechanically assisted calculation could work with six digits and could carry digits across columns. Although this initial calculator worked, and was the first device to calculate numbers for people, rather than simply being an aid to their calculating the numbers themselves, it never made it beyond the prototype stage.

Blaise Pascal, noted mathematician and scientist, in 1642 built yet another mechanical calculator, called the Pascaline. Seen using his machine in Figure 1.2, Pascal was one of the few to actually make use of his novel device. This mechanical adding machine, with the capacity for eight digits, made use of the user's hand turning the gear (later, people improving on the design added a crank to make turning easier) to carry out the calculations. In Pascal's system, a one-tooth gear (the ones' place) engaged its tooth with the teeth in a gear, with ten teeth each time it revolved. The result was that the one-tooth gear revolved 10 times for every tooth, and 100 times for every full revolution of the ten-tooth gear. This is the same basic principle as the original odometer (the mechanical mechanism used for counting the number of miles, or kilometers, that a car has traveled), in the years before odometers were computerized. This Pascaline calculator not only had trouble carrying, but it also had gears that tended to jam. Because Pascal was the only person who was able to make repairs to the machine, breakage was a time-consuming condition to rectify and was part of the reasons that the Pascaline would have cost more than the salaries of all of the people it replaced. But it was proof that it could be done.

Gottfried Leibniz, in 1673, built a mechanical calculating machine that not only added and subtracted (the hard limits of the initial machines), but also multiplied and divided.

Although not a direct advancement in computing and calculating machines, the discovery, in 1780, of electricity by Benjamin Franklin has to be included in the important developments of computing history.

Figure 1.2   Pascal and the Pascaline. (From http://www.thocp.net/hardware/ pascaline.htm.)

Although steam was effective in driving the early machines, and brute-force man power was also an option, electricity would prove to be far more efficient than any of the alternatives.

In 1805 Joseph-Marie Jacquard invented an automatic loom that was controlled by punch cards. Although this was not a true computing advance, it proved to have implications in the programming of early computing machines.

The early 1820s saw the conception of a difference engine by Charles Babbage (Figure 1.3). Although this difference engine (Figure 1.4) was never actually built past the prototype stage (although the British government, after seeing the 1822 prototype, assisted in working toward its completion starting in 1823), it would have been a massive, steam-powered, mechanical calculator. It would have been a machine with a fixed instruction program used to print out astronomical tables. Babbage

Figure 1.3   Charles Babbage. (From http://www.math.yorku.ca/SCS/Gallery/images/portraits/babbage.jpg.)

Figure 1.4   The difference engine. (From http://www.weller.to/his/img/babbage.jpg.)

attempted to build his difference engine over the course of the next 20 years only to see the project cancelled in 1842 by the British government.

In 1833, Babbage conceived his next idea, the analytical engine. The analytical engine would be a mechanical computer that could be used to solve any mathematical problem. A real parallel decimal computer, operating on words of 50 decimals, the analytical engine was capable of conditional control, built-in operations, and allowed for the instructions in the computer to be executed in a specific, rather than numerical, order. It was able to store 1000 of the 50-decimal words. Using punch cards, strikingly similar to those used in the Jacquard loom, it could perform simple conditional operations. Based on his realization in early 1810 that many longer computations consisted simply of smaller operations that were regularly repeated, Babbage designed the analytical engine to do these operations automatically.

Augusta Ada Byron, the countess of Lovelace (Figure 1.5), for whom the Ada programming language would be named, met Babbage in 1833 and described in detail his analytic engine as a machine that weaves

Figure 1.5 Augusta Ada Byron, the countess of Lovelace. (From http://www.uni-bielefeld.de:8081/paedagogik/Seminare/moeller02/3frauen/Bilder/Ada%20 Lovelace.jpg.)

algebraic patterns in the same way that the Jacquard loom weaved intricate patterns of leaves and flowers. Her published analysis provides our best record of the programming of the analytical engine and outlines the fundamentals of computer programming, data analysis, looping structures, and memory addressing.

While Tomas of Colmar was developing the first successful commercial calculator, George Boole, in 1854, published *The Mathematical Analysis of Logic*. This work used the binary system that has since become known as Boolean algebra.

Another advancement in technology that is not directly related to computers and computing, but that had a tremendous impact on the sharing of information, is the invention of the telephone in 1876 by Alexander Graham Bell. Without it, the future invention of the modem would have been impossible, and the early Internet (ARPANet) would have been highly unlikely.

A giant step toward automated computation was introduced by Herman Hollerith in 1890 while working for the U.S. Census Bureau. He applied for a patent for his machine in 1884 and had it granted in 1889. The Hollerith device could read census information that was punched onto punch cards. Ironically, Hollerith did not get the idea to use punch cards from the work of Babbage, but from watching a train conductor punch tickets. As a result of Hollerith's invention, reading errors in the census were greatly reduced, workflow and throughput were increased, and the available memory of a computer would be virtually limitless, bounded only by the size of the stack of cards. More importantly, different problems, and different kinds of problems, could be stored on different batches of cards and these different batches (the very first use of batch processing?) worked on as needed. The Hollerith tabulator ended up becoming so successful that he ultimately started his own firm, a business designed to market his device. Hollerith's company (the Tabulating Machine Company), founded in 1896, eventually became (in 1924) known as International Business Machines (IBM).

Hollerith's original tabulating machine, though, did have its limitations. Its use was strictly limited to tabulation, although tabulation of nearly any sort. The punched cards that he utilized could not be used to direct more complex computations than these simple tabulations.

Nikola Tesla, a Yugoslavian working for Thomas Edison, in 1903 patented electrical logic circuits called gates or switches.

American physicist Lee De Forest invented in 1906 the vacuum tube, the invention that was to be used for decades in almost all computers and calculating machines, including ENIAC (Figure 1.6), Harvard Mark I, and Collosius, which we will look at shortly. The vacuum tube worked, basically, by using large amounts of electricity to heat a filament inside

Figure 1.6   ENIAC. (From http://ei.cs.vt.edu/~history/ENIAC.2.GIF.)

the vacuum tube until the filament glowed cherry red, resulting in the release of electrons into the tube. The electrons released in this manner could then be controlled by other elements within the tube. De Forest's original device was called a triode, and the flow control of electrons was to or through a positively charged plate inside the tube. A zero would, in these triodes, be represented by the absence of an electron current to the plate. The presence of a small but detectable current to the plate represented a 1. These vacuum tubes were inefficient, requiring a great deal of space not only for the tubes themselves, but also for the cooling mechanism for them and the room in which they were located, and they needed to be replaced often.

Ever evolutionary, technology saw yet another advancement in 1925, when Vannevar Bush built an analog calculator, called the differential analyzer, at MIT.

In 1928, Russian immigrant Vladimir Zworykin invented the cathode ray tube (CRT). This invention would go on to be the basis for the first monitors. In fact, this is what my first programming teacher taught us that the monitor that graced the Apple IIe was called.

In 1941, German Konrad Zuse, who had previously developed several calculating machines, released the first programmable computer that was designed to solve complex engineering equations. This machine, called the Z3, made use of strips of old, discarded movie films as its control mechanism. Zuse's computer was the first machine to work on the binary system, as opposed to the more familiar decimal system.

The ones and zeros in a punch card have two states: a hole or no hole. If the card reader read a hole, it was considered to be a 1, and if no hole was present, it was a zero. This works admirably well in representing things in a binary system, and this is one of the reasons that punch cards and card readers remained in use for so long. This discovery of binary representation, as we all know, was going to prove important in the future design of computers.

British mathematician Alan M. Turing in 1936, while at Princeton University, adapted the idea of an algorithm to the computation of functions. Turing's machine was an attempt to convey the idea of a computational machine capable of computing any calculable function. His conceptual machine appears to be more similar in concept to a software program than to a piece of hardware or hardware component. Turing, along with Alonzo Church, is further credited with founding the branch of mathematical theory that we now know as recursive function theory.

In 1936, Turing also wrote *On Computable Numbers*, a paper in which he described a hypothetical device that foresaw programmable computers. Turing's imaginary idea, a Turing machine, would be designed to perform structured, logical operations. It would be able to read, write, and erase those symbols that were written on an infinitely long paper tape. The type of machine that Turing described would stop at each step in a computation and match its current state against a finite table of possible next instructions to determine the next step in the operation that it would take. This design would come to be known as a finite state machine.

It was not Turing's purpose to invent a computer. Rather, he was attempting to describe problems that can be solved logically. Although it was not his intention to describe a computer, his ideas can be seen in many of the characteristics of the computers that were to follow. For example, the endless paper tape could be likened to RAM, to which the machine can read, write, and erase information.

Computing Machines

Computing and computers, as we think about them today, can be traced directly back to the Harvard Mark I and Colossus. These two computers are generally considered to be the first generation of computers. First-generation computers were typically based around wired circuits containing vacuum valves and used punched cards as the primary storage medium. Although nonvolatile, this medium was fraught with problems, including the problems encountered when the order of the cards was

Figure 1.7   Mark I. (From http://inventors.about.com.)

changed and the problem of a paper punch card and moisture and becoming bent or folded (the first use of do no bend, fold, spindle, or mutilate). Colossus was an electronic computer built at the University of Manchester in Britain in 1943 by M.H.A. Neuman and Tommy Flowers and was designed by Alan Turing with the sole purpose of cracking the German coding system, the Lorenz cipher. The Harvard Mark I (developed by Howard Aiken, Grace Hopper, and IBM in 1939 and first demonstrated in 1944) was designed more as a general-purpose, programmable computer, and was built at Harvard University with the primary backing of IBM. Figure 1.7 is a picture of the Mark I and Figure 1.8 shows its creators. Able to handle 23-decimal-place numbers (or words) and able to perform all four arithmetic operations, as well as having special built-in programs to allow it to handle logarithms and other trigonometric functions, the Mark I (originally controlled with a prepunched paper tape) was 51 feet long, 8 feet high, had 500 miles of wiring, and had one major drawback. The paper tape had no provision for transfer of control or branching. Although it was not the be all and end all in respect of speed (it took three to five seconds for a single multiplication operation), it was able to

Grace Hopper   Howard Aiken

Figure 1.8   Grace Hopper and Howard Aiken. (From http://inventors.about. com.)

do highly complex mathematical operations without human intervention. The Mark I remained in use at Harvard until 1959 despite other machines surpassing it in performance, and it provided many vital calculations for the Navy in World War II.

Aiken continued working with IBM and the Navy, improving on his design, and followed the Harvard Mark I with the building of the 1942 concept, the Harvard Mark II. A relay-based computer that would be the forerunner to the ENIAC, the Mark II was finished in 1947. Aiken developed a series of four computers while working in conjunction with IBM and the Navy, but the Mark II had its distinction in the series as a discovery that would prove to be more widely remembered than any of the physical machines on which he and his team worked. On September 9, 1945, while working at Harvard University on the Mark II Aiken Relay Calculator, then LTJG (lieutenant junior grade) Grace Murray was attempting to determine the cause of a malfunction. While testing the Mark II, she discovered a moth trapped between the points at Relay 70, Panel F. The operators removed the moth and affixed it to the computer log, with the entry: "First actual case of bug being found." That event was henceforth referred to as the operators having *debugged* the machine, thus introducing the phrase and concept for posterity: "debugging a computer program."

Credited with discovering the first computer bug in 1945, perhaps Grace Murray Hopper's best-known and most frequently used contribution to computing was her invention, the compiler, in the early 1950s. The compiler is an intermediate program that translates English-like language instructions into the language that is understood by the target computer. She claimed that the invention was precipitated by the fact that she was lazy and ultimately hoped that the programmer would be able to return to being a mathematician.

Following closely, in 1946, was the first-generation, general-purpose giant Electronic Numerical Integrator and Computer (ENIAC). Built by John W. Mauchly and J. Persper Eckert at the University of Pennsylvania, ENIAC was a behemoth. ENIAC was capable of performing over 100,000 calculations per second (a giant leap from the one multiplication operation taking five seconds to complete), differentiating a number's sign, comparing for equality, making use of the logical "and" and the logical "or," and storing a remarkable 20 ten-digit numbers with no central memory unit. Programming of the ENIAC was accomplished by manually varying the switches and cable connections.

ENIAC used a word of ten decimal digits instead of the previously used binary. The executable instructions, its core programs, were the separate units of ENIAC, plugged together to form a route through the machine for the flow of computations. The path of connections had to be redone for each different problem. Although, if you stretch the imagination, this made ENIAC programmable, the wire-it-yourself way of programming was very inconvenient, though highly efficient for those programs for which ENIAC was designed, and was in productive use from 1946 to 1955.

ENIAC used over 18,000 vacuum tubes, making it the very first machine to use over 2000. Because of the heat generated by the use of all of those vacuum tubes, ENIAC, along with the machinery required to keep the cool, took up over 1800 square feet of floor space, 167 square meters. That is bigger than the available floor space in many homes. Weighing 30 tons and containing over 18,000 electronic vacuum valves, 1500 relays, and hundreds of thousands of resistors, capacitors, and inductors, ENIAC cost well over $486,000 to build.

ENIAC was generally acknowledged as being the very first successful high-speed electronic digital computer (EDC).

In 1947, Walter Brattain built the next major invention on the path to the computers of today, the transistor. Originally nearly a half inch high, the point contact transistor was the predecessor to the transistors that grace today's computers (now so small that 7 million or more can fit on a single computer chip). These transistors would replace the far less efficient and less reliable valves and vacuum tubes and would pave the way for smaller, more inexpensive radios and other electronics, as well as being a boon to what would become the commercial computer industry. Transistorized computers are commonly referred to as second-generation computers and are the computers that dominated the government and universities in the late 1950s and 1960s. Because of the size, complexity, and cost, these are the only two entities that were interested in making the investment in money and time. This would not be the last time that universities and government would be on the forefront of technological advancement. Early transistors, although definitely among the most significant advances, had their problems. Their main problem was that like any other electronic component at the time, transistors needed to be soldered together. These soldered connections had to be, in the beginning, done by hand by a person. As a result, the more complex the circuits became, and the more transistors that were on an integrated circuit, the more complicated and numerous were the soldered connections between the individual transistors and, by extent, the more likely it would be for inadvertent faulty wiring.

The Universal Automatic Computer (UNIVAC) (Figure 1.9), developed in 1951, can store 12,000 digits in random-access mercury delay lines. The first UNIVAC was delivered to the Census Bureau in June 1951. UNIVAC processed each digit serially with a much higher design speed than its predecessor, permitting it to add two ten-digit numbers at a rate of nearly 100,000 additions per second. It operated at a clock frequency of 2.25

Figure 1.9   UNIVAC. (From http://www.library.upenn.edu/exhibits/rbm/
mauchly/jwm11.html.)

MHz, an astonishing speed for a design that relied on vacuum tube circuits
and mercury delay-line memory.

The Electronic Discrete Variable Computer (EDVAC) (Figure 1.10) was
completed for the Ordinance Department in 1952, the same year that G.W.
Dummer, a British radar expert, proposed that electronic equipment could
be manufactured as a solid block with no connecting wires. Because
EDVAC had more internal memory than any other computing device in
history, it was the intention of Mauchly and Eckert that EDVAC carry its
program internal to the computer. The additional memory was achieved
using a series of mercury delay lines through electrical pulses that could

Figure 1.10   EDVAC. (From http://lecture.eingang.org/edvac.html.)

be bounced back and forth to be retrieved. This made the machine a two-state device, or a device used for storing ones and zeros. This mercury-based two-state switch was used primarily because EDVAC would use the binary number system, rather than typical decimal numbers. This design would greatly simplify the construction of arithmetic units. Although Dummer's prototype was unsuccessful, and he received virtually no support for his research, in 1959 both Texas Instruments and Fairchild Semiconductor announced the advent of the integrated circuit.

In 1957, the former USSR launched Sputnik. The following year, in response, the United States launched the Advanced Research Projects Agency (ARPA) within the Department of Defense, thereby establishing the United States' lead in military science and technology.

In 1958, researchers at Bell labs invented the modulator-demodulator (modem). Responsible for converting the computer's digital signals to electrical (or analog) signals and back to digital signals, modems would enable communication between computers.

In 1958, Seymour Cray realized his goal to build the world's fastest computer by building the CDC 1604 (the first fully transistorized super-computer) while he worked for the Control Data Corporation. Control Data Corporation was the company that Cray cofounded with William Narris in 1957.

This world's fastest would be followed very shortly by the CDC 6000, which used both 60-bit words and parallel processing and was 40 times faster than its immediate predecessor.

With the third generation of computers came the beginnings of the current explosion of computer use, both in the personal home computer market and in the commercial use of computers in the business community. The third generation was the generation that first relied on the integrated circuit or the microchip. The microchip, first produced in September 1958 by Jack St. Claire Kilby, started to make its appearance in these computers in 1963, not only increasing the storage and processing abilities of the large mainframes, but also, and probably more importantly, allowing for the appearance of the minicomputers that allowed computers to emerge from just academia, government, and very large businesses to a realm where they were affordable to smaller businesses. The discovery of the integrated circuit of transistors saw nearly the absolute end of the need for soldering together large numbers of transistors. Now the only connections that were needed were those to other electronic components. In addition to saving space over vacuum tubes, and even over the direct soldering connection of the transistors to the main circuit board, the machine's speed was also now greatly increased due to the diminished distance that the electrons had to follow.

The 1960s

In May 1961, Leonard Kleinrock from MIT wrote, as his Ph.D. thesis, the first paper on packet switching theory, "Information Flow in Large Communication Nets."

In August 1962, J.C.R. Licklider and W. Clark, both from MIT, presented "On-Line Man Computer Communication," their paper on the galactic network concept that encompasses distributed social interactions.

In 1964, Paul Baran, who was commissioned in 1962 by the U.S. Air Force to conduct a study on maintaining command and control over missiles and bombers after nuclear attack, published, through the RAND Corporation, "On Distributed Communications Networks," which introduces the system concept, packet switching networks, and the idea of no single point of failure (especially the reuse of extended redundancy as a means of withstanding attacks).

In 1965, MIT's Fernando Corbats, along with the other designers of the Multics operating system (a mainframe time-sharing operating system that was begun in 1965 as a research project and was in continued use until 2000, and was an important influence on operating system development in the intervening 35 years), began to envision a computer processing facility that operated much like a power company. In their 1968 article "The Computer as a Communications Device," J.C.R. Licklider and Robert W. Taylor anticipated different Grid-like scenarios. And since the late 1960s, there has been much work devoted to developing efficient distributed systems. These systems have met with mixed successes and continue to grapple with standards.

ARPA, in 1965, sponsored a study on time-sharing computers and cooperative networks. In this study, the computer TX-2, located in MIT's Lincoln Lab, and the AN/FSQ32, located at System Development Corporation in Santa Monica, CA, were directly linked via direct dedicated phone lines at the screaming speed of 1200 bps (bits per second). Later, a Digital Equipment Corporation (DEC) computer located at ARPA would be added to form the Experimental Network. This same year, Ted Nelson coined two more terms that would impact the future, *hypertext* and *hyperlink*. These two new terms referred to the structure of a computerized information system that would allow a user to navigate through it nonsequentially, without any prestructured search path or predetermined path of access.

Lawrence G. Roberts of MIT presented the first ARPANet plan, "Towards a Cooperative Network of Time-Shared Computers," in October 1966. Six months later, in a discussion held at a meeting in Ann Arbor, MI, Roberts led discussions for the design of ARPANet.

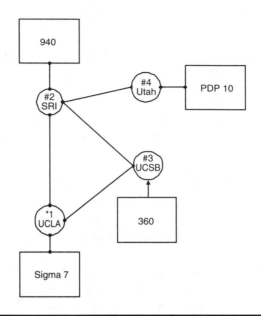

Figure 1.11 ARPANet original four-node network. (From http://www.computer-history.org.)

In October 1967, at the ACM Symposium on Operating Systems Principles in Gatlinburg, TN, not only did Roberts present his paper "Multiple Computer Networks and Intercomputer Communication," but also members of the RAND team (Distributed Communications Networks) and members of ARPA (Cooperative Network of Time-Shared Computers) met with members of the team from the National Physical Laboratory (NPL) (Middlesex, England) who were developing NPL data network under the direction of Donald Watts Davies. Davies is credited with coining the term *packet*. The NPL network carried out experiments in packet switching using 768-kbps lines.

In 1969, the true foundation of the Internet was born. Commissioned by the Department of Defense as a means for research into networking, ARPANet was born. The initial four-node network (Figure 1.11) consisted of four Bolt Beranek and Newman, Inc. (BBN)-built interface message processors (IMPs) using Honeywell DDP-516 minicomputers (Figure 1.12), each with 12K of memory and each connected with AT&T-provided 50-kbps lines. The configuration and location of these computers are as follows:

■ The first node, located in UCLA, was hooked up on September 2, 1969, and functioned as the network measurement center. As its operating system, it ran SDS SIGMA 7, SEX.

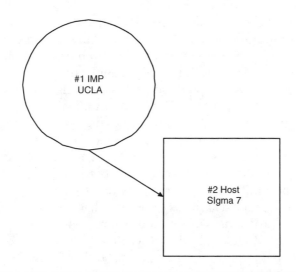

Figure 1.12   Interface message processors (IMPs). (From http://www.computer-history.org.)

- The second node, located at Stanford Research Institute, was hooked up on October 1, 1969, and acted as the network information center. It ran the SDS940/Genie operating system.
- Node 3 was located at the University of California–Santa Barbara and was hooked up on November 1, 1969. Node 3 was running the IBM 360/75, OS/MVT operating system.
- The final node, node 4, was located at the University of Utah and was hooked up in December 1969. It ran the DEC PDP-10, Tenex operating system.

Charley Kline sent the first packets on the new network on October 29 from the UCLA node as he tried to log in to the network: this first attempt resulted in the entire system crashing as he entered the letter G of LOGIN.

Thomas Kurtz and John Kemeny developed the Beginners All-Purpose Symbolic Instruction Code (BASIC) in 1963 while they were members of the Dartmouth mathematics department. BASIC was designed to allow for an interactive and simple means for upcoming computer scientists to program computers. It allowed the use of print statements and variable assignments.

Programming languages came to the business community in 1960 with the arrival of the Common Business-Oriented Language (COBOL). Designed to assist in the production of applications for the business world at large, COBOL separated the description of the data from the actual program to be run. This approach not only followed the logic of the likely programmer candidates (separation of data from code), but also allowed for modular programming and component reuse because programmers could separate out these descriptions and eventually whole sections of code that could be used later in many programs.

Nillaus Wirth, Swiss computer scientist, in the late 1960s released his first programming language, Pascal. Oddly, in this case, the scientific and academic language followed the business language. Although academia had been programming in machine language for decades, this was the first of what we consider to be higher-level programming languages. Pascal forced programmers to write programs in both a structured and logical fashion. This meant that the programmers had to pay very close attention to the different type of data in use and to what they needed to do with the flow of the program. Wirth would follow his release of Pascal with future releases of Modula-II and Modula-III.

Highly important to business computing, in April 1964, IBM introduced the IBM 360 and the commercial mainframe was born. Over the coming decades, the 360 and its descendants would become one of the major moneymakers for IBM and the mainstay of computing in hundreds of businesses.

In 1965, a typical minicomputer cost about $20,000. An integrated circuit that cost $1000 in 1959 cost less than $10 in 1965.

In the 1960s, once computers became more cost effective and viable for smaller private companies, and once the storage capacity of computers became such that more data and programs could be loaded into memory, databases became an option. The first manner that was used for data storage was accomplished in the computer system through the use of file processing. In file processing systems, data is partitioned into separate files; each has its own different format and each application has its own separate program.

The initial forays into databases (where the data is centrally integrated into a database with common format and managed) were made in 1964 with NASA's Apollo moon project. One of the computer advances that was spurred by the space project led to the development of GUAM (Generalized Update Access Method) by IBM. Although this was not a commercially available database, it laid the foundation for those that would follow.

Access to the data stored in the database was accomplished through low-level pointer operations linking records. Storage details depended on the type of data to be stored, and adding an extra field to your database required completely rewriting the underlying access and data modification manner. The emphasis was naturally on the records to be processed, not the overall structure of the system. A user or programmer would need to know the physical structure of the database to query, update, process, or report on the information.

Many of us know the content, if not the origin, of Moore's law. Gordon Moore made the observation in 1965 (just four years after the first integrated circuit) that the number of transistors per square inch in an integrated circuit would double, on average, every year. Although the timeframe has been adjusted somewhat, the law per se has withstood the test of time, with the number of transistors still doubling, on average, every 18 months. This trend is expected to continue for at least another decade and maybe more.

In 1966, IBM released the first commercially available database management system, the Information Management System (IMS) based on the hierarchical data model. The hierarchical data model organizes data in an inverted tree structure where there is a hierarchy of parent and child data segments. This structure implies that every record can have repeating information stored in the child data segments. The data is stored in a series of records, each record having a set of field values attached to it, collecting every instance of a specific record together as a record type. To create the links between these record types, the hierarchical model uses parent–child relationships and pointers, often bidirectional pointers, to ensure ease of navigation. Although the model was very popular for two decades, and many people have for the last 15 or 20 years been foreseeing its demise, IMS remains a core data storage manner for many companies.

GE was soon to follow in 1967 with the development of the Integrated Data System (IDS). IDS was based on the network data model.

In 1968, Doug Engelbart demonstrated what would become three of the most common computer programs/applications. He showed an early word processor, an early hypertext system, and a collaborative application. This same year, Gordon Moore, along with Robert Noyce, founded Intel, one of the companies most responsible for upholding Moore's law in the reinvention of the technology every 18 months.

In 1969, the Conference on Data Systems Languages (CODASYL) Database Task Group Report set the standards for network database products. The popularity of the network data model coincided with that of the hierarchical data model; however, fewer companies invested as heavily in the technology. Some data is naturally modeled with more than one parent per child, and the network model permits the modeling of these many-to-many relationships in data. The basic data-modeling construct in the network model is the set theory, wherein a set consists of an owner record type, a set name, and a member record type. The member record type can have the member record type role in more than one set, allowing for support of the multiparent concept. Not only can a member record type be a member of more than one set, but it can also be a an owner record type in another set, and an owner record type can be either a member or an owner type in another set. The CODASYL network model is based on mathematical set theory.

The 1970s

The year 1970 saw the introduction of the 256-bit RAM chip by Fairchild Semiconductor, and later the 1-kilobyte RAM chip by Intel. Intel also announced the 4-bit microprocessor, the 4004.

Also in 1970 Dr. E.F. Codd, IBM researcher, proposed a relational data model in a theoretical paper promoting the disconnection of the data access and retrieval methods from the physical data storage. Because of the highly technical and mathematical nature of Codd's original article, its significance was not widely recognized immediately; however, it would become one of the bases on which database systems would be based. This model has been standard ever since.

The supercomputers of the1970s, like the Cray 1, which could calculate 150 million floating point operations per second, were immensely powerful.

Although processing power and storage capacities have increased beyond all recognition since the 1970s, the underlying technology of large-scale-integration (LSI) or very-large-scale-integration (VLSI) microchips has remained basically the same, so it is widely regarded that most of today's computers still belong to the fourth generation.

The first reports out of the ARPANet project started to appear on the scene in 1970. The first publication on the Host–Host Protocol by C.S. Carr, S. Crocker, and V.G. Cerf, "HOST-HOST Communication Protocol in the ARPA Network," was presented in the AFIPS Proceedings of SJCC. "Computer Network Development to Achieve Resource Sharing" was also presented at AFIPS. During this same year, ARPANet started using the Network Control Protocol (NCP), the first host-to-host protocol, and the first cross-country link between two entities was created, installed by AT&T at 56 kbs (this initial link would be replaced by one between BBN and RAND), and the second line between MIT and Utah.

The next advance, in November 1971, was the Intel release of the very first microprocessor (the 4004), and the fourth generation of computers was born. Using these microprocessors, much of the computer processing abilities are located on a single small chip. Although this microprocessor was capable of only 60,000 instructions per second, the future was born, and future releases of these processors would see far greater increases in speed and power.

Intel further pushed the advancement of these fourth-generation computers by coupling the microprocessor with its newly invented RAM chip, on which kilobits of memory could be located on a single chip.

Norman Agramson at the University of Hawaii developed the first packet radio network, ALOHAnet. Becoming operational in July 1970, ALOHAnet connected to ARPANet in 1972.

In 1971, Intel released the very first microprocessor: a highly specialized integrated circuit that was able to process several *bits* of data at a time. The new chip included its own arithmetic logic unit. The circuits used for controlling and organizing the work took up a large portion of the chip, leaving less room for the data-handling circuitry. Computers up until now had been strictly relegated to use by the military, universities, and very large corporations because of their preventative cost for not only the machine, but also the maintenance of the machine once it was in place.

The UNIX Time Sharing System First Edition V1 was presented on November 3, 1971; version 2 came out seven months later.

In 1972, Cray left Control Data Corporation to found the Cray Research Company, where he designed the Cray 1 in 1976. The Cray 1 was an 80-megahertz machine that had the ability to reach a throughput stream of 100 megaflops (or 1 gigaflop) of data.

Holding with Moore's law, in 1972, Intel announced the 8008, an 8-bit microprocessor.

In 1975, the cover of *Popular Electronics* featured a story on the "world's first minicomputer kit to rival commercial models ... Altair 8800." The Altair 8800 was produced by Micro Instrumentation and Telemetry Systems (MITS) and retailed for $397. This modest price made it easily affordable for the small but growing hacker community, as well as the intrepid few souls destined to be the next generation of computer professionals.

Furthering the area of networking, ARPANet was expanded to include 23 nodes, including: UCLA, SRI, SCSB, University of Utah, BBN, MIT, RAND, SDC, Harvard, Lincoln Lab, Stanford, UIUC, CWRU, CMU, and NASA/Ames. BBN started to use cheaper Honeywell 316 systems to build its IMPs and, because the original IMP could support only four nodes, developed the more robust terminal IMP (TIP) that would support an amazing 64 terminals. In Washington, D.C., at the International Conference on Computer Communications (ICCC) in 1972, ARPANet using the terminal interface processor was demonstrated, now with 40 nodes.

Ray Tomlinson of BBN invented an e-mail program to send messages across a distributed network, deriving the original program from a combination of an intramachine e-mail program (SENDMSG) and an experimental file transfer program (CPYNET). Tomlinson modified his program for ARPANet and it became a quick success. This initial foray into e-mail was when the @ sign was chosen as the character from the punctuation keys on Tomlinson's Model 33 Teletype machine for the meaning "at" in an e-mail address. Several months later, Lawrence Roberts wrote the first e-mail management program to list, selectively read, file, forward, and respond to messages, adding deeper functionality to Tomlinson's creation.

The first computer-to-computer chat took place in 1972, at UCLA, and was repeated during the ICCC in Washington, D.C.

Specifications for TELENT (RFC 318) rounded out the eventful year.

The Altair was not designed for typical home use, or for your computer novice. The kit required extensive assembly by the owner, and once assembled, it was necessary to write the software for the machine because none was commercially available. The Altair 8800 needed to be coded directly in machine code — ones and zeros (accomplished by flipping the switches that were located directly on the front of the machine) — and had an amazing 256 bytes of memory. This made its onboard memory about the size of a paragraph.

Two young hackers who were intrigued by the Altair, having seen the article in *Popular Electronics*, decided that the Altair needed to have software available commercially and contacted MITS owner, Ed Roberts, and offered to provide him with BASIC that would run on the Altair.

The boost that BASIC would give the Altair would be considerable, so Roberts said he would pay for it, but only if it worked. The two hackers, Bill Gates and Paul Allen, worked feverishly and diligently and finished the product barely in time to present it to Roberts. It was a huge success and the basis on which they would design not only BASIC for many other machines, but also operating systems for a wide variety of machines.

In 1973, ARPA was renamed the Defense Advanced Research Projects Agency (DARPA). Development, under the new DARPA, started on the protocol that would later be known as TCP/IP (a protocol that allows diverse computer networks to not only communicate, but also to interconnect with each other), by a group headed by Vinton Cerf from Stanford and Bob Kahn from DARPA. ARPANet was using the NCP to transfer data and saw the very first international connections from University College of London in England.

Harvard Ph.D. candidate Bob Metcalfe, in his thesis, outlined the idea of what would become Ethernet. The concept was tested out on Xerox PARC's Alto computers. The first Ethernet network was called the Alto Aloha System. In 1976, Metcalfe developed Ethernet, allowing a coaxial cable to move data rapidly, paving the way to today's local area networks (LANs).

Kahn suggested the idea of an Internet and started an internetting research program at DARPA. Cerf sketched a potential gateway architecture on the back of an envelope in a hotel lobby in San Francisco. The two later presented the basic Internet idea at the University of Sussex in Brighton, United Kingdom.

The year 1976 saw IBM's San Jose Research Lab developing a relational database model prototype called System R. AT&T developed UUCP (UNIX to UNIX CoPy) that would be distributed with UNIX in 1977. DARPA started to experiment with TCP/IP and shortly determined that it would be the standard for ARPANet. Elizabeth II, the Queen of the United Kingdom, sent an e-mail on March 26, 1976, from Royal Signals and Radar Establishment (RSRE) in Malvern.

Dr. Peter Chen, in 1976, proposed the entity-relationship (ER) model for database design. The paper "The Entity-Relationship Model: Toward a Unified View of Data," later to be honored as one of the most influential papers in computer science, provided insight into conceptual data models providing higher-level modeling that allows the data architect or the database designer to concentrate on the use of the data rather than the logical table structure.

The Altair was not the only commercial kid on the block for long. Not long after its introduction, there came an avalanche of more personal type computers. Steve Jobs and Steve Wozniak started this avalanche in 1977 at the First West Coast Computer Fair in San Francisco with the unveiling of the Apple II. Boasting the built-in BASIC language, color graphics, and a screaming 4100 characters of board memory, the Apple II sold for $1298. Further, programs could be stored, starting with the Apple II, on a simple everyday audiocassette. During the fair, Jobs and Wozniak secured firm orders for 300 of their new machines.

Also introduced in 1977 was the home computer, the Tandy Radio Shack's TRS-80. Its second incarnation, the TRS-80 Model II, came with an amazing 64,000-character memory and another odd new invention, a disk drive on which to store programs and data. With the introduction of the disk drive, personal computer applications started to take off at a similar rate as the computer. A floppy disk remained the most convenient publishing medium for distribution of software for well over a decade.

Not to be outdone, IBM, a company geared to creating business machines and who, up to this time, had been producing mainframes and minicomputers primarily for medium- to large-size businesses, made the decision to get into the new act. It started working on the Acorn, later called the IBM PC (and the term was born). The PC was the first computer designed especially for the home market and featured a modular design. This meant that pieces could easily be added to the architecture either at the time of purchase or later. It is surprising to note that most of the PC's components came from outside of IBM, as building it with IBM parts would have made the resulting machine's cost entirely too much for nearly anyone in the home computer market. When it was first introduced, the

PC came with 16,000 characters of memory, the keyboard from an IBM electric typewriter, and a connection for a cassette tape recorder (for program and data storage), and it listed for $1265.

In 1978, TCP/IP was split into TCP (Transmission Control Protocol) and IP (Internet Protocol).

USENET, a decentralized new group network initially based on UUCP, was created in 1979 by graduate student Steve Bellovin and programmers Tom Truscott and Jim Ellis at the University of North Carolina. The first message was sent between Duke and UNC.

Again, not to be outdone, IBM created BITNET (Because It's Time Network), introducing the store-and-forward network that would be used for e-mail and listservers.

DARPA established the Internet Configuration Control Board (IICB) to assist in the management of Internet activity. The ICCB would later (1983) be disbanded and replaced by Task Forces and yet later by the Internet Activities Board (IAB) (formed from the chairs of the Task Forces).

On the lighter side, also getting its start in 1979 was the interjection of emotion into an e-mail message. Kevin MacKenzie e-mailed the Msg-Group, on April 12, the suggestion that adding emotion into dry text could be accomplished by using characters such as -), suggesting that the referenced sentence was intended as tongue in cheek. MacKenzie found himself flamed by the masses at the suggestion, but as millions can attest, emoticons have since become widely used.

In the late 1970s and early 1980s there were special database machines that offloaded database management function onto special processors with intelligent storage devices or database filters. These machines had a high cost of customized hardware and limited extensibility.

The 1980s

In 1981, IBM released the first commercially available database product based on the new relational model, the Structured Query Language/Data System (SQL/DS), for its mainframe systems. The Relational Database Management System (RDBMS) is based on the relational model developed by E.F. Codd. This structure allows for the definition of the data structures, storage and retrieval operations, and integrity constraints with the data and relationships between the different data sets organized into tables (a collection of records with each record containing the same fields). Properties of these tables, in a true relational model, include the fact that each row is unique, columns contain values of the same kind, the sequences of the columns and rows within the table are insignificant, and each column has a unique name. When columns in two different tables contain values from the same set (the columns may or may not have the same names), a joint operation can be performed to select all of the relevant information, and joining multiple tables on multiple columns allows for the easy reassembly of an entire set of information. The relational database model is based on relational algebra and, by extension, relational calculus.

Also in 1981, Ashton-Tate released dBase II for microcomputer systems.

CSNET (Computer Science NETwork, later to become known as Computer and Science Network) was also built in 1981 by a collaboration of computer scientists from the University of Delaware, Purdue University, the University of Wisconsin, RAND Corporation, and BBN to provide networking services (initially the primary use would be e-mail) to university scientists with no access to ARPANet.

DB2, produced by IBM in 1982, was an SQL-based database for its mainframes with a batch operating system. DB2 remains one of the most popular relational database systems in business today, now available for Windows, UNIX, Linux, mainframes, and the AS-400 computer systems.

DCA and DARPA established TCP and IP as the protocol suite, commonly known as TCP/IP, for ARPANet, and the Department of Defense determined it to be the standard. This establishment would lead to one of the first definitions of an Internet being a connection of sets of networks, primarily a set using TCP/IP. By January 1, 1982, TCP and IP replaced NCP entirely as the core Internet protocol for ARPANet.

Also in 1982, Larry Ellison's Relational Software, Inc. (RSI, currently Oracle Corporation) released the C-based Oracle V3, becoming the first database management system (DBMS) to run not only on mainframes and minicomputers, but also on PCs.

The following year, Microrim created the R:BASE relational database system based on NASA's mainframe product RIM using SQL.

In 1983, the University of Wisconsin created the first Domain Name System (DNS), which freed people from the need to remember the numbers assigned to other servers. DNS allowed packets to be directed from one domain to a domain name, and that name to be translated by the destination server database into the corresponding IP address.

By 1984, both Apple and IBM had come out with new models. At this time, Apple released the first-generation Macintosh computer, which was the first computer to come with both a graphical user interface (GUI) and a mouse. The GUI interface would prove to be one of the most important advances in the home computer market. It made the machine much more attractive to home computer users because it was easier and more intuitive to use. Sales of the Macintosh soared like nothing ever seen before. IBM, not to be outdone, released the 286-AT. This machine came with real applications, like a spreadsheet (Lotus 1-2-3) and a word processor

(Microsoft Word). These early applications quickly became, and remained for many years, the favorite business applications.

The division of ARPANet into MILNET (designated to serve the needs of the military) and ARPANet (supporting the advanced research components) occurred in 1984.

Speed was added to CSNET, also in 1984, when MCI was contracted to upgrade the circuits to T1 lines with speeds of 1.5 Mbps (25 times as fast as the previous 56-kbps lines). IBM pitched into the project by providing routers, and Merit managed the new network that would now be referred to as NSFNET (National Science Foundation Network). The old lines would remain in place, and the network still using those lines would continue to be referred to as CSNET.

In 1984, William Gibson published *Neuromancer*, the novel that launched the cyberpunk generation. The first novel to win not only the Hugo Award but also the Nebula Award and the Philip K. Dick Award, *Neuromancer* introduced the rest of the world to cyberspace.

In 1985, the American National Standards Institute (ANSI) adopted SQL as the query language standard.

Exactly 100 years to the day (1885–1985) of the last spike being driven into the cross-country Canadian railroad, the last Canadian university became connected to NetNorth. The one-year effort to have coast-to-coast Canadian connectivity was successful.

Several firsts rounded out 1985. Symbolics.com was assigned on March 15, making it the first registered domain. Carnegie Mellon (cmu.edu), Purdue (purdue.edu), Rice (rice.edu), UCLA (ucla.edu), and the MITRE Corporation (mitre.org), a not-for-profit that works in the public interest, working in systems engineering, information technology, operational concepts, and enterprise modernization, all became registered domains.

Cray 2 was built in 1985 and was again the fastest computer of its time.

The first Freenet came online in 1986 under the auspices of the Society for Public Access Computing (SoPAC). The National Public Telecommuting Network (NPTN) assumed the Freenet program management in 1989, the same year that the Network News Transfer Protocol (NNTP) was designed to enhance USENET news performance running over TCP/IP.

BITNET and CSNET merged in 1987 to form the Corporation for Research and Education Networking (CREN), yet another fine work of the National Science Foundation. This was at the same time that the number of hosts on BITNET broke the 1000 mark.

Also in 1987, the very first e-mail link between Germany and China was established using the CSNET protocols, and the first message from China was sent September 20.

The T1 NSFNET backbone was completed in 1988. The traffic increased so rapidly that plans began immediately on the next major upgrade to the network. Canada, Denmark, Finland, France, Iceland, Norway, and Sweden connected to NSFNET that year.

The Computer Emergency Response Team (CERT) was formed by DARPA in response to the needs that became apparent during the Morris Worm incident. The Morris Worm, released at approximately 5 P.M. on November 2, 1988, from the MIT AI laboratory in Cambridge, MA, quickly spread to Cornell, Stanford, and from there on to other sites. By the next morning, almost the entire Internet was infected. VAX and Sun machines all across the country were rapidly being overloaded by invisible tasks. Users, if they were able to access machines at all, were unable to use the affected machines effectively. System administrators were soon forced to cut many machines off from the Internet entirely in a vain attempt to limit the source of infection. The culprit was a small program written by Robert Tappan Morris, a 23-year-old doctoral student at Cornell University. This was the year of the first great Internet panic.

For those who enjoy chat, 1988 was the year that Internet Relay Chat (IRC) was developed by Jarkko Oikarinen.

Cray Computer Corporation, founded by Seymour Cray, developed Cray 3 and Cray 4, each one a gigaflop machine based on the 1-gigahertz gallium arsenide processor (the processor developed by Cray for super-computers).

In 1989, the *Cuckoo's Egg* was published. The *Cuckoo's Egg* is a Clifford Stoll novel recounting the real-life drama of one man's attempts to track a German cracker group who infiltrated U.S. facilities by making use of little-known backdoors. A cuckoo lays an egg in another bird's nest; it hatches first and pushes the other eggs out of the nest, forcing the mother of the nest to care for the imposter hatchling. The egg in the book was a password-gathering program that allowed the crackers to get into many systems all over the United States. The year of the *Cuckoo's Egg* saw Australia, Germany, Israel, Italy, Japan, Mexico, the Netherlands, New Zealand, Puerto Rico, and the United Kingdom joining those already connected to NSFNET.

By the middle of the 1980s it had become obvious that there were several fields where relational databases were not entirely practical due to the types of data involved. These industries included medicine, multimedia, and high-energy physics. All of these industries need more flexibility in the way their data was represented and accessed.

This need led to research being started in the field of object-oriented databases, where users can define their own methods of access to data and the way that it is represented and manipulated.

This object-oriented database research coincided with the appearance of object-oriented programming languages such as C++.

In the late 1980s, there were technological advancements resulting in cheap commodity disks, commodity processors and memories, and software-oriented database management system solutions. Large-scale multi-processor systems with more than 1000 nodes were shipped, providing more total computing power at a lower cost. Modular architecture now began to allow for incremental growth and widespread adoption of the relational model for database management systems.

The 1990s

NSFNET's T3 backbone was constructed in 1990. During the construction, the Department of Defense disbanded the ARPANet and replaced it and its 56-kbs lines with NSFNET. ARPANet was taken out of service.

Also in 1990, Argentina, Australia, Belgium, Brazil, Chile, Greece, India, Ireland, Korea, Spain, and Switzerland joined the NSFNET's T1 network.

In 1991, CSNET and its 56-kbps lines were discontinued. CSNET fulfilled its early role in the provision of academic networking services. One of CREN's defining features is that all of its operational costs are met through the dues paid by its member organizations.

By the early 1990s, the first object-oriented database management systems had started to make an appearance, allowing users to create database systems to store the vast amounts of data that were the results from research at places such as CERN, and to store patient records at many major medical establishments.

In 1991, Oracle Corporation, with its two-year-old Oracle 6.2, not only brought to the market clustering with Oracle Parallel Server, but reached the 1000 transactions per second mark on a parallel computing machine, becoming the first database to run on a massively parallel computer. Wide area information servers (WAIS) invented by Brewster Kahle, Gopher released by Paul Linder and Mark McCahall, Pretty Good Privacy (PGP) released by Phillip Zimmerman, and World Wide Web (WWW) released by CERN were all important services that came on to the computing and networking scene in 1991.

Finally, in 1991, Croatia, the Czech Republic, Hong Kong, Hungary, Poland, Portugal, Singapore, South Africa, Taiwan, and Tunisia connected to NSFNET.

Veronica, a search tool for Gopher space, was released by the University of Nevada in 1992, the year that NSFNET's backbone was upgraded to T3, making the network's speed nearly 45 Mbps.

The first MBONE audio and video multicast also occurred in 1992. MBONE is a service provided by the Distributed Systems Department Collaboration Technologies Group of the Computing Science Department of Berkeley Lab. Currently still somewhat experimental, MBONE's video-conferencing services are not yet available for all operating systems.

Zen and the Art of the Internet, by Brendan Kehoe, was published in 1992. Now available at http://www.cs.indiana.edu/docproject/zen/zen-1.0_toc.html, this book has been a useful tool to many beginners coming to the Internet and has been on the textbook list for university classes.

Antarctica, Cameroon, Cyprus, Ecuador, Estonia, Kuwait, Latvia, Luxembourg, Malaysia, Slovakia, Slovenia, Thailand, and Venezuela all joined NSFNET in 1992, pushing the number of hosts to over 1 million.

CAVE Automatic Virtual Environment, also developed in 1992 by the Electronic Visualization Laboratory at the University of Illinois at Chicago, can also be defined as a virtual reality theatre display or a spatially immersive display. CAVE is now being produced commercially by FakeSpace Systems.

In 1993, the National Science Foundation created InterNIC to provide Internet services. AT&T provided directory and database services, Network Solutions, Inc., was responsible for registration services, and General Atomics/CERFnet provided information services for the new venture.

The same year, Marc Andreessen, of the University of Illinois and the National Center for Supercomputing Applications (providers of *A Beginners Guide to HTML*, available at http://archive.ncsa.uiuc.edu/General/Internet/WWW/HTMLPrimer.html), introduced a graphical user interface to the World Wide Web called Mosaic for X. Through this browser, one could view the pages for the U.S. White House and the United Nations, which both came online in 1993.

Also in 1993, Bulgaria, Costa Rica, Egypt, Fiji, Ghana, Guam, Indonesia, Kazakhstan, Kenya, Liechtenstein, Peru, Romania, the Russian Federation, Turkey, Ukraine, UAE, and the U.S. Virgin Islands joined the NSFNET's T3 network.

In 1994, the World Wide Web became the second most popular service on the Net, edging out Telnet and sneaking up on FTP, based on the number and percentage of packets and bytes of traffic distributed across NSFNET. Helping to add to these percentages, Algeria, Armenia, Bermuda, Burkina Faso, China, Colombia, Jamaica, Jordan, Lebanon, Lithuania, Macao, Morocco, New Caledonia, Nicaragua, Niger, Panama, the Philippines, Senegal, Sri Lanka, Swaziland, Uruguay, and Uzbekistan added their names to those connected to the NSFNET.

The National Science Foundation, in 1995, announced that it would no longer allow direct access to its NSF backbone, contracting with four other companies to provide access to the backbone indirectly, selling connections to groups and organizations. This allowed NSFNET to revert back to a research network linking the supercomputing centers of NCAR, NCSA, SDSC, CTC, and PSC.

In 1994, the World Wide Web was second in the percent of packets sent over NSFNET's backbone; in 1995, it became the number one service based on both packets and byte count.

CompuServe, America Online, and Prodigy began, in 1995, to provide dial-up online Internet access.

Just in time for the Supercomputing 95 conference, the I-WAY (Information Wide Area Year) was unveiled, with over 60 applications running on the platform. This proved to be the beginnings of the Grid infrastructure and provided the basis for the first generation of the modern Grid research projects.

Netscape had its NASDAQ IPO on August 9, 1995. Although several Net-related companies had their initial public offering this year, Netscape was the hands-down leader, with the third largest IPO ever, and the single largest of the 1990s, capitalizing over $2.6 billion.

May 23, 1995, Sun launched Java, formally announcing both Java and HotJava at Sun World '95. At the same time, Netscape announced its intention to license Java for use in its Netscape browser. In December of that year, Sun announced Javascript, the scripting language based on Java and designed to allow nonprogrammers to make use of many of Java's features. December also saw IBM announcing a licensing agreement with Sun for the use of Java, as well as Microsoft announcing its intent to license Java.

In 1996, the Internet Society, the group that controlled the Internet, was trying to figure out a new TCP/IP scheme that would be able to have billions of addresses, an improvement on the xxx.xxx.xxx system. The problem facing them was trying to determine if the new and old systems could interact and work together during a transition period between the two.

The controversial Communications Decency Act (CDA) became law in 1996. This act was brought about to prohibit the distribution of indecent materials over the Net. The Supreme Court unanimously ruled most of it unconstitutional in 1997.

The year 1996 was one to note in the browser wars. Microsoft and Netscape fought these wars online, releasing quarterly new releases via the Internet, allowing eager users to be the first to start trying out the beta versions of the browsers.

Also in 1996, at the age of 71, Seymour Cray died. To his credit, Cray had either invented or contributed to the invention of Cray 1, vector resistor technology, various cooling systems, the gallium arsenide processor, semiconductor technology, and the RISC (Reduced Instruction Set Computing) Architecture.

ARIN (the American Registry for Internet Numbers) was established in 1997 to handle the administration and registration of IP numbers to the geographical areas that were handled by InterNIC.

The first of the file-sharing (peer-to-peer) clients started to appear in early 1999 and reached mainstream popularity within just a few months. Despite media hype to the contrary, peer-to-peer usage has not subsided, but rather grown consistently. Although how it is used is as varied as the different peers that connect together, it is a fact that peer-to-peer is here to stay.

May 1999 is when the launch of Napster is credited — the first global peer-to-peer file-sharing fad. It was at its peak in February 2001, when it saw over 29 million registered users who contributed to the sharing of over three quarter billion files in a single month (http://www.cachelogic.com/p2p/p2phistory.php#).

The 21st Century

Web size is estimated to have surpassed 1 billion indexable pages in 2000.

March 2000 saw the publication, on Slashdot, of an article by Nullsoft that divulged the secrets behind the Napster phenomenon. Peer-to-peer companies are still constantly evolving their applications to ensure that their technology not only continues to grow, but also takes advantage of the continued rise in broadband adoption.

That brings us up to nearly the present. Although the digital divide still exists, many people now have their own home personal computers, and nearly everyone has access to one through the local library system, schools, or other convenient locations. In fact, many people have several computers in their home. The average computer that a person might have in his or her home today is several times more powerful than the massive and impressive ENIAC. The computer revolution has been growing fast, and there continue to be innovations and leaps every year.

Chapter 2

Definition and Components

I am only one; but still I am one. I cannot do everything, but
still I can do something. I will not refuse to do the something
I can do.

—Helen Keller

What better place to start a chapter on the definition of a Grid environment
and its components than with a definition of what is considered to be the
characteristics of Grid environments in general? A Grid is considered to be
a decentralized system spanning multiple administrative domains, encom-
passing multiple platforms and systems, that provides a nontrivial quality of
service to a broad audience of clients, where both the set of users and the
total set of resources can (and do) vary dynamically and continuously. It
handles a large number of hardware and software systems in order to perform
functions and computations on high volumes of data. Uniform and transparent access to heterogeneous systems (again hardware and software) are
provided to both the end user and the users' applications. It is a flexible
mechanism through which one can locate and manipulate resources based
on a user's needs combined with a set of rules and permissions.

The benefits that Grid is most likely to bring to an organization are,
in part, as follows:

■ Grid will help enable more effective and nearly seamless collaboration of often widely dispersed communities. This is true for both scientific communities and commercial endeavors.

■ Grid will assist with enabling large-scale applications, and the combining of up to tens of thousands of computers to perform single or many hundreds of tasks.

■ Grid can provide transparent access to high-end resources and power that can approach that found in supercomputing environments from end users' desktops. These resources are often on the scale that would be prohibitive otherwise.

■ Grid can provide a uniform look and feel to a wide range of resources. This uniform interface will allow users to access files and other resources from a mainframe environment, Windows servers, open systems, and Linux systems without having to be concerned with the syntax and idiosyncrasies involved with each different environment. The front end that end users are presented with allows them to manipulate the data and the information in a uniform environment (often a browser-based interface).

■ Grid can allow for visualization location independence. Computational resources can be separated from data and data can be widely separated (in geography as well as in disparate operating systems) from other pieces of data.

Additionally, Grid computing will allow companies to form partnerships in entirely different ways, enabling them to work more closely and efficiently with colleagues, partners, and suppliers. This can be extended to more than simple partnerships between one core company and its suppliers. The extension can encompass the suppliers' suppliers and on out. This collaboration can take on the following characteristics:

■ Resource aggregation will allow participating organizations to treat geographically dispersed systems as one virtual supercomputer with efficient resource management.

■ Secure database sharing can allow participants to access any remote database within the Grid. This has proven particularly useful for Grids connected to the life science companies sharing human genome data and for those groups mining data of weather data-gathering databases. Although there is going to be distinct separation between the information and data that a company is willing to share and those pieces of information that they choose to keep private, the publicly shared data will benefit all parties involved.

■ Widely dispersed organizations or groups of organizations, using the Grid to allow for collaboration, will be able to work together on a project, sharing everything from engineering blueprints to software applications. This can extend to far more than sharing information across what is typically considered to be computer systems.

The Web has proven, and will continue to prove, to be a good test bed for computing and, in particular, Grid computing. In many ways, peer-to-peer computing (P2P) can be viewed to have been a small step in the direction of Grid computing. Although P2P does not provide the level of security, authentication, or the virtual access to machine architecture that many of the academic, research, and commercial Grids do today, it does allow for working across different platforms and enables applications and file sharing.

P2P

P2P computing is the natural offspring of decentralized software and available technology. Many of the trends of the past decade or so have tended away from huge centralized systems and toward more distributed systems. Although management of the decentralized model has, historically, been more difficult than its centralized cousin (and this has stood partly in the way of a far more widespread acceptance of the model), the immense growth of the Internet, the availability of powerful networked computers, more affordable means to acquire larger amounts of bandwidth, and the rise of business-to-business transactions, distributed computing, in one model or another, is becoming popular with people interested in file sharing, and that is becoming a necessity for more and more corporations. While the idea of file sharing in this model brings to mind pirated music or movies, the collaboration on scientific data or on stores of financial information also proves advantageous.

Peer-to-peer refers to a communication model that includes computing devices (desktops, servers, palm tops) linked directly with each other over a network and including the associated technology. They can include any number and combination of interconnections. Often people think of P2P as associated with their popular use, enabling users to trade music files directly over an Internet connection, without requiring a direct connection to either the central database or file server.

Social issues have impacted the popularity of peer-to-peer computing.

When the World Wide Web first began to emerge, people would put up a page and link to other pages. In turn, those pages would return the link. Without the hyperlink and the WWW, the Internet would likely not be where it is today, good, bad, or indifferent.

The arrival of Napster and other file-sharing environments spawned the development of new and different technology to allow a user to more easily find those files that he wants to find, and others to find those files that he wants to share. Lawsuits aside, the idea is sound and is not likely to die.

Napster

Napster has become arguably one of the most infamous peer-to-peer models. Trading music computer to computer, originally for free and more recently charging for the songs, Napster provides the means for computers to connect directly to each other and exchange files. Lawsuits pitting peer-to-peer file-sharing software companies against the entertainment industry groups not only threatened the company, but also could have extended that threat to the model. Courts did find that peer-to-peer networks, regardless of what users choose to do to use or abuse the system, have legitimate uses, not the least of which is the swapping of public domain media and distribution of open-source software.

Gnutella

Since its inception with ARPANet, the Internet's central premise has been file and information sharing. Many people do not realize that this is the underlying history and premise, but only see and understand the World Wide Web as it is today. Gnutella provides the Internet community with a means by which people can use much of the Internet to get back to these basics.

Where Napster was based on a centralized network agent, Gnutella is a public and completely decentralized network. Nobody owns it and there is no central server available on which it relies. In a true peer-to-peer model, every user's computer is a server and every user's computer is a client. Every user contributes to keeping the network not only alive, but also healthy, wealthy, and wise.

Gnutella works with two types of clients, Leaf (low-capacity users who do not have enough bandwidth, CPU power, or memory to handle and route general traffic, but can process queries, search results and can provide files shared over the network) and Ultrapeers, which take care of most of the Gnutella traffic, form the core of the network (allowing any Leaf the ability to connect close to the core), and protect the Leaves from excessive traffic. Ultrapeers may not be sharing files, but they have plenty of bandwidth (512 kbps in both directions). Ultrapeers will typically connect together in groups of five to ten, with hundreds of Leaves connected to each Ultrapeer, making a several hundred or thousand computer cluster. In this way, everyone contributes.

The same people who created Winamp at Nullsoft created Gnutella. The protocol was first developed in 1999. When AOL (soon to become AOL Time Warner) acquired Nullsoft, it decided that it could not continue to develop a technology that could become a threat to the parent company's primary industry. Although this was likely a gut reaction to the Napster court cases and many saw the entire premise of peer-to-peer as a threat, particularly to the music industry, Gnutella and the peer-to-peer concept is not a threat to any industry. Partly in the same way that guns are blamed for killing people, Napster was blamed for being the vehicle used to allow those trading music freely over the Internet to do so. But in the same way that guns do not kill people, people kill people, and if a person is determined to kill someone, not having access to a gun will not stop them, people who really want to have access to music that is covered by copyright laws will always find a way to do something if they want to do it badly enough. Copying a CD to cassette or burning it to another CD, zipping an MP3 file and e-mailing it — these are not the fault of the technology, but of what people choose to do with it.

Running Gnutella software and connecting to a node in the Gnutella network allows you not only to bring with you the information that you have on your computer and are willing to make public (and the choice of what to make public is always entirely within your control), but also to see the information that others have on their computers and have decided to make public.

Unlike the Napster ilk of file-sharing software, where the applications, if not the files, are centralized and use central servers, and where it is much easier to snoop traffic and hack one central location, Gnutella allows you to search for your information anonymously from a network of independent servers from where you pull information (information is never pushed to you) that you have independently searched for.

The peer-to-peer model is a lot like Kevin House (the very first hospitality house in the United States, a memorial by Mr. and Mrs. Cyril Garvey from Sharon, Pennsylvania, for their 13-year-old son, who lost his life battling cancer) where my family stayed when my aunt went for appointments or treatment at Roswell Park Cancer Institute in Buffalo, NY. The house was a family-like community (or maybe a commune-like community) where guests were given a private room to put their clothes and other personal belongings that they did not want everyone to share or have access to. This was their private space.

There was a communal pantry for donated grocery items as well as groceries that guests were willing to share with others staying in the house. Linens, laundry supplies, flatware, and other supplies that people had donated or were willing to share were put into the communal locations.

Books and magazines that people were willing to share were left in the living room or the library.

P2P works in generally the same way. After downloading and installing a software program that allows you to access the system (the keys to the door of the house in Buffalo) and connect to the network of other users who have downloaded and installed the same software (other people in Buffalo visiting the cancer hospital), *you* decide what information on your hard drive you want to make public (what you want to put into the library and into the pantry) and what you want to keep private. You can then work with your own information or access that information that other people have put into their own public locations.

Peer-to-peer could mean an end to people sending big files as e-mail attachments and depending on bandwidth, connection speed, and a central server to process them. These attachments can be intercepted, allowing for potential security breeches for businesses that find themselves in this situation. Business and E-Commerce could both benefit from peer-to-peer models of file sharing, providing secure and expedient means of file sharing for its members.

Types

But peer-to-peer is only a kind of subset of what can be seen as constituting the Grid. There are many views of what the Grid is and what it can be, and each of these views is applicable to a different business issue, a different problem that it can solve.

Computational Grid

Word Spy (http://www.wordspy.com/words/computationalgrid.asp) defines a computational Grid as "a large collection of computers linked via the Internet so that their combined processing power can be harnessed to work on difficult or time-consuming problems. (Also called *community computation*.)" These Grids provide supercomputing-like power on demand, just as a power grid provides electricity on demand, and frequently the resources and many of the users of them are geographically separated.

Typically when people start talking about Grid and Grid computing, they are most often referring to computational Grids. With the advent of processors that obtain higher and higher performance metrics and the emergence of open-system operating systems such as Linux, inexpensive clusters of multiple-processor systems for medium- and higher-scale computations and efficiency in utilizing the distributed computing resources are more possible and cost effective. Even though a highly significant percentage of personal computers, and nearly all servers, are powered on and operating virtually all of the time in companies around the globe, much of the time that they are powered on is spent with the computer's CPU sitting idle or nearly idle. Surfing the Web, word processing, spreadsheet manipulation, or other typical day-to-day jobs are not computationally taxing jobs and often only require the memory on the computer, with very little use of the actual CPU. The extra horsepower is nice when it comes to being able to open several programs at once and seeing quicker response times, but it would be more productive if a way to harness these spare CPU cycles was found.

Enter computational Grids. Computational Grids allow you to harness the extra CPU cycles available on your network and apply those CPU cycles to other, more resource intensive purposes.

Computational Grids have been built from disparate collections of independent services brought together to achieve a unified environment, allowing for collaboration and cooperation.

Distributed Servers and Computation Sites

Obviously, one of the most key components in any computational Grid will be the servers, or the source of CPU cycles. These servers may or may not meet the traditional definition of server. A mainframe computer, a supercomputer, or another conventional type of server can be the source. However, a PC can also be a source of CPU cycles, as can the newer technology of a blade server.

Remote Instrumentation

Scientific instruments used to gather data are integral in many computational Grid environments. Because of the historical background of the Grid, finding its start in particle physics, bioinformatics, and the genome projects, among other highly scientific information, telescopes, electron microscopes, and other remotely accessible resources are often included as data sources for the Grids in question. In Grids that are in place in the sciences, this instrumentation is often one of the primary (if not the single) sources of data.

One grand vision for remote instrumentation is that data can be captured from arrays of sensors or other data gatherers that are deployed throughout the global environment, whatever that environment is, and integrated with other data sources. Later that data is accessed on a global scale in ways that allow it to be visualized, manipulated, and shared from any location. Although we may need to reevaluate the way we capture and store the measurements from these instruments due to the existing design, there are ways to accomplish the necessary changes.

Remote access of telescopes and satellites has been a reality for quite some time, but there remain many types of instrumentation that are less commonly or rarely accessed remotely via a computer network.

One of the places where there are a lot of possibilities is the area of telemedicine and telecare. With telemedicine, the trend is toward the increased growth in the range of locations where advanced medical care has to be available and delivered. The goal of telemedicine and telecare is to increase the reliable availability of medical care. Reducing demand on hospital services is one of the primary long-term goals, along with improving long-term care and the ultimate quality of life for the patients. Grid technology could go far to facilitate online monitoring of patients and the reliable delivery of the remote data from healthcare sites. Although ultimately this will be a business decision, as nothing will be put into place that could cause a financial loss, it will also mean a higher quality of life for those on the remote end of the collection devices. If a person can be adequately taken care of in his own home instead of having to be hospitalized far away from where he is comfortable, he will be less reticent to accept the help, and it will be less costly for him and his family to receive quality care.

There remain several technical issues standing in the way of elegant implementation of these remote medical locations. One of the issues will be to process signals from the remote devices such that significant events can be monitored and data on these events gathered and processed.

Communication facilities (wireless and other mobile technology) need to be in place to allow remote access across a variety of bandwidths. These communication channels need to be both reliable and as small a bottleneck as possible.

Security mechanisms will have to be in place to allow for the delivery of the information to and from a vast number and array of types of devices to the collecting areas, while maintaining the privacy and anonymity of the patients. Although the Health Insurance Portability and Accountability Act (HIPAA) of 1996 is only a major legal issue in the United States, there will naturally be concerns everywhere. No one wants to think of his medical information being freely accessible to anyone who is dedicated enough to hack the network.

Data Archives

Typically, the data on which scientists and researchers have operated has been stored, primarily, in flat files on file systems. These file systems are likely to be located across many machines and many countries.

The digital archival process demands a reliable storage system for digital objects, well-organized information structures for content management, and efficient and accurate information retrieval services for a variety of users' needs. This information, hundreds of petabytes of data, now with the continued collection of information at a rate of several petabytes a year, is disbursed all over the Internet, on hundreds of servers. How do researchers turn that information into knowledge? How can they efficiently access that information? How can that information be stored in such a way that it is both stable and accessible to as many people as possible, so that the information can be turned into knowledge?

A digital object is defined as something (an image, sound clip, text document, movie clip, astrological data, seismic or map information) that has been digitally encoded and integrated with some form of metadata to support the discovery. It deals with the use and storage of those objects with the goals of being able to not only protect the original, but also duplicate that original for longevity. Archives need to be flexible to facilitate search and retrieval from both heterogeneous and homogeneous sources, and also to facilitate the ease of access for resource sharing. Archives also have to provide lower costs of maintenance and dissemination for the owner as well as for the end user.

Networks

In a system where several dozen to several thousand computers are linked together to more quickly perform jobs, the interconnection between these servers takes on increased importance. Not only is it critical to have a reliable network connecting the pieces, but it is also important to remember that the fastest response time in any system is the slowest piece in the system, and it is important that this network have as low latency as possible. This may be difficult to achieve because of the extreme heterogeneous nature of the components that make up the Grid environment, but in a system that is within the control of a single company or even a multinational organization, the network can be controlled enough that as much latency as possible can be removed. When and if the Grid becomes a true utility, computing the way it has been suggested, this will be one of the major hurdles to overcome.

Portal (User Interface)

As in any well-designed system, a user, client, or customer should not need to understand or care about the complexities and intricacies of the system on which they are functioning; they should only see a well-designed interface through which they can complete their work.

User interfaces can take many forms, and are often application specific; they can (in a broad sense) be seen as portals. In fact, the user interface in a Grid environment is often a portal on a Web page.

Webopedia (http://www.webopedia.com/TERM/W/Web_portal.html) defines a portal as follows:

> Commonly referred to as simply a *portal*, a Web site or service that offers a broad array of resources and services, such as e-mail, forums, search engines, and on-line shopping malls. The first Web portals were online services, such as AOL, that provided access to the Web, but by now most of the traditional search engines have transformed themselves into Web portals to attract and keep a larger audience.

Many Internet users today understand the concept of a Web portal, where the browser provides a single unified interface through which a user launches applications that will use services and resources, but is not required to do anything other than perform its job. From this perspective, the user sees nearly any system as a virtual computing resource. A portal service on the Grid is little different than this conceptual model.

Security

A major requirement for Grid computing is security. At the base of any Grid environment, there must be mechanisms to provide security, including authentication, authorization, data encryption, and so on. The Grid Security Infrastructure (GSI) component of the Globus Toolkit provides robust security mechanisms. The GSI includes an OpenSSL implementation. It also provides a single sign-on mechanism, so that once a user is authenticated, a proxy certificate is created and used when performing actions within the Grid. When designing your Grid environment, you may use the GSI sign-in to grant access to the portal, or
you may have your own security for the portal. The portal will then be responsible for signing in to the Grid, either using the user's credentials or using a generic set of credentials for all authorized users of the portal.

Security, because it is such a major concern in Grid computing and in database design in general, will be covered more extensively in Chapter 4.

Broker

A broker is a master scheduler. It allows a user or a process to request resources from one or more machines for a job. It may perform load balancing across multiple systems. Brokers discover resources for a job, select appropriate systems, and submit the job. There are metaschedulers, superschedulers, and simple brokers. The metaschedulers take care of load balancing. Superschedulers discover the resources and select and submit the jobs. Basic brokers quote resources or discover resources and distribute data and computations based on the determined cost model.

Once a user is authenticated to the network, she will be launching one application or another. Based on which application, and potentially on what other parameters are provided by the user, next the system needs to identify appropriate available resources to make use of within the Grid. A broker can carry out the task of identification of resources. The Globus Toolkit does not directly provide the facility for a resource broker, but does provide the framework and tools to add a broker service.

One such service is the Grid Resource Broker (GRB). One of the current Globus projects of the High Performance Computing (HPC) Lab of the Center for Advanced Computational Technologies at the University of Lecce in Lecce, Italy (http://www.informatica.unile.it/laboratori/lab-hpc/), GRB is a general framework Grid portal that allows those users who are trusted or authenticated to access and work within computational Grids making use of a simple graphical user interface (GUI).

The user's Web browser must be configured to accept cookies. Authentication to GRB makes use of MyProxy (a credential repository for the Grid). You need to store, inside one of the MyProxy servers, your proxy and authentication information. GRB will retrieve the authentication and proxy information using your password and authenticate you using your unique name and information.

User Profile

When a user starts the GRB, she authenticates herself to the system by means of a log-in name and her password. This log-in and all subsequent transactions make use of the HTTPS (Secure Sockets Layer [SSL] on top of HTTP) to encrypt the user's password, thereby avoiding the transmission of the information over an insecure channel. Once the user is authenticated, the user can start a GRB session. The session will last for a specified number of hours (this number of hours is specified at proxy creation time) or until the user logs out. Before using the GRB, there has to be a user profile containing information about those computational resources on the Grid that that particular user can use. For each machine on which the user has permissions, the profile contains the host name and the path to her favorite shell, and the conceptual cost per hour for that resource (the weighting factor to assist in the automatic determination of what computer to use for a given job). If a particular computational resource becomes unavailable for an extended period, it should be removed from the profile so that the broker does not attempt vainly to access that resource, wasting time in the contact attempt. Once a profile is set up for a user, the user can view the information stored in the file. Ideally, GRB and other resource brokers will eventually contain additional information to allow for more complex scheduling algorithms.

Searching for Resources

Grid Index Information Service (GIIS) is a Lightweight Directory Access Protocol (LDAP) server that collects the information related to every Grid Resource Information Service (GRIS) server available in the organization. This can be seen as a basic broker resource. It allows users or processes to find, if available, those computing resources and their particular features, such as memory and number and speed of processors.

GRIS then acts as a superscheduler. Computational resources can be periodically queried about their features and status if a server is running Globus. This is because a GRIS is listening on a port. GRIS is a small LDAP server that stores static (and semistatic) information, as well as dynamic information about available Grid hardware and the system software associated with it. GRIS can be looked at as an active index that allows for the simple central retrieval of a machine's main features. GRB or any other resource broker can tap into this information and make use of it when looking at what resources to schedule for any given batch or real-time job.

Batch Job Submittal

A user submits a batch job to be worked on by the Grid through the GRB (then acting as a metascheduler) by entering a machine's host name and the name of the executable to be run (the complete path name if the executable is to be staged from another machine). If needed, we also allow the use of GSI-FTP servers (Globus Security Infrastructure File Transfer Protocol) to copy the executable as well as the input and output files to the machine that the user selected. The job is then submitted to the scheduler, and if the submission is successful, the user can use his browser to verify that the job is in the queue. The GRB stores the information related to the user's jobs automatically. This information can be used later to allow the user to check the job status.

But what about jobs that the user does not want to run in batch? What about the jobs that need to be run interactively? When dealing with interactive jobs, you use GSI-FTP to copy both the executable and the input files to the target machine, and the output is sent directly back to the browser for the user to access and act upon.

What happens then if you do not know what machine you want to run the job on, or if you do not really want to leave that decision entirely up to the end user? The GRB tool is a generic resource broker that allows the user's machine to search the Grid system to find an available computational resource suitable for the submission of the current job, and to submit a batch job on resources that are found to match the specified criteria. If the decision of on which machine to run is taken out of the hands of the user, scheduling automatically gets performed by GRB, which takes into account the cost information for all nodes found available and routes the job at hand to the machine or machines that will perform the task in the most cost effective manner that the rules allow for.

After submitting a batch job, a user typically wants to monitor the job's progress. GRB allows users the ability to check on the status of any batch jobs previously submitted. This status checking exploits the information that gets saved at job submission time. A job can have at any time any one of five statuses: pending, active, suspended, failed, or done. A pending job is still sitting in a queue waiting to be executed. Active means actively executing. A suspended job may be temporarily suspended because a job with a higher priority enters the system and is making use of the required resources. The suspended job will become either active (when the resource becomes available again) or failed (if something goes wrong in the processing). Failed jobs fail for any number of reasons. Normal completion of the job results in a done status. When the job receives a done status, GRB transfers the output file to the selected repository machine using GSI-FTP, if this is the action that the user requested.

Sometimes users need to run the same executable with different sets of input. This is true in what if scenarios or when working on a parameter study. GRB allows them elegant means to accomplish this end.

This resource broker (acting as the basic broker) provides the means for the user to transfer files between machines using GSI-FTP. GRB supports both single-file transfer and whole-directory transfer.

The GRB service allows the administrator the ability to centrally check the status of the Globus daemons installed on each machine in the Grid.

Although most users know that they should always log out of a system when they are done, this is not always done. There are many reasons that users do not like to log out of a system. Often the steps needed to log back in feel redundant to the user. Users just feel that if the system is always there when they need it, it will save them time in the end. GRB allows for automatic log-out settings that will take the decision to log out of a system out of the hands of the users after a period, and their session will expire automatically. This is important for security and resource management.

Credential Repository

Rather than storing your Grid credentials on each machine you use to access the Grid, you can store them in a credential repository, for example, a MyProxy repository, and retrieve the credentials from the repository when needed.

Storing your Grid credentials in a repository allows you to retrieve your credentials whenever and from wherever they are needed. A credential repository will allow users to do all of this without having to be concerned with maintaining local private keys and certificate files locally.

Using any standard Web browser, regardless of your choice of browser, you can connect to the Grid portal to retrieve a user's proxy credential to access Grid resources on his behalf. Further, that user can also allow trusted servers to renew his proxy credentials so that his long running interactive and batch tasks will not fail simply because of an expired credential. Further, a well-managed credential repository can supply both a more secure and less corruptible storage location for Grid credentials than any typical local end-user systems could hope to.

MyProxy provides a set of flexible authorization mechanisms for controlling access not only to the Grid resources, but also to the repository itself. Serverwide policies allow an administrator to control how end users, programs, and programmers use the repository. Policies can allow users to specify how each or any credential may be accessed. Certificate-based authentication is required to allow the browser to retrieve credentials from the MyProxy server. If any credential is stored with a passphrase or password, the private key is encrypted with that word or phrase in the repository.

Scheduler

Once the resources have been identified and the permissions on those resources established, the next logical step is to schedule the individual jobs to run on those resources. If users submit stand-alone jobs with no interdependencies between them to be run, then no specialized scheduler is likely to be required. If, however, the more likely scenario occurs, and a user or set of other processes needs a specific resource, or needs to ensure that the different jobs within the job stream from the application run concurrently (if, for example, there is a need for them to communicate with each other's interprocess), then it becomes necessary for a job scheduler to be used to coordinate the execution of these jobs. A broker may or may not be able to handle the complex scheduling.

The Globus Toolkit does not include such a complex scheduler. There are several schedulers currently available. These have been tested with Globus and can be used in a Globus Grid environment. Different levels of schedulers can also be used within the Grid environment. A cluster could be represented as a single resource and could have its own scheduler to help manage the nodes that it contains. Another higher-level scheduler (the metascheduler referred to in the broker section earlier) might be used to schedule work to be done on the total cluster, while the cluster's single scheduler would handle the actual scheduling of work on the cluster's individual nodes.

Data Management

If any data — including application modules — must be moved or made accessible to the nodes where an application's jobs will execute, then there needs to be a secure and reliable method for moving files and data to various nodes within the Grid. The Globus Toolkit contains a data management component that provides such services. This component, know as Grid Access to Secondary Storage (GASS), includes facilities such as GridFTP. GridFTP is built on top of the standard FTP, but adds additional functions and utilizes the GSI for user authentication and authorization. Therefore, once a user has an authenticated proxy certificate, he can use the GridFTP facility to move files without having to go through a log-in process to every node involved. This facility provides third-party file transfer so that one node can initiate a file transfer between two other nodes.

In a computational Grid, most of the machines are high-performance servers.

Figure 2.1 shows a model of what a computational Grid may look like. The user, in this case in accounting, logs in to the system by means of a portal running on the application server to run his or her application. That application server directs the request to the broker or the scheduler, which then distributes the jobs to the available resources that are necessary to complete those jobs. The results are returned to where the user can pick them up, again via the portal interface.

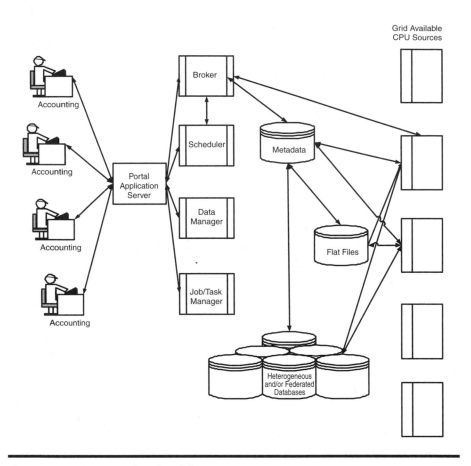

Figure 2.1   Computational Grid components.

Data Grid

A data Grid is typically responsible for the housing of the access provisions to data across multiple organizations. Users of the data need not ever be concerned with where this data is located as long as those users have access to the data that they require. Picture, for example, two universities doing life science research: each with unique data may, through a data Grid, share and manage its data and the security issues associated with such sharing, like who has access to what data. Or two departments within a multinational corporation, one on the U.S. West Coast and one in the United Kingdom, have a need to access data located in proprietary systems that belong to the different departments. Each of these departments could access the other's data across the Grid and still maintain control over their own.

There are several unique characteristics of data Grids that are not necessarily components of the others.

Storage Mechanism Neutrality

Grid architecture is designed to be as independent as possible because much of the information and data (as well as the metadata) could potentially be stored on low-level devices. This can also apply to lower-level transfer media. Achieving mechanism neutrality can be accomplished by defining data access, providing third-party data movement capabilities, and allowing for catalog access as well as other interfaces that minimize the peculiarities of the different systems and data transfer algorithms.

Policy Neutrality

Because of the nature of the Grid and the nature of end-user direct interaction with the data, access methods and access paths can be taken out of the hands of the users and encapsulated in the application. This has significant performance implications, as anyone who has dealt with dynamic query tools (like Business Objects, Oracle Discoverer, or Cognos's Power Play) can attest. Data movement and the cataloging of replicated information are possible and provided as basic operations for which you can substitute parameters as a user or through application code.

Compatibility with Other Grid Infrastructure

Because data Grids do not necessarily exist in a vacuum and are rarely implemented independent of other Grid components, anything that is configured as a data Grid needs to be compatible with the other components already in place or destined to be put into place. This compatibility needs to extend as far as enabling the ability to adapt to system conditions at runtime, regardless of when runtime is. This has definite implications to not only the hardware of which the system is comprised, but also the data model.

Storage Systems

An administrator may or may not have any control over what kind of storage system on which the data resides, or what characteristics those storage devices have. Although it is important that the end user never have to know or care about the storage, it does remain an important feature and something that both the administrators and programmers have to take anything that might come into contact with. Storage at the Grid level no longer has physical attributes; rather, it has logical attributes. Physically, how it is implemented is less important (as the data can literally be placed on any storage technology) than the ability for it to support the required access functions. A distributed file system manages files that are distributed over multiple physical storage devices or multiple sites rather than files placed physically on disk.

Files, in a data Grid, are also a conceptual construct that is a little bit different than what many people typically consider it to be. A file in this instance is also logical rather than physical, and can be what we typically think of as a file (a flat file stored in a file system) or data stored in a database, or other means that allow us to store data in an electronically accessible format. A data Grid implementation might use a storage resource broker (SRB) system to access data stored within a hierarchical database management system (like IMS) or a relational database system (like DB2, Oracle, or MySql) or an object-oriented or object-relational database management system that can store data in different kinds of constructs.

Access or Collaboration Grid

An access Grid is not really what anyone considers to be a Grid environment. It is an assembly of resources that support and facilitate group-to-group interaction across a Grid environment. This includes highly distributed meetings, collaborative work sessions with individuals who are geographically distributed, seminars, distance lectures, and training (including lecturer-assisted computer-based training). The primary difference between this and the other types of Grids is that they focus on computational resources of one ilk or another, and the collaboration Grid focuses on individuals and communication.

Currently, an access Grid is in place and in use at over 150 different institutions around the world. It was, interestingly, even in use at Hibbing Community College in northern Minnesota in the year 2000. I took a manufacturing class through Bemidji State University's distance learning program and sat with four other students in one of two access Grid-enabled classrooms at Hibbing Community College.

The components of an access Grid are therefore different as well.

Large-Format Displays

These displays could be wall-mounted liquid-crystal display (LCD) panels that take up the majority of the wall space in a conference room (Figure 2.2) or what could pass for a wide-screen television (Figure 2.3). These

Figure 2.2   Large-format display.

displays allow for face-to-face interaction between participants at different ends of the earth.

Presentation Environments

Presentation environments include presentation software that we would typically think of, like PowerPoint, but they also include book cameras (Figure 2.4) that allow everyone in the meeting session to look at the exact same book over the connection. This can save on shipping of materials from one location to another and the need to have a dozen copies of a publication in every location for the purpose of teaching one lesson from the book.

Interfaces to Grid Middleware

Because an access Grid can become an intricate piece in connection with other Grid implementations, interfaces to the Grid middleware are needed to facilitate this interaction. For departmental or enterprise Grids, this will be (initially) true. People working on a project who are located at different locations can meet face-to-face rather than over a typical teleconference.

Figure 2.3 Teleconferencing display.

They can meet far more frequently than they would be able to if they were to have to invest in airfare — and all in the comfort and familiarity of their own offices.

Others

There are other components that will be important to an access Grid implementation, depending on the purpose of the Grid and the type of business or research involved. Particle physics will need different components than a distance education lecture hall.

Scavenging Grid

A scavenging Grid is typically a configuration of a large number of desktop machines. All of the machines are scavenged for available CPU cycles and other free resources. The owners of the machines, or the users of them, are given control of when their resources are and are not available to participate in the Grid environment. If the user does not set up a specified schedule for the scavenging of resources, anytime that machine would

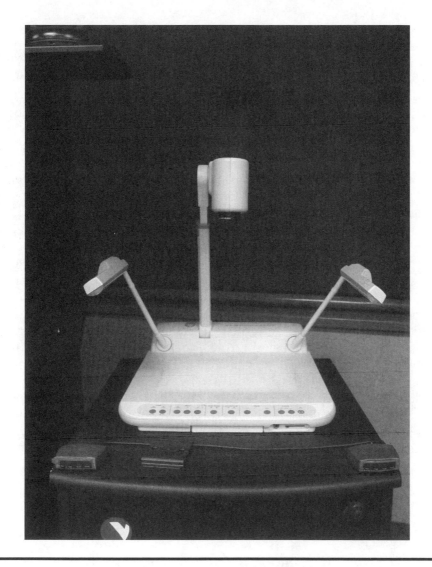

Figure 2.4 Book camera.

become idle, its status would be reported to the central management server and its node added to the database of accessible nodes.

Scavenging Grids are in place in many computer labs on university campuses around the world. These desktop systems have periods when they are in heavy use (during programming classes, when term papers are coming due, or when the majority of students are out of classes and are chatting, gaming, or surfing the Internet), but also extended periods when they are idle. During these idle periods, and during the times when any given computer is not being accessed, its CPU could be added to those available resources.

Cycle scavenging has been around for a long time under the SETI@home project without the computer having to be connected to a network or actively registered with a central server's database. SETI (the Search for Extra Terrestrial Intelligence) is based out of the University of California–Berkley and creates a virtual supercomputer to analyze the data collected from the Arecibo radio telescope in Puerto Rico. The analysis searches for signs of extraterrestrial intelligence. Using the Internet (to distribute the packets of data for each computer to process and analyze), SETI has managed to bring together the CPUs and processing power of 3 million or more personal computers from around the world.

SETI@home (Figure 2.5) is simply a screen-saver type of program that works behind the scenes without any deleterious impact to the normal use of the computer. Any owner of a PC anywhere in the world (PC in this case is a loose definition, as the machine in question can be running MAC, Windows, or Linux) can download the program from the Web and set his computer free to analyze data. These different PCs (the nodes of the loosely defined Grid) with their different speeds and different capabilities all work simultaneously, each on different parts of the whole problem. When each task is complete, the result set is passed back to the central system and the personal system can then retrieve more chunks of data from the Internet to process. The success of SETI has inspired many other applications of similar types. These include protein-folding simulations (Figure 2.6) for sifting potential future drugs, filters for astronomical data searching for pulsars, evolutionary programs that attempt to analyze problems in population dynamics, and many others with their own purposes.

Grid Scope

Project Grid, Departmental Grid, or Cluster Grid

The simplest and lowest form of a Grid environment is typically at the departmental level. Used for multiple projects, either at the team or departmental level within an organization, a departmental Grid is usually where a company that already has an infrastructure in place, with programs and systems already in play, would start.

The major features of a departmental Grid include maximizing the utilization of departmental resources, with allocation based primarily on priorities, with rules and weights assigned to projects and resources to balance out the priorities and allow for the equitable distribution of (and accounting for) the communal resources.

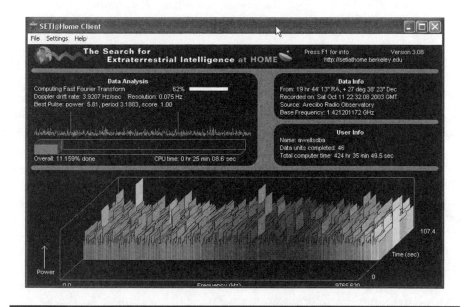

Figure 2.5   SETI@home.

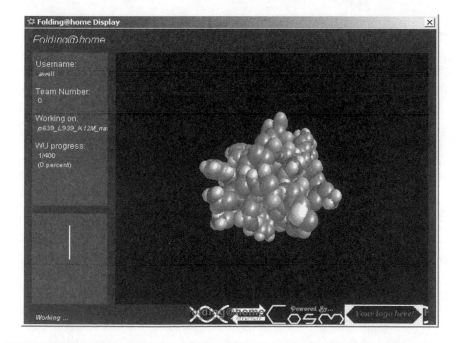

Figure 2.6   Protein folding.

Enterprise Grid or Campus Grid

An enterprise Grid is often what companies foresee when they first start looking at implementing a Grid infrastructure. In an enterprise Grid, all major computing resources are shared with every department and project in the entire enterprise. Policies are implemented to ensure computing on demand and allow for the multiple groups' seamless access to the enterprise's resources.

This may be the ultimate goal of many companies attempting a Grid initiative, but it is more typical and realistic for companies to end up starting with a departmental Grid. This allows the company to learn from the experience and build on its starts (not only from the technology perspective, but also from the learning curve and people perspective).

An enterprise Grid is made up of several departmental Grids, clustered around a central single Grid. The central Grid needs to be capable of handling the needs (computing, data and personal) of multiple departments, each potentially (and quite likely) working on multiple projects all sharing the same computing resources. The entire enterprise Grid is located inside the corporate firewall and accessible only by those with the authority to access any other information within that firewall.

Global Grid

In a global Grid environment, resources will be shared over the Internet or other widely distributed networking environment. It will provide a unified global view of widely distributed datasets. It may be at an international organizational level (this would likely be made available via an intranet, rather than an Internet) or at an interest level or any other level that unifies a group of interested parities. Multiple groups of people, in a global Grid environment, will be working on multiple projects and sharing a central set of resources. In this phase, companies (if that is the level of globalization) will gain a global view of the distributed databases.

Extending this idea to its penultimate extent, many resources will be made commercially available much in the same way that electricity, water, phone service, and natural gas are currently available to the public. A person, company, or group would subscribe to the service and draw upon the computing resources, as those resources are required.

Chapter 3

Early Adopters

> Humans are allergic to change. They love to say, "We've always done it this way." I try to fight that. That's why I have a clock on my wall that runs counter-clockwise.

> **—Rear Admiral Grace Murray Hopper**

The Grid can be a tremendous advantage to anyone who finds that he has periods when he is running short on CPU cycles, or is coming dangerously close to that point. There are industries that are inherently more apt to make early use of the immerging technology.

Computational and Experimental Scientists

Computational scientists are groups of people who are disbursed but who also have the preexisting need to interact either with each other or with remote resources. These resources can be computing resources or telescopes, particle accelerators, and electron microscopes. Computational scientists (those who are more directly connected to the theory) will be interested in making use of the ability to visualize applications in realtime; experimental scientists (the more numerous group and the group connected to the observations) will make even more extensive use of the remote instrumentation in gathering data and the large-scale CPU power and visualization devices, like the Computer Augmented Virtual Environment (CAVE) virtual reality modeler.

Bioinformatics

Bioinformatics involves applying considerable computer technology to biology and medicine. It seeks to integrate genomics, postgenomic (the genome mapping projects), and proteomic disciplines in an attempt to use these as a tool to seek the cure to cancer. There are several organizations around the world that seek to implement Grid systems, often on series of supercomputer systems to make these resources available to bioinformatics users. These supercomputers will likely play a very large part in providing the glue and shared memory structures for the Grid-enabled distributed computing applications.

One major location of life science applications is North Carolina Bioinformatics Grid Project in Research in Triangle Park, NC. Although its projects did not start out with the defined goal of building a Grid, the Grid architecture grew out of a natural need by several organizations for significant amounts of computing resources. Based on organizations' requirements for not only high-performance computing and extensive scalability, but also a simple model providing a single unified user interface, the Grid system spans a number of computers at three separate universities, several large commercial and government research facilities, and the North Carolina Supercomputing Center.

Corporations

Corporations are increasingly more global. The Web has allowed for the extensive adoption of corporate intranets for even modest-size companies. These two facts together make corporations a target for Grid technologies. Portals allow for the presentation of interfaces through the intranet browser, and the global nature of many organizations means that the wide distribution could make extensive use of the underlying technology.

Okay, so these are the kinds of groups who will make extensive use of the Grid in the future, but who are the daring souls who have made the decision to be on the cutting edge and become among the first companies and groups to adopt the Grid infrastructure?

Academia

As with most of the major advances in technology, academia is where the Grid has its earliest adopters. There is a deep and impressive amount of research and data connected with Grid implementations in this area.

University of Houston

The University of Houston's High Performance Computing group, formed in 1999, provides the faculty and students with a centralized parallel computing environment that is more powerful than any of the resources that would have been available to any of the individual departments.

Previously, the university had relied on a conventional infrastructure, but the total cost of ownership was becoming prohibitive and the infrastructure was not providing the performance and scalability that were needed.

So the university installed several Sun Fire servers, Blade servers, and StorEdge storage arrays, as well as Sun Open Net Environment (Sun ONE) Grid Engine and the Solaris operating system, to better meet its needs.

The impact of the Grid at the University of Houston will be far reaching all over the state of Texas. The institution is a part of the High Performance Computing Across Texas (HiPCAT), a consortium of Texas that is dedicated to using advanced computing, visualization, data storage, and networking technologies to enhance research and educational activities. It is through HiPCAT that the university is involved with the Texas Internet Grid for Research and Education (TIGRE) project. TIGRE will allow for the sharing of computing resources, instruments, and data that will allow for the creation of massive scientific simulations and analyses.

The University of Houston will also be corroborating with Texas A&M's weather experts to work on developing an accurate air quality model for the Houston region.

This new infrastructure will allow for the fostering of partnerships, rather than competitions, within the university systems of the state.

University of Ulm Germany

The University of Ulm, located in Ulm, Germany, is one of Germany's premier medical, scientific, and mathematical institutions and, as such, demands a tremendous amount of computing power. To help with supporting such intensive computing, in 2001, the University of Ulm partnered with Stuttgart University to implement a four Sun Fire 6800 server cluster to run the Sun ONE Grid Engine as a batch system for workload management and allow researchers throughout the region from different universities, as well as industrial partners, to experiment using the high-performance distributed computing capabilities. The project was aptly named Sun Center for Excellence for Computational Chemistry.

The White Rose University Consortium

The White Rose University Consortium is made up of the University of Leeds, the University of York, and the University of Sheffield to share technological resources. These resources include computers, data, applications, and storage and network resources. To facilitate this sharing, the consortium turned to Sun to obtain a unique solution to build the joint infrastructure for scientific computing. The project, called the White Rose Grid, utilized Sun Fire servers (Sun Fire 6800, Sun Fire V880, Sun StorEdge array, and Sun Blade 100) at each of the three locations and utilized Grid computing technology to allow for on-demand computational capacity available to not only the participating universities, but also an even wider commercial and academic market.

The White Rose Grid has contributed extensively to the development of business and commerce use of Grid technology in the United Kingdom.

Science

Particle Physics

As recently as 1990, Centre European pour Recherche Nucléaire (CERN), the major European international accelerator lab located near Geneva, Switzerland, in combination with a few other particle physics labs made up the entire World Wide Web. Originally, it was designed at CERN to help facilitate the exchange of information between scientists who were each working on separate computers, often at widely dispersed sites. The United Kingdom has always played a significant role in these revolutionary developments. The Grid is no exception.

The World Wide Web is aimed at an efficient and effective exchange of information. Grid is, in these cases, concerned with the exchange of computing power, storage of data, and access to very large databases without the users having to deliberately search for the resources manually. Once connected to the Grid, the users see the computing resources as one huge computer system. It is a viable and practical solution to data intensive problems that scientists must overcome if they are to continue to make the historic advancements over the coming years.

Still among the leaders, U.K. physicists are currently preparing themselves for the Large Hadron Collider (LHC), which will be turned on in 2007 at CERN. It will produce an enormous stream of data (to the tune of millions of gigabytes per year). That stream of data must be stored and processed. The processing of data to this extent could utilize computing power approaching 100,000 processors — a scale that no single computer center has or will be able to provide to the dedication of both the storage and computing requirements of the entire LHC operation. This is where Grid computing can thrive. The distribution of computation and data via the Grid for a project of this magnitude is essential. The United Kingdom expects to continue to play a significant role in the emerging technology and the analysis of data from the LHC. Many new and exciting discoveries are anticipated.

U.K. physicists are also participating in a number of projects, although not on the scale of the LHC, using Grid developments to hone their skills and learn through experience how to use the Grid as a tool for doing day-to-day analysis today.

The cartoons available at http://www.gridpp.ac.uk/cartoon.html depict an excellent example of what this Grid will mean to scientists in the United Kingdom. Although these distributed resources are available, they have to be negotiated and manipulated by each individual scientist as needed, and each scientist requires a separate account on each system and an account for every system, making the management of just his or her accounts almost a full-time occupation. Once the accounts are managed, the jobs have to be submitted individually and the results of those jobs collected by the scientist manually. The Grid will enable the scientists to treat these resources as if they are a signal integrated computer system, with a single sign-on and middleware handling all of the details and allowing the scientists to concentrate on science.

Industries

Many industries are currently prime for getting on the Grid. These industries are computational and data intensive and ready to make the change from the conventional to something that passes for (to many people's thinking) bleeding edge.

Gaming

The online gaming industry is one of the first places where a new technology is going to start making commercial inroads if that technology is going to "make it." Ironically, through the gaming industry, the immerging technology will touch many millions of people who have no idea on what hardware they are running and furthermore do not care. Millions of dedicated game console platforms are already in homes worldwide, including Playstations, Xboxes, and Game Cubes, as well as the less exciting PC. These dedicated consoles, together with the PC gaming market, form a multibillion dollar industry. Games have become a serious business, and the Grid has become one of the means by which provider companies have started to flesh out the worlds in which the games take place and ensure that the game field is not only wide and diverse, but always available, worldwide, whenever any of the millions of subscribers want to play.

But online gaming, as it has existed, has faced its hurdles. The computer systems, the game systems, and environments are very complex, not only to create and manage, but also to play. Not only are they complex, they have notoriously been very expensive to create and operate because the game publisher has to invest in new systems (hardware, operating systems, and supporting software) for each and every new game that is launched. Another drawback to buying the gaming service is that it is frequently taken offline, often for several hours at a time, for server maintenance. Conventional technology dictates that game providers need to run several identical copies of the virtual world, each copy called a shard or server, to segment different players onto separate servers (a player can typically choose the shard on which he or she wants to interact) or separate shards, thereby limiting much of the possible intercharacter interaction (by forcing a player's character to exist on exactly one server at any one time) and further exacerbating reliability and support problems because of the additional hardware, and therefore the additional server maintenance downtime. Although this copying of the system allows for load balancing of users (each server environment allows only a certain number of concurrent users), it severely limits what those users can do while online, because it limits the number of other players they can interact with.

A prime example of what a huge phenomenon online gaming is EverQuest. EverQuest is notorious for dedicated players who not only play and play seriously, but also use online auction sites like EBay to sell characters, secrets, and equipment from the virtual game world, and are reported to have a virtual economy that makes its setting one of the largest economies in the world, real or virtual.

The Grid has begun to overcome many of these issues and provide added flexibility, reliability, and added depth of gaming world features.

The Butterfly.net Grid is the first commercial Grid system that has the capability of processing online virtual video games across a network of server farms, thus allowing the most efficient utilization of computing resources for extremely high-performance three-dimensional immersive game worlds.

One of the expenses that a game developer incurs is when it lays out upwards of $3 million for the development of a game and its underlying infrastructure, anticipating 100,000 people turning out and only a tenth of that signing up and playing. Although not as much of a problem from the accounting perspective, but a problem from the player's perspective, is when the same game is anticipated to draw 100,000 players and instead draws half a million players and the servers are not scaled to handle the load. With Butterfly.net, these issues are not part of the picture. Because it is a service provider and its infrastructure is always available and almost infinitely scalable, the game developers making use of the service can concentrate on developing deep and robust games, how to organize and orient people within the game, and how to scale the game so that when the people come, the game will be rich enough to hold the attention. This challenge is more fun and interesting than trying to determine how to support exactly the number of players who decide to subscribe.

From Butterfly.net's perspective, the hardware that it is using is low-cost commodity type systems. But that is not the only cost savings; another important area is in standardization. Launching multiple games on one Grid can allow for the scaling back of games that are unpopular, while allowing the computing and communications resources to be diverted to those with more popularity. Operating all games together with no mirror universes, the less popular as well as the big hits, becomes much easier and profitable. What is more is that it allows all administrators to learn one platform, limiting the learning curve.

In the Grid configuration, a three-tiered architecture utilizes a gateway to switch people between servers when necessary; the experience is unique. Because the model is entirely on the server, many different kinds of interfaces to the game can be created, allowing people with many different kinds of gaming platforms to interact with the same game, together. With such a small footprint on the client machine, and the vast majority of the processing occurring on the servers, from a network perspective, it is extremely efficient, with much smaller packets being sent and received and very low latency, meaning that narrowband dial up works just as efficiently as broadband connections. This means that everyone, regardless of connection speed, can enjoy a very rich and exciting gaming experience.

Extend this concept and its findings to the corporate environment and consider what this could mean in those environments. Where with conventional configurations, high volumes of data are transferred across the network and a single server or small cluster is responsible for all of the processing, with this new configuration, all of the servers can take on a smaller chunk each of the problem and return a result set in a much more efficient manner.

Financial

The Grid is a wonderful platform on which to perform high-intensity financial market calculations. Typically, these calculations include considerable what if scenarios and are a means by which the suggestions provided to the customer are based.

Wachovia

The fixed-income derivative trading unit at Wachovia received a computing boost when it installed the Grid computing solution designed by Data-Synapse. Before the implementation of the new environment, it took 15 hours to run the simulations. Since the Grid environment has been installed, taking advantage of the underutilized servers and desktops, those same simulations now take 15 minutes. Wachovia is putting it to work in areas such as financial derivatives, wherein large corporate customers can hedge their risks on foreign exchange transactions or stock index futures.

Wachovia's trading volumes, under the new system, increased several hundred percent, and the number of simulations that they were able to run increased over 2000 percent. As a result of these two improvements, Wachovia can make larger, less risky, and more complex trades than ever before, making both their clients and their company more money. Their Grid computing adoption has been driven by the need for the company to optimize resources, lower their computing costs, and the increased need for disaster prevention and disaster recovery systems.

RBC Insurance

RBC Insurance, one of North America's largest diversified financial services companies, took an existing application and Grid enabled it. It now runs this application on a Grid platform that is based on the IBM eServer xSeries. This new computing solution has allowed RBC Insurance to reduce time spent on job scheduling by nearly 75 percent, and the time spent actually processing an actuarial application by as much as 97 percent (again, reducing jobs that once took several hours to mere minutes). Based on the stellar performance seen in the initial trials, RBC Insurance is looking forward to expanding the Grid computing environment to take advantage of these kinds of savings with even more applications and business units. Being able to virtualize its applications and infrastructure, RBC will be able to deliver higher-quality services to its clients even faster than ever before, making the Grid system a significant component in the company's competitive edge (http://www-1.ibm.com/grid/grid_success_stories.shtml).

Charles Schwab

Computer World, on December 19, 2003, reported the Charles Schwab–IBM partnership in the Schwab Grid venture (http://www.computerworld.com/).

Schwab and IBM worked together to connect 12, two Intel processor servers together in the Phoenix data center to launch the Schwab Grid system, built to improve the performance of an investment management application. It has already shown improvements in the short time that it has been operational.

It took Schwab's 15-member team working with IBM nearly a year to build the system that utilizes the Globus Toolkit 2.0 running on servers with the Red Hat Linux operating system running on them (leveraging open sources to improve the total quality of customer service) and the DB2 database, WebSphere (IBM's application server), along with the BEA Systems' WebLogic application server.

Schwab anticipates ramping up its Grid presence in 2004 by rolling out even more applications on Grid technology by combining well over a thousand commodity servers, providing the spare CPU cycles to speed up even more of Schwab's computationally intensive applications, thereby not only speeding up processing, but also lowering the total cost of ownership and making the Grid one of the competitive advantages for the company. Although hard numbers are not being touted, because Schwab wants to be able to keep its competitive edge, it has been suggested that the company has been able to minimize times for customer planning that used to range up to several days to minutes and seconds. The retirement planning tool, now running successfully on the Grid, can calculate portfolio scenarios that are based on retirement goals and take into account risk tolerances and the client's preference in investment plans. These what if scenarios are historically computationally intensive and can take a long time on a traditional architecture.

Prior to adopting this new architecture, Schwab had to scale its computing capacity at twice or more of the average required load so that it had the ability to handle the peak loads without missing processing windows. But this meant that the company often had significant excess capacity laying nearly idle on a less than peak trading day. With Grid computing, Schwab is able to funnel this unused capacity in a far more efficient manner.

The master server breaks up the computationally intensive processes into a series of smaller jobs to be run in parallel and sends those smaller jobs to the other resources on the Grid for processing. When all of the result sets are in, the master node reassembles all of the pieces and presents the unified result set to the requesting manager to help assist with the clients' requirements.

Life Science

The American Diabetes Association

One of the initial forays into a somewhat commercial use of Grid technology that impacts the lives of many thousands of people every day is the use of Gateway, Inc.'s Grid (backed by United Device's Grid MP Alliance platform) by the American Diabetes Association (ADA). Making use of this platform to run computationally intensive applications designed to accelerate diabetes-related research, the ADA can create a robust environment in which it can run analysis on several variables at once when researching the different aspects of diabetes care and when running clinical studies. Cross-correlations between patients with high blood pressure and diabetes or other coincidental co-occurring conditions can be drawn with analysis of the pros and cons of administering different dosages of medicines to patients based on age, weight, and other variables far faster than if the same analysis was to be done using a traditional architecture.

By using processing on demand, the American Diabetes Association has already experienced dramatic improvements in the time that it takes to process a single component of diabetes-related research, from nearly two days down to one hour (less than 25 cents in computing expense), and it is expecting even further reductions in time through this improved efficiency. These calculations previously would have stretched the limits of a normal computing environment, causing delays in the results of the calculations, and thus causing delays in the finding of potential new treatments or even cures.

Gateway, Inc. (better known for the Holstein-colored boxes that its commercial PCs ship in than for Grid technology) has begun linking thousands of PCs nationwide to create a Grid computing environment that is capable of scaling to nearly 11 teraflops in performance (ranking the Gateway Processing on Demand Grid among the top ten largest supercomputers in the world when compared on the amount of raw processing power). Its processing-on-demand initiative, when unveiled, made available the computing power of over 6000 PCs to research institutions (such as the ADA) as well as to universities, government agencies, and businesses. This initiative allowed companies to concentrate on the core competencies while allowing those with excess computing power to provide those cycles, at a charge that would be less than it would cost to create that excess capacity and knowledge base in house (less than 25 cents per hour for unlimited computing power and 1 trillion floating point operations per second). Compare this cost to the hundreds of thousands of dollars that it would cost to perform similar computations and calculations on rented supercomputer time, and you can easily see the cost benefit to making use of a Grid environment. This is the ultimate utility computing model that the Grid intends to eventually become.

North Carolina Genomics and Bioinformatics Consortium

Members of the North Carolina Genomics and Bioinformatics Consortium, a group of more than 70 academic and commercial organizations, created the NC BioGrid using Avaki's technology and Grid software.

Avaki's technology will allow researchers and educators to use a unified research environment that will not only simplify their ability to share computing and data resources, but also improve their ability to do data mining and analysis and modeling of biological data.

The NC BioGrid combines genetic mapping information, information on protein folding and protein synthesis as it is related to genetic transcription, and other related protein and genetic data from around the world with software and hardware provided by the North Carolina Supercomputing Center, the North Carolina Research and Education Network, and the NC Network Applications Center, along with the Avaki Grid software, thereby allowing researchers to utilize a unified environment that will allow them to focus on their research, because it masks the complicity of managing the data that is stored at different locations and on different types of hardware protected by a variety of security models.

This production Grid will likely become one of the cornerstone research resources for the researchers involved, and they will remain unaware of its inner workings; that is the beauty of the system.

Spain's Institute of Cancer Research

The Institute of Cancer Research at the University of Salamanca, Spain, has installed a Grid system. This system is based on the technology that was developed by GridSystems, a Majorcan company that works to optimize the computer resources available at the customer site. The Institute of Cancer Research is using this infrastructure change to help it investigate the genes that may be involved in the development of tumors.

In the first phase, the Grid will be used to analyze experiments that allow for the identification of genes that are linked with the development and evolution of different types of tumors. In future phases, researchers will use the distributed computing infrastructure to analyze the protein folding.

Petroleum

Royal Dutch Shell

IBM has been working with Royal Dutch Shell to build Grid-enabled software that will run on a Grid infrastructure that the company is using, initially, for applications that interpret seismic data. Royal Dutch Shell, running Linux on IBM xSeries servers with Globus Toolkit, cut its processing time of seismic data while improving the quality of the resulting data. This allows the employees to focus on key scientific problems rather than double-checking the validity of data and waiting on computations to complete.

Utilities

Kansai Electric Power Co., Inc.

Kansai Electric Power Co., Inc. (KEPCO), Japan's second largest electric utility, has been working with IBM to develop an information-based Grid that will allow it to federate various data sources and to virtualize these sources across the enterprise. The KEPCO IBM Grid solution will integrate the information that has been traditionally distributed across departments and other affiliated companies to enable information sharing. This Grid will allow KEPCO to not only use its existing systems (thereby cutting time for implementation) but also develop new businesses and business processes more rapidly at a minimum cost.

Manufacturing

Ford Motor Company

Ford Motor's Engine and Transmission Groups, when requested to cut information technology costs, invested in nearly 500 dual-processor Sun Blade workstations from Sun Microsystems, Inc., for use by their designers and engineers. The dual-processor configuration might initially seem to be overkill for workstations for typical individual users, but engineers often need considerable horsepower at their disposal to complete their jobs. Consider, however, that the cost of these scaled-up workstations was less expensive than two single-processor workstations would have been. Also, when the investment in these workstations was made, they were bought with their being key components in a Grid computing environment in mind. During the day, when engineers are hard at work, one of the processors is dedicated for the user's local computer-aided design jobs (typically interactive mechanical computer-aided design [MCAD] jobs), while the second processor is made available to the Grid for Grid-based mechanical computer-aided engineering (MCAE) jobs. When users leave for the day, Ford effectively has 1000 CPUs to run MCAE batch jobs in the Grid.

For Ford, Grid computing was a low-cost way to harness the spare CPU cycles of the group of workstations. Grid computing put to work all of the available CPUs at idle workstations, virtually doing away with the need for powerful servers and, in many cases, supercomputers.

Saab Automobile

Since the middle of 1999, Saab Automobile AB has been using Sun's free ONE Grid Engine to create a pool out of 100 Sun workstations for use in external aerodynamics and other simulations. Saab now uses this Grid environment as a relatively inexpensive virtual supercomputer, using 24 hours a day, 365 days a year. Originally built for Solaris and Linux, ONE has since grown to encompass open-source versions for nearly all flavors of Unix and for the Mac OS X operating system as well.

Motorola

Motorola Semiconductor uses Grid-enabled software to allocate additional CPU cycles to individual projects as deadlines approach. It had nearly 400 workstations in a heterogeneous environment plus several servers that could be clustered together into a server farm, with each server powered with anywhere from two to ten processors and upwards of a half dozen to a dozen gigabytes of memory. Seeing these resources lying idle at night and on weekends, as they are in thousands of offices around the world, officials decided that it might be worthwhile to try to borrow some extra computing power there. They found a way, Sun's Grid software (Sun ONE), to maximize the resources that they already had, and share them among different groups.

Engineers now just send their computationally intensive engineering jobs to the Gus One Grid Engine and let it find the most appropriate systems on which to run them, allowing engineers to run more regression tests in a shorter amount of time than ever before, making the risk of poor quality far lower than they thought easily achievable.

Government

Governmental agencies have extensive computationally complex requirements as well, and they too are making use of this emerging technology.

In the federal government, there is great demand for high-performance computing resources. Teams of scientists and researchers seek access to computers powerful enough to execute their large-scale projects, and Grid computing is a powerful operation concept that will allow them to find greater efficiencies and better leverage existing computing resources.

NASA

NASA acquired the Information Power Grid, its Grid environment, to help manage its combined scientific computing and engineering computing workloads. Applications that simulate wing design can now be easily linked with engine simulation software in another part of the country, and the results of the simulations and analysis can then be delivered back to one computer. It lets scientists create tests that have never been practical or possible before the Grid.

NASA's Grid solution extends the distributed resource management capabilities by coordinating the scheduling of the computing resources between the different NASA centers in a high availability solution, without requiring NASA to purchase additional new hardware and without the users and programmers having to learn or implement any new job submission language or queuing system.

Before implementing the new Grid environment, users at both centers were constrained by the limited capacity of their local server farms. Although these resources were optimized, users often required more processors or access to processors that had different performance characteristics. This was particularly true for structural analysis applications used in aerodynamics and propulsion projects requiring prompt access to highly intensive computing resources. The implemented Grid system and the accompanying Linux clusters have helped to solve these issues.

Not only have the original issues been solved, but NASA is now considering new opportunities and interagencies for additional uses of Grid computing.

U.S. Department of Defense

IBM, United Devices, and Accelrys have all joined efforts to help the U.S. Department of Defense in the fight against bioterrorism in a search for a smallpox cure, linking the power of over 2 million computers to assist in the effort. The project will scavenge spare CPU cycles, otherwise idle, that will be donated from millions of computer owners around the world in a massive research Grid, looking for new drugs. Results from the Smallpox Research Grid Project not only will be used by hospitals in the event of a smallpox outbreak, but also will be delivered to the secretary of defense.

Smallpox, once considered to be eradicated, currently has no specific treatment and the only prevention has been vaccination. Many people in the United States still bear the vaccination mark, having been required to be vaccinated prior to entering elementary school. Routine vaccination was discontinued several years ago.

The Smallpox Research Grid Project will allow researchers at facilities around the world to access excess computing power that is needed to identify the new antiviral drugs necessary to fight this disease.

Individuals worldwide can participate in the project by downloading a screen saver at www.grid.org. Similar to the SETI project's screen saver, the Smallpox Research Grid screen saver will patiently wait for more slack periods of time when your computer is able to donate idle processing power and link it into a worldwide Grid. The net effect will be that the connected computers will act as a virtual supercomputer — a supercomputer that is capable of analyzing billions of molecules in a fraction of the time it would ordinarily take in a laboratory. Once a piece of the processing is complete, the next time the processing computer connects to the Internet, the resident program will send results back to the central data center and will request new data to analyze. And the cycle begins again.

European Union

Europe has decided that the Grid is a competitive advantage and is going about taking that advantage. Although American universities often lead in technology, it is often difficult for these new technologies to get put into widespread general use, partly because the government has a more or less hands-off process when it comes to implementing industrial policies. This is a mixed blessing.

Because European governments have traditionally been effective in the deployment of unified standards and in concentrating on technologies that offer a significant economic advantage, the Europeans working in this area have the advantage of having a clearer road map than their counterparts in the United States, where any planning for large-scale computing and networking infrastructures is scattered throughout the federal government. Europeans see the Grid as such a serious advance in computing that they have a ten-year strategic plan.

In early 2004, the European Union was preparing to launch two major Grid initiatives. The first one, called Enabling Grids for E-Science and Industry in Europe, is going to attempt to build the largest international Grid infrastructure to date. It will operate in more than 70 institutions throughout Europe and will provide 24X7 Grid services and a computing capacity that is roughly comparable to nearly 20,000 of the most powerful existing personal computers. The other project is a distributed supercomputing project that is being led by France's National Center for Scientific Research. In this project, the center will connect seven supercomputers throughout Europe on an optical network (high-speed interconnects).

What is more is that the British government is helping its country to be among those taking the lead by supporting several different projects, not the least of which is the Diagnostic Mammography National Database project, which is using Grid computing to store, scan, and analyze mammograms. Because it has governmental backing, the project is more likely to make it into integration with the national healthcare system.

The United States is making strides in deployment of computing Grids for computationally intensive scientific applications (studying earthquake risks or analyzing weather patterns). Even CERN is not supposed to catch up to these efforts until some time in 2005.

Flemish Government

In a December 2003 article, *Primeur Monthly* writes about the emerging Flemish Grid that is being assisted by the Flemish government (http://www.hoise.com/primeur/04/articles/monthly/AE-PR-01-04-84.html).

The Flemish government is helping to fund the BEGrid computational Grid initiative to assist researchers in gaining experience with Grid technologies and to work toward connecting to other international Grids. With applications like astronomy, astrophysics, bioinformatics, chemistry, climatology, genomics, and high-energy physics, it will not take long for this Grid to join with other computational Grids to make even more strides in the research community.

BEGrid will become a part of the pan-European computing and data Grids. This will allow them to join with the Enabling Grids for E-Science and Industry in Europe's Integrated Infrastructure Initiative (a project designed to create and deploy Grid technologies throughout the European research area to enable E-science applications).

Ironically, when the Flemish government surveyed potential users in universities and other educational institutions, it found that half of the respondents did not know what the Grid and Grid computing was, although of those that do know, most of them believe that it is important for them and for the future of computing.

Suggested barriers to Grid implementation include shortage of personnel, lack of required hardware and software, and lack of an existing knowledge base.

Benefits

The benefits to these early adopters are broad. As with research universities, commercial ventures that adopt the Grid as a central technology solution can hope to find as benefits business virtualization, added flexibility in infrastructure, instant access to data resources, and leveraging of their capital investments. These fancy buzzwords sound great, but what do they really mean, and what can they mean for your organization?

Virtualization

In servers such as storage area networks (SANs) or network attached storage (NAS), virtualization is the key concept, with large arrays of individual physical devices working together on a high-speed network and, under control of clever software, acting as a single, powerful, and highly flexible resource.

Virtualization enables a company or other organization to balance the supply and demand of computing cycles and other computing and electronic resources by providing users with what appears to be a single, transparent, aggregated source of computing power. It provides the ability for the organization to lower the total cost of computing by providing on-demand, reliable, and transparent access to any and all available computer resources.

This means that these organizations can leverage investments in current existing heterogeneous resources, increasing return on investment and return on assets, enabling organizations to do more with less. It can mean reduced infrastructure and other operational costs, including hardware and software resources. Because the user has a single interface, it can lead to improved user productivity with faster response time, faster time to answer, and more reliable results, not only often leading to a time benefit to the company, but also often increasing revenues and profits.

THE PARTS AND PIECES

Let us be patient with one another,
And even patient with ourselves.
We have a long, long way to go.
So let us hasten along the road,
The road of human tenderness and generosity.
Groping, we may find one another's hands in the dark.

—Emily Greene Balch   Nobel Peace Prize winner, 1946

Just what will be involved in building a Grid system? Grids will be built to support different sets of user communities. Each of the systems, based on the user requirements, will be built with different components. There is not likely going to be a one-size-fits-all, one-form, off-the-shelf product that will be dropped into place. There will be some basic pieces that will be included in most, if not all configurations.

Scale

One of the most differential pieces of any Grid project will be the scope and scale of the project and the resulting Grid. Many companies will look at implementing an entire Grid system. This is not likely to be the end product, unless there is no existing infrastructure. What is more likely to be the situation is that smaller projects will spring up, introducing Grid systems in pockets inside organizations, and as those projects succeed, they will expand to fill the vacuums and will prove to be successful in many applications.

Section 2 provides the description of what is entailed in defining a Grid environment. There are new paradigms that must be looked through when defining a Grid environment and a different kind of mindset in administering something that is very fluid in its definition.

One thing is constant: with the replication of processing and data across resources, the Grid and its replication need to have a few characteristics.

Robust

Each file must be successfully and confidently replicated in at least two sites. Although one of these sites must have read/write/update access, so that one or more processes can make alterations to the data, the others may be read-only versions. It is not only possible, but suggested that this be the case.

Not only does the data need to be replicated and replicable, but it is also important that there be multiple sites in the Grid system that can be available to process any given application. Although with open source this is not as big of a concern, there will be applications in the Grid system that are operating system dependent or hardware dependent, and resources have to be available on which these pieces can be processed.

Efficient

To increase the efficiency of the Grid environment, files (database files, replication members, flat files, or other resources) should be located as closely as possible to where they are to be used. In the case of high-powered telescopes and other remote instrumentation, they need to be located in places where they can most efficiently perform their functions. Data should be located in locations where it can be easily accessible to the applications that are acting upon it.

Transparent

It is important that the users not have to know or care where or how the data is stored, or where or how the application is running. They should not have to care or worry about how the Grid is constructed, where the components are located, or on what operating system the processes are running.

Fault Tolerant

Without a doubt, one of the most important features of a Grid environment is its fault tolerance. There should be no single point of failure. Although there does need to be one central controlling thread that makes sure that all of the nodes are working and answering to polls when sent, that thread can run on virtually every system, each checking for the others to determine that they are available.

If a node does fail, an e-mail can be sent to the administrators of the Grid system, and the control threads can start to redistribute the processing, applications, and information that were located on the failed node to others in the system, so that even in fault conditions, transparency is maintained.

These threads need to be maintainable so that a node can be disabled if there needs to be maintenance on that resource, without the control thread attempting to redistribute existing loads based on that resource's unavailability.

The replicas of the central control thread can back up the metadata and configuration files, as well as provide alternative paths into the Grid for the purpose of not only assuring availability, but also load balancing and ease of control, if not ease of administration all of the time.

Centralized Distributed Control

Because much of the Grid and its processing rely on a Web interface into the system — for application access not only from the users, but also by the administrators to maintain the system — the Web (intranet, Internet, and extranet) is a key component in the system. These interfaces allow you to administer or access the Grid from virtually anywhere on the planet that you have Internet access, and that access extends to being able to access the interface.

This distributed control allows users to access the Grid and its processing in ways that might be difficult in other circumstances (mobile technology, highly remote access, administrators on the road and without direct access to the network) and can provide more flexible avenues for access to match the more flexible infrastructure. It also means that a thin client or other Web-enabled front end can process requests, limiting the need to invest in as many high-end components for all of the people to use just to allow them the disk space necessary to complete the typical processing (making even more components available over which distribution of CPU cycles can be farmed, and pushing data access out to those components that have that as part of their descriptions).

This means that the Grid will become even more flexible as time passes and applications are built to be accessed in the ultimate distributed mechanism, the Web browser. More and more applications are being built to take advantage of this architecture (Oracle E-Business Suite, for example), and with this emerging infrastructure, more and more will continue to be built.

Onward

The Grid has been prevalent in academia for several years; it has also started to make its presence felt in the business community, as more companies not only need to throw more horsepower at more complex problems, but are also being asked to do more with less. Budgets are tight, and in many cases getting tighter. Resources are thin; in particular, skilled human capital can be scarce, undertrained, or expensive. Many companies have an overall overabundance of idle computing power for the majority of the time, often utilizing only 10 to 20 percent of their available capacity — however, having pockets of time or areas where processing is a little on the thin side (Monday night processing of accumulated data, month's end accounting closing processes, or a four-hour job to calculate the what if scenario for a client). But companies are looking at the free and idle cycles that are going unused in some areas and determining that it might just be possible to reallocate those cycles elsewhere, rather than having to invest in still more hardware to get those taxed resources over their difficult moments.

The companies with taxed resources do not need more power connected to those resources; what they need is more equitable distribution of the existing processing, more efficient processing with what they already have that is sitting idle. There needs to be a way to tie these machines together into a single pool of available labor that can be drawn against to get over tight times. If we can accomplish this, work will get done faster, more efficiently, and often with fewer errors, and can become a competitive advantage while all the time cutting expenses.

As you look at Figure II.1, keep it in mind for the following chapters (refer back to it from time to time to keep it fresh in your mind). You will be better able to see how the components fit together and how they can interconnect. In many cases, the lines blur in the model, because many pieces overlap and stretch into neighboring areas (for example, security can be a component of nearly every level).

Open standards and protocols have become an essential part of the backbone of the Grid, with services enabling users to get their job

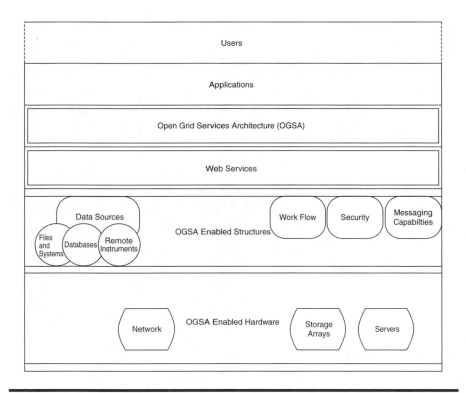

Figure II.1   Grid overview.

done and those services interacting seamlessly together to accomplish the following:

- Information queries
- Network bandwidth allocation
- Data extraction
- Data management
- Request processing
- Session management
- Workload balancing
- Processing distribution

A good service, however, is not just limited to what tasks it can accomplish for the user (be that user a human or another Grid component), but it can also help enable virtualization, or the appearance that the Grid system is simply one big system that can be seen as a whole, and not thought of as a sum of its parts. It is this ability that many see as the ultimate future of the Grid, the future that will take it to the extent of commodity computing, where computing resources are as available and purchasable as water, gas, and electric utilities are in many parts of the world today. You will no more care from where your CPU cycles originate than you now care where the electricity that runs your toaster, TV, or computer comes from. You only care that it works. If Grid computing is taken to its ultimate end, and there are many people who believe that it will be, it will be taken just as much for granted as the other utilities in our lives today.

Chapter 4

Security

Life was simple before World War II. After that, we had systems.

—Rear Admiral Grace Murray Hopper

Security .

Security, at its highest level, is simply preventing unauthorized disclosure of or modification to data and ensuring that there remains continued operation of the system.

This is a hard enough feat when you are looking at a simple network configuration.

When you look at a configuration that allows access to a large number of computers, data, and other resources from nearly anywhere, security takes on increased significance. In a world where there are new virus threats nearly every month, and hackers are able to get into almost any system that they set their sights on, it is important that an understanding of the security issues and potential solutions be addressed.

Computer and network security can be broken down into significant chunks. These logical chunks have their own sets of issues. Security deals with authentication, access control, accounting, and data integrity.

Authentication

Authentication deals with one party gaining the assurance that the identity of another is declared and true, preventing impersonation. Entity authentication is the process of one party in the communication process being ensured through quantitative evidence that the identity of a second party in the communication process is correct and allowed. Identification or authentication can either be accepted or terminated without being accepted (or rejected).

Authentication, at its root, is the process of confirming an identity. This identity can be attributed to the user of the system, but in a Grid environment, the identity can be attributed to any component accessing any other component. In the context of any network interactions, authentication involves the ability of one party to confidently identify another party. Authentication over networks (and nearly all communication today takes place over networks) can take many forms. Later in the chapter we will look at how certificates are one way of supporting authentication.

In a Grid environment, authentication is critical not only for users that are authenticating when they log in to the Grid system, but also, even more importantly, when a new resource joins the Grid environment, it needs to be authenticated to the system. Although it may be a welcome sight to have more and more resources joining themselves to your system, the authentication at this level is even more important because there is a possibility that a computer with nefarious purposes may try to join your Grid. It is in the best interest of your environment to make sure that anyone volunteering to donate resources has honest intentions. And even if he or she has the best of intentions, it is important to know the sources of the resources and the level of security that those resources have as well.

Network interactions typically are seen to take place between a client, for example, browser software running on a personal computer, and a server, the software and hardware used to host a Web site. Remember that in the Grid, at any time a computer in the system can be acting as either a client or a server, or both. Client authentication is identification of a client by a server such that the server is then confident that the client is who it claims to be. Server authentication is identification of a server by a client such that the client is then certain that the server is what it claims to be.

Verifying the identity of a participant to an operation or request is what authentication boils down to in a Grid environment. A principal or claimant is the participant under whose authority an operation is performed or authorized. This principal can be a user logged on to a remote system on whose behalf the application is running. It can be a local user logged directly into the server. The principal can be the server itself.

The basis of the identification can be something known (personal identification numbers [PINs] or secret keys whose knowledge is demonstrated in a challenge–response protocol) or something possessed (physical accessory, passport-like in function). These could be magnetic-strip cards, like a credit card, chip cards or smart cards containing physically embedded microprocessor or password generators (providing time-variant passwords), or something that is inherent to a human or an electronic entity (signatures, fingerprints, vice or retinal patterns).

Identification protocols differ significantly from one another, but they do have several similar properties.

Reciprocity of Identification

One of these common properties is reciprocity of identification. This means that either or both parties may (and may have to) corroborate their identity to the other using either unilateral or mutual identification techniques. These can be fixed-password schemes; however, this may be susceptible to another entity posing as the principal, having gained access to the password by illicit means.

In the case of computer-to-computer authentication and the premise of reciprocity of identification, one way for the computers to definitely identify themselves to each other in a network, and in the Grid, is by use of the unique media access control (MAC) address with which they are created. MAC is a hardware address that uniquely identifies each node of a network. The MAC address is your computer's unique hardware number. On an Ethernet local area network (LAN), the MAC address is the same as your Ethernet address. When your computer is connected to the Internet, a correspondence table determines the Internet Protocol (IP) address that has been assigned to your computer's physical (MAC) address.

Computational Efficiency

Computational efficiency is another potentially common identification protocol property. This property includes the number of operations that are required to execute the protocol. An authentication protocol is not going to work well in any network if it is not computationally efficient. This means that you need to find the best possible authentication method that allows you to fully and comfortably recognize each and every resource in the Grid while still maintaining an efficient enough network to allow work to actually get done in it. It has to be robust enough that it is difficult to hack, and simple enough to be elegant.

Communication Efficiency

Communication efficiency includes the number of passes that a message may have to exchange and the total bandwidth (total number of bits required to be transmitted) that is expended in its travels though a network. Again, if any message has to pass through many different points in its travels through the network, it is inefficient. If it has to go searching node to node, or has to be proven as authentic at each node, then this is not necessarily an efficient means of determining that the message is destined for the given machine or the given network. It is important to make sure that messages are as authentic as the physical constructs in the Grid, whether that message is external to the network or a request for a job that originates within the Grid itself, but the determination has to be tempered with the knowledge that it is important that efficiency be taken into account. You can have a perfectly safe network on which nothing can be accomplished because it takes too many resources, too many passes through the network, and too much bandwidth expended on the communication of the authenticity of the message.

Third-Party Real-Time Involvement

The real-time involvement of a third party may be a necessary property in many identification protocols. The third party could be an online trusted third party that acts to distribute symmetric keys to all of the communicating parties for the purpose of authentication. An online untrusted directory service could also be used for distribution of public key certificates, as can an offline certification authority. More details on the two different means of keys will be dealt with later in the chapter in the section on cryptography.

Further, the nature of trust required of a third party is another potential protocol property. Included in this property could be the trusting of a third party to correctly authenticate each of the parties and bind each entity's name to a public key. This third entity could be also trusted with the private keys of the entities.

Nature of Security

Security is not simply a component of a distributed system that can be added after the system is built, as an afterthought. Security is an inherent quality that a system has, or does not have, with regard to both the information that is resident in the system and the processing that is done on, to, and with that information. Because it is such a central component and because it is something that is inherent to a system, security has to be designed into a system from the beginning. The nature of security guarantees is yet another property that can be included in the protocol definition. Provable and zero-knowledge properties are included.

Secret Storage

Finally, storage of secrets, including the location and method used to guarantee the storage of critical key material and information, is one of the protocols that may be necessary in the different security protocols that are used.

But what specific methods are used to ensure that only authenticated users and servers access resources?

Passwords

Historically, one of the most common and conventional schemes that has been used for authentication is a password. Passwords provide weak authentication, with one password tied to each user or entity in the communication link. Typically passwords are strings of four to ten characters (the more characters, the less easy it is supposed to be to guess) that a user can memorize.

Passwords can be considered one component for users to computer security, even in a Grid system. There has to be a simple way for users to be authenticated to the computer and, by extension, to the network. Because many systems, and one of the ideals suggested in the Grid environment is Lightweight Directory Access Protocol (LDAP) (a set of protocols for accessing information directories), and the ability to do single sign-on to a system (sign on once, having your security identified at that time and having the system be responsible for understanding what that security means), it is important to be able to definitely identify the given user to a system, but the method used to uniquely identify the user has to be practical enough in reality to allow the user to be able to do his job efficiently and effectively. Single sign-on eliminates the need for multiple passwords in a system and allows a user to have to remember far fewer than he would have to otherwise. It also means that if anyone were to compromise that one password, then she would have far easier access to all of the resources that the owner of the password had, without his knowledge. It is the proverbial double-edged sword.

By their very nature, passwords are weak, as people are more apt to have a password that is some variation on something that can be associated with them. If a password is sufficiently complicated as to not be easily guessable, it then becomes difficult to remember. When this happens, people find other ways of remembering their passwords. This can take the form of Post-it Notes attached to computer monitors or taped under the keyboard or to the slide-out writing drawer on a desk.

So there has to be a better way, but what?

Private Key

One of the basic problems of cryptography (a process associated with scrambling plaintext into ciphertext in a process known as encryption, and back into plaintext again, decryption) is that it is usually either very complicated or less robust. Cryptography concerns itself with:

- Confidentiality — Keeping the information known only to those for whom it was intended
- Integrity — Keeping the information unaltered or unalterable either while it is being stored or while it is being transmitted,
- Nonrepudiation — Making sure that the creator or sender of the information is unable to later deny the data was deliberately sent or created
- Authentication — The sender and receiver can verify each other's identity, as well as the origin and destination of the information, allowing for secure communication over an insecure channel

User A wants to send a secret or sensitive message to User B over what may be an insecure communication channel (a tapped line, a channel open to packet sniffing). Traditionally, the common solution to this situation is private key encryption. Users A and B agree on both an encryption and decryption algorithm and a secret key to the algorithm. Although an intruder may be able to figure out the algorithm, the unavailable secret key allows the encoded message to remain secret. Private key algorithms are also referred to as symmetric or synchronous algorithms (communication events that are coordinated in time).

Traditionally, in private key cryptography, the sender and receiver of any message know and use the same private (secret) key. The sender uses the private key to encrypt the message, and the receiver uses the same key to decrypt the message. This is known as symmetric cryptography or secret key cryptography. One of the main challenges is getting both the sender and receiver to agree on the secret key without anyone else being able to find out about the key. If they are in separate physical locations, a courier must be trusted (phone system or other transmission medium) to prevent the disclosure of the key. If anyone were to in any way intercept the key, he or she can later use the key to read, modify, or forge other messages that are encrypted or authenticated using that particular key. The generation, transmission, and storage of these keys is called key management, and cryptosystems must deal with these key management issues. This is most particularly true with a large number of users or in an open system.

There are advantages and disadvantages to private key cryptography (Table 4.1).

Block Ciphers

A block cipher is a symmetric key encryption algorithm that is applied to a fixed-length block of data (for example, 64 or 128 contiguous bits) at one time, taking the group as a single unit rather than one bit at a time. The resulting ciphertext is identical in length to the plaintext version of the message. To ensure that identical blocks of text are not encrypted the same way every time they are in a message, making the cipher easier to break, it is common to use the text in one block as part of the key for the encryption of subsequent blocks. A random number is used, combined with the text of the first block, along with the key, to ensure that the subsequent block's encrypting bears no resemblance to the previous blocks. This is called block chaining.

The implementation of the block cipher in a Grid environment is usually the same as in any other environment in a network. Distribution has little effect on this implementation.

Stream Ciphers

The main alternative to block ciphers, although used less frequently, is stream ciphers. Stream ciphers encrypt each individual character of a plaintext message or individual bits (or bytes) of a data stream, one at a time, using the encryption transformation. The transformation algorithm varies over time. Stream ciphers are typically faster than block ciphers at the hardware level and are also more appropriate in some telecommunications applications, when buffering space is limited or when individual characters have to be processed, rather than allowing blocks of data to be decrypted at one time. Stream ciphers have little or no error propagation, so they may also be advantageous in situations where transmission errors are highly possible. Stream ciphers are sometimes referred to as state ciphers, as the encryption of any particular bit is dependent on the system's and bit's current state. Most of the ciphers that are used in this type of encryption consist of a pseudorandom number generator. XORing each plaintext bit with the corresponding key bit in the keystream accomplishes encryption. This means that if a single bit of error is introduced

Table 4.1   Advantages and Disadvantages of Private Key Cryptography

Advantages:

Symmetric algorithms can be designed to facilitate high rates of data throughput. When you consider that every request and much of the data not only have to travel through the network to the brokers and schedulers that make up the services that are the Grid, but from there also have to be distributed throughout the system, it is important to note that throughput can be one of the major issues in this kind of distributed system.

Keys for symmetric algorithms are typically relatively short.

Symmetric algorithms can be employed as primitives (or building blocks) to construct various other cryptographic mechanisms. The more advanced constructs include stronger ciphers, pseudorandom number generators, hash functions, and computationally highly efficient digital signature schemes, among others. Simple transformations are typically easy to analyze and, by extension, break, but grouped together they can be used to build much stronger end products.

Disadvantages:

The key must remain secret at both ends of every communication channel. In a Grid, where there is no real end, only stopping points along the way, this means that the secret has to be kept in even more locations and that, for this reason, there is a somewhat greater chance that the secret will get out.

As the number of connections in the network increases (and with the Grid, this could potentially become nearly limitless), so does the number of key pairs that must be managed. As a result of this increase, management is often accomplished through the use of an unconditionally trusted third party (TTP). Any time you add an extra person to the mixture, there is an increased risk of discovery. The risks must be weighed against the potential benefits. As the number of nodes increases, so does the benefits of seeking assistance.

To ensure that private key security in networks remains viable, the key has to be changed frequently. This frequency can often approach the need to change with every communication session. This adds further management issues and complexity. In a Grid system where there is great concern about security (as in medical, insurance, or financial institutions), this can aid the maintenance complexity. But with complexity come both the literal security of the system and the implied security — the security that you have in the knowledge that your data and information are secure. In a two-party communication between entities A and B, sound cryptographic practice dictates that the key be changed frequently and perhaps for each communication session.

Digital signatures that arise as a result of symmetric algorithms require large keys (often prohibitively long in comparison to the amount of data associated with each message packet) or (again) the use of a TTP.

to the data, it results in a single bit of error in the decrypted message, not the entire block, or worse, the remainder of the message. This also means, however, that stream ciphers are more prone to a type of attack known as bit fiddling, where causing a bit to be dropped can result (depending on the bit) in complete garbage (this is particularly true in self-synchronizing stream ciphers where the encryption of the current bit is dependent on the encryption of the previous several ciphertext bits). Fortunately, the garbage caused by the interference lasts only as long as that bit's influence on the message remains. Synchronous stream ciphers encrypt each bit independently of every other bit.

The implementation of the stream cipher in a Grid environment is usually the same as in any other environment in a network. Distribution has little effect on this implementation.

Public Key

Public key cryptography, first described by Diffe and Hellman in 1976, is another cipher. In this one, the encryption and decryption keys are different from each other, where private keys have to be the same, and the knowledge of the encryption method lends no clue to the decryption method. Public key cryptography is based on a one-way or trapdoor function. This kind of function is a transformation of text that is simple to implement and apply; however, it is less easy to reverse. If you look at an example mathematically, it is simple to multiply two very large prime numbers together and come up with the product; however, given the product, it is not as easy to arrive at the original factors.

Public key cryptography answers the problem encountered when one person has a message that he wants his friends to be able to read, but wants no one other than those for whom it was intended to understand. If he were to use private key cryptography, all of his friends would have to know the key, and in order for them all to have the key, the key would have to be distributed over a secure channel. However, if he had a secure channel, he would not need cryptography to ensure the secrecy of the message. In public key cryptography, he only has to publish the public key and the security is not in doubt.

Because Grid environments are accessed typically through a portal, how every Web browser handles cryptography and authentication is a vital detail to have uppermost in your mind, particularly if you are a Grid administrator. Because there is not necessarily any way to absolutely guarantee what browser a user will choose to use to access the portal, all browsers and their idiosyncrasies should be taken into account when implementing this and all security.

Utilizing a public key infrastructure enables an organization to provide authentication, as well as access control, confidentiality, and nonrepudiation to its networked applications. It, along with its related standards and techniques, underlies the security features of many products, including Netscape and Apache, including single sign-on and the Secure Sockets Layer (SSL) Protocol.

Because all Internet and intranet communication uses Transmission Control Protocol (TCP)/IP (the *de facto* standard), information is sent from one computer to another over often separated networks and through a variety of intermediate computers before it reaches its ultimate destination. Under normal circumstances, these computers allow messages to pass without interfering with the transmission in any way. At the same time, the ability for a message or data packet to hop from network to network and computer to computer to get from its source to its destination is a flexibility feature of TCP/IP, meaning that information that is sent from one computer *will* travel over disparate networks and through several dozen to hundreds of computers, any one of which is a potential place for someone to interfere with the communication in any of the following ways:

- Eavesdropping
  - In eavesdropping, the information remains intact; only its privacy is compromised. In this way, nefarious individuals can learn your credit card number, your bank account number, or other classified or sensitive information.
  - Because one of the primary components for the Grid and its environment is the network, it is important that eavesdropping be taken into account when the Grid administrator or security administrator is designing the security of the overall system.
- Tampering
  - In tampering, information (while it is in transit) is changed (or replaced) and then allowed to proceed to the intended recipient. In this way, someone could alter an order for goods (either changing what was ordered or where the order would be shipped) or change information in a contract before allowing that contract to reach its destination.
  - Depending on the scale and scope of your Grid, this may or may not be a serious concern. If your data passes outside of your firewalls in any way, outside of your ability to control the data and access to the network, there is the possibility of tampering. This is not any different in the Grid, except in that there is more data traveling over the network and therefore

more that could be tampered with, including the jobs, job streams, and tasks.

▪ Impersonation
  ▪ Impersonation means that as information passes through the network, it passes to a person who is pretending to be the intended recipient. This can take two forms:
    ▪ Spoofing
      ▪ In spoofing, a person simply pretends to be someone else. A person can pretend to have a spoofed e-mail address (highly common in the ever popular spam and virus mailing) or a computer can spoofingly identify itself as a site or computer that it is not.
      ▪ If we look back at authentication, it is important, particularly in a Grid environment, to be mindful that spoofing can occur and take measures to be alerted to its existence.
    ▪ Misrepresentation
      ▪ As with any organizational misrepresentation, one person or one organization can misrepresent itself by making a claim to be one thing (a legitimate business, a low-price retailer, or something else that is perfectly above board) while it is, in fact, only processing credit card payments without actually providing the service advertised. This would be similar to someone on a street corner selling Rolex watches, but the spelling on the watch face is Rollex or Rolax.
      ▪ Misrepresentation is similar to spoofing in that it is possible for a component to misrepresent itself when attempting to join or access the Grid. Although it is not likely that IBM's Unix, the Advanced Interactive Executive (AIX) server would attempt to represent itself as an Intel Windows server, or vise versa, someone with less than honorable intentions could represent himself or one of his components to gain access.

Public key cryptography makes it relatively easy to take precautions with messages and information that may be sensitive in nature, while allowing it to travel freely of TCP/IP or other protocol networks. Encryption and decryption are easily addressed with public key cryptography. It allows both of the communicating parties (regardless of how many pairs, or how many people are communicating with a single resource) to disguise the information that they are sending to each other. Although the sender can encrypt the information and the receiver decrypts it, during the time that the message is in transit, the information is completely unintelligible to an intruder. If someone were able to tamper with the information and modify it in any way, the attempt at modification or substitution would be easily detected. But it goes further than just making sure that the information gets from point A to point B without interruption, it also allows the recipient to determine where the information originated (the identity of the sender) and prevents the sender from being able to claim later that the information that was received was never actually sent.

Where private key cryptography was symmetric encryption, public key encryption is asymmetric and involves a pair of keys, one of which is still a private key, but the other is a public key. Both of these keys are associated with an entity that needs the ability to digitally sign and encrypt its data. The public keys are published, and the private key of both the sender and receiver (not the same secret key as in private key encryption) is kept secret and is the means by which the receiver decrypts the message.

If you compare the computational effort required for public versus private key asymmetric, public key encryption requires more computational effort, and is therefore not always the best solution for large amounts of data.

It is possible to use public key encryption and to send an additional symmetric key, which can then be used to encrypt additional data. This is the approach used by the SSL Protocol.

This still may not be a desirable way to encrypt sensitive data, however, because anyone with your public key, which is by definition published, could decrypt the data. In general, logically the strength of the encryption is directly related to the difficulty of discovering the key. Discovering the key in turn depends on both the cipher that is chosen and the length of the key. The difficulty of discovering the key for one of the most commonly used ciphers for public key encryption depends on the difficulty of factoring large numbers, a well-known mathematical problem. This is one of the reasons that encryption strength is often described in terms of the size of the keys (in number of bits) used in the encryption of the data (with the longer keys providing the stronger encryption algorithm). Different ciphers use different key lengths to achieve the same level of encryption, based on the mathematics used in the algorithm. This is another reason that private key cryptography is considered stronger; it can use all possible values for a given key length rather than a subset of the values.

What is worse is that what is currently considered to be sufficiently strong encryption is strong only relative to the time when it is discussed. Sixty-four-bit encryption used to be considered sufficiently strong for asymmetric cryptography (public key cryptography), and now, for many purposes, 512 bits is required, and that may soon not be strong enough.

Advantages of public key cryptography include:

- The public key is published, although authenticity must be guaranteed. The private key part must, however, still be kept secret. This will simplify much of the key management in the massively distributed environment that is the Grid.
- Network key administration can be accomplished through trusted third parties, but they do not have to be unconditionally trusted and may be able to be utilized in an offline manner, rather than in real-time. Being able to put the burden of as much management off on these other sources will allow Grid administrators to concentrate on other parts of the environments. It is important to note, yet again, that care must be taken in deciding who should maintain your keys, as this responsibility is great and the potential losses or compromises are many.
- Depending on how they are used, the key pairs can remain unchanged for long periods. This can mean an extended number of sessions, or even several years.
- Public keys can typically be fewer in number (depending on the size of the network, this can be significant) than the private keys in a symmetric algorithm.

Disadvantages of public key encryption include:

- Public key encryption's throughput rates are significantly slower than simple private key encryption's. Again, because the network is such a big part of the Grid environment, anything that makes the system significantly slower or that takes an inordinate amount of bandwidth will have an impact on the overall efficiency of the system.
- Key sizes are often significantly larger than those in private key encryption.
- Public key algorithms have not been found to be unbreakably secure. So far, no encryption has proven completely unbreakably secure, and when you have a massive amount of computing power to throw at an encryption scheme (based on math), as in a Grid environment, you can see that it becomes possible to use the Grid to compromise the Grid. Because they are based on a finite set of mathematical functions, and computers are good at math, encryptions, given enough computing resources, can still in theory be broken.

A digital certificate is an attachment to an electronic packet, similar to an attachment to an e-mail. Where e-mail attachments are designed to carry additional information that you want the receiving party to know, the certificate carries additional information that you want the receiver's computer to know, information that is used for security purposes. The certificates are based on the combination of public key and private key encryption. Each key is like its own unique encryption device, as no two keys are ever identical. This is why a digital certificate can be used as a digital signature to identify its owner.

Encryption and decryption together address the problem of network snooping and eavesdropping. Eavesdropping on the contents of network packets is one of the main security issues that need to be addressed, but encryption and decryption by themselves do not address either tampering or impersonation. Public key encryption and cryptography address the issues of eavesdropping and tampering as well as impersonation. Tamper detection relies on a mathematical function called a one-way hash. A one-way hash, a number of a fixed length, has a unique value for a given set of hashed data. Any change in the data, even the deletion or alteration of a single character in the hashed data, would result in a completely different value. What is more is that the contents of the hashed data cannot be deduced from the hashed data (this is why it is called one way).

Digital Signature

Digital certificates allow us to help automate the process of distributing public keys as well as exchange the resulting security information. Once you have installed the digital certificate either on your computer or on the server, the machine on which it is installed or the Web site on the server through which people are accessing the information now has its own private key. Although it is possible to use your private key for encryption of data and your public key for decryption, it would not be desirable to follow this encryption-and-decryption scheme for the encryption of really sensitive data; it is one of the main pieces for digitally signing any data. Rather than encrypting the data itself, signing software creates a one-way hash of the data, and then uses the private key to encrypt the hash. This encrypted hash then, along with other information (including hashing algorithms), is what is known as a digital signature.

Figure 4.1 shows one simple way that the resulting digital signature can be used as a means to validate the integrity of signed data.

As shown in Figure 4.1, items are transferred from the source to the recipient. The messages that are moving from one to the other are of signed data, and contain both the original data (a one-way hash of the original data) and the digital signature that has been encrypted with the

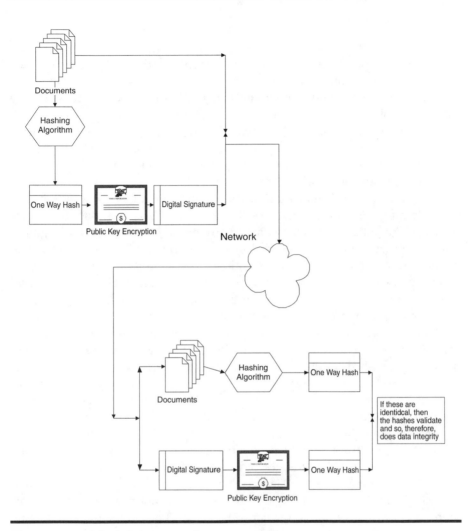

Figure 4.1 Digital signature and one-way hash.

signer's private key. To validate the data's integrity, the receiving computer's software first uses the original signer's public key to decrypt the hash, resulting in an unencrypted and easily readable set of data. The receiver's computer then uses the same hashing algorithm that was used to generate the original hash to generate yet another new version of the one-way hash of the same data. This rehashing is possible because information about the original hashing algorithm used is sent along with the digital signature. The receiving computer's software, once the new hash has been calculated, compares the new hash value against the original hashed dataset. If the two hashes match, there can be absolute certainty that data had not been changed since it was signed and sent. If they do not match, the data may have been tampered with since it was signed, corruption may have occurred in transit, or the signature may have been created with a private key that does not correspond directly to the public key that was presented by the signer.

If the hashes match, the recipient can have confidence in the certainty that the public key used to decrypt the digital signature corresponds to the private key that was used to create the digital signature. This confirms directly the identity of the signer. However, this also requires that there be some way of confirming that the original public key belonged to a particular person or to some other entity.

In this way, the significance of the digital signature is comparable to a handwritten signature. Once you have signed data, it is difficult, if not nearly impossible, to later deny having any part in the creation and signing. Assuming that the private key had in no way been compromised, or that it never had been in any way outside of the signer's control, this same certainty has crossed to the computer and other digital devices. A digital signature is often as legally binding as a handwritten signature, enabling it to provide a high degree of nonrepudiation.

To exchange information using a digital certificate, the sender accesses the certificate that contains the public key. That user's computer or server then validates the identity of the owner of the certificate and, if the user proves to be verified, encrypts the data that the sender wants to share with the owner of the public key using SSL, using the receiver's public key. Only the receiver's private key can then decrypt that message, data, or information.

X.509 is the most widely used and the *de facto* standard for digital certificates. Because X.509 is not officially sanctioned by the International Telecommunications Union (ITU), only recommended by it, the standards are not always followed in the same way by all vendors over all platforms; there are occasions when idiosyncrasies occur. This means that a certificate that is created by one application may or may not be strictly understood or readable by other kinds or brands of applications.

A digital certificate is an electronic document, similar to a driver's license, passport, voter's registration card, or other identification that is used to identify an individual, but is also used to uniquely identify a server, company, or any other entity, and to associate that unique identity with a unique public key. In this way, public key cryptography is used in certificates to address the problem of impersonation.

To get a driver's license, passport, or voter's registration card, you need to apply to a government agency, which verifies your identity, your ability to drive (for a driver's license), your address, and other information before issuing the identification. Certificates work a lot like any of these more familiar forms of identification. Certificate authorities (CAs) are the entities that validate identities and issue the certificates (similar to the government entities, but not affiliated with any agency for any government). These CAs can be either independent trusted third parties or internal organizations running their own certificate-issuing software. The methods that are used to validate an identity can vary depending on the particular policies of the given certificate authority. Before issuing a certificate, the CA uses its published verification procedures to ensure that the entity requesting a certificate is who it claims to be.

Because a digital certificate binds a particular public key to the name of the entity (person, server, or other entity), the certificate can help prevent the attempted use of fraudulent public keys for the purpose of impersonation. Only the certified public key will encrypt a message that can be decrypted by that person's private key. What's more, the public key and certificate always include the name of the entity that it identifies, an expiration date, the name of the CA who issued the certificate, and a serial number so that you can be sure the entity with whom you are sharing information is who you believe it to be. This allows the certificate to be the official introduction for users who know and trust the CA, but who do not necessarily know or trust the entity that is identified by the certificate.

Certification authorities will create valid and reliable certificates as they are bound by legal agreements. There are several commercially available CAs, including VeriSign (one of the most popular and common 40- and 128-bit encryption CAs), Thawte (128-bit encryption), and Entrust (128-bit encryption).

X.509 is the most widely used digital certificate definition standard. It describes the writing down of the data format. An X.509 certificate contains the following components:

- *Version* —Identifies which version of the X.509 standard applies to the contents of the certificate. The version affects what information can be contained within it. There have been three versions to date:
  - *X.509 Version 1* first became available in 1988. It is widely deployed and is the most generic version.
  - *X.509 Version 2* was the version that introduced the concept of subject name and issuer-unique identifiers to handle the possibility of reuse of either subject or issuer names over time. Version 2 certificates are not widely used.
  - *X.509 Version 3* became available in 1996 and supports the idea of extensions (additional security inclusions in a certificate).
- *Serial number* — Assigned by the entity that created the certificate. The serial number distinguishes it from other certificates that the entity has issued. One of the most useful features of a serial number

is when a certificate is revoked, the serial number is placed on a
certificate revocation list.

- *Signature algorithm identifier* — Identifies the algorithm that was
  used by the certificate authority to sign the certificate.
- *Issuer name* — The name of the entity that signed the certificate.
  This issuer is typically a certificate authority. Using the certificate
  implies that you are trusting the entity that signed this certificate.
- *Validity period* — Because each certificate is valid only for a limited
  amount of time, the validity period is described by a start date and
  time and by an end date and time. The difference in this time
  period and can be as short as a few seconds or almost as long as
  several decades. The validity period chosen depends on several
  factors, such as the strength of the private key used to sign the
  certificate and the amount that the person contracting with the
  authority is willing to pay for a certificate. The validity period is
  the amount of time that entities can expect to be able to rely on
  the public value, and is trustable as long as the certificate's associated private key has not been compromised.
- *Subject name* — The name of the entity that the public key
  certificate identifies. This name is intended to uniquely identify an
  entity across the Internet or across any other network.
- *Subject public key information* — The public key of the entity
  named, as well as an algorithm identifier that specifies to which
  public key cryptography system this specific key belongs and any
  associated key parameters required by the certificate.

The goal of a Grid environment is not only to prevent unauthorized
access and to protect itself from the users (intended inappropriate access
as well as accidental), but also, just as important, to ensure the mutual
authentication of servers to each other. This is critical to ascertain that the
resources and data that are provided by any given server are not provided
by a hacker, attacker, or intruder.

And not only do the users and servers have to be authenticated, but
the users also have to be reasonably comfortable that the data on which
they are working is clean and secure. Data origin authentication is how
this is accomplished. It is the assurance that any given message, data item,
or executable object actually originated with a particular principal. To
accomplish this, information is used to determine if a program was
modified by or sent by an attacker with the intent to compromise the
resource that the program was accessing. This, however, by itself, does
not ensure that the data that is sent by a principal is intact and unaltered,
only that at some point in its lifetime it was generated by the principal.
Packet interception, alteration to the data, and forwarding of the data to

an intended destination could potentially occur. These are among the challenges of data security in the Grid.

In a Grid environment, remote authentication is accomplished by verification of a cryptographic identity in a way that establishes trust that there has been an unbroken chain from the relying party to a named human, system, or service identity, and from that named entity back to the relying party. This trust is accomplished through an essential sequence of trusted steps, each of which occurs in an essential order from the accepting of a remote user on a Grid resource back to the named entity in question.

Delegation is accomplished by generating and sending a proxy certificate along with its private key to any remote Grid system so that the remote system in question may be allowed to act on behalf of the user. This is the basis of what single sign-on accomplishes in a Grid: the user or entity proves its identity once, when it signs in, and then proceeds to delegate its authority to the remote systems for any subsequent processing steps.

The trust establishment process involves:

1. Binding an entity identity to a distinguished name, or the subject name, in an X.509 identity certificate.
2. Binding a public key to the distinguished name (generating an X.509 certificate).
3. Ensuring that the public key that is presented to the system actually represents the user that it is supposed to be representing. This is accomplished through the cryptography algorithms and the protocols of public key infrastructure.
4. Ensuring that messages originating from an entity, and therefore tied to that entity that is maintaining the distinguished name, could only have originated with that entity.
5. Mutual authentication, accomplished when the two ends of a communication channel agree on each other's identity.
6. Delegation of identity to the remote Grid systems through the cryptographic techniques and protocols that are used for generating and managing the proxy certificates (directly derived from the certificate authority that issued identity certificates).

Authorization

Authorization, in a computer network, is the permission for a user or system to access a particular object (computer, resource, data, or program). Authorized users should, in practice, be the only ones allowed to access specific data or resources. Details of who is or is not authorized to do what is usually maintained in special access control lists (ACLs).

Because of the large number of objects that a user or a resource can access in a Grid environment, these access control lists can become very large and complicated. Even if these lists are stored in such a manner as to allow them to be accessed and maintained in as simple and elegant a manner as possible, they can soon become unwieldy.

Traditionally, authorization is based on authenticated identity of the requesting user and on information that is local to the server. An individual is identified as authorized to perform an operation after that user's identity and permissions associated with the particular files, services, directories, and operations requested are verified. The authorization mechanisms in the Grid will be similar to those in any other arena, only there will be more options for access permissions.

Access to a file in a data repository, access to reserve network bandwidth, and access to allow for running a task on a given node are examples of accesses granted via access control lists. The ability to run a given task on a given machine may be based on not only the identity of the user (the principal), but also the identity of the task or the application to be run and the machine on which it has been requested to be run. Access control lists may contain names or checksums of those authorized programs, together with the names of principals authorized to invoke the programs and the machines on which the function was requested to be run.

Delegation of Identity

Grid environments have the need for authorization of user processes running in an unattended manner. They also have the need for both local and remote processes to be able to run on behalf of a user with all of the authorization that the user has. Grid Security Infrastructure (GSI), a part of the Globus Toolkit, allows for short-term proxy certificates that are stored with unencrypted private keys. The given user delegates his identity to these unencrypted keys, which are accurately formatted X.509 certificates in all respects other than they are signed by an entity other than the one attempting to run the given process.

The choice of taking this action is the trade-off that must be made between allowing long-running jobs to continue and complete as authenticated entities and mitigating and limiting the damage that might be done in the event that a proxy is compromised.

Proxy certificates with restricted rights are one way of limiting the potential damage that might be done by a compromised proxy.

Delegation of Authority

Delegation of authority is the means by which a user process that is authorized to perform operations on given machines can grant that authority to perform those operations to another process on its behalf. Delegation of authority is more restrictive than delegation of identity, and it is an important service for tasks that will run remotely on the Grid, but it must make calls to read or write remotely stored data.

Accounting

Tracking, limiting, and charging for consumption of resources fall under the umbrella of accounting. Being able to accurately account for the use and allocation of resources in the Grid environment is critical for fair allocation of resources. Accounting is closely tied in with authorization. It is important, particularly in a Grid environment with its fluid form, that there be a means of payment for use of resources (even if that payment is inferred rather than explicit), and that the usage of these resources be tracked carefully and accurately so that a user is charged accurately for the consumption of resources. The accounting information can also be used for planning for future capacity and for when there will likely be peaks in demand. Accounting is not intended to be punitive, but rather is an attempt at a means to ensure that computing resources are available when and where needed, an incentive to make judicious use of the resources.

Because it is possible for a user or several users to all be connected to one area or department, quotas and limits need to be put into place to ensure that runaway processes or other processes that put unexpected demands on the system are found and stopped.

There needs to be a distributed mechanism in place that is designed to maintain the prescribed quotas across all systems in the Grid environment, to ensure that users are not exceeding the resource limits simply by spreading the access out over different pieces of the system.

Accounting, in the Grid computing paradigm, is an emerging field, and there is little currently in place, other than rules, to make sure that users do not overstep their authority, even inadvertently.

Audit

Although the word *audit* conjures up thoughts of the IRS and being called on the carpet for something that you did that might be perceived as wrong, *audit* is not punitive, but more of a record-keeping mechanism.

True, it is used for providing a way to determine what went wrong if something does go wrong, but it can also be used for much more. If there is a problem in the system, auditing is a means to determine what may have gone wrong. If there is an intrusion into the system, it can assist with its detection and tracking. Again, because of the nature of the Grid environment, it must be a distributed mechanism.

One of the challenges with auditing in the Grid environment is in the scope of intrusion detection. Grid administrators need to maintain a record, or log, of all accesses and all log-able events in a manner that allows for analysis to be done later, but also so that, if need be, analysis can be started immediately concurrently with the logging. The logs and their record need to be protected to ensure confidentiality and inalterability of audited data. Great care needs to be taken to make sure that the record is in no way open to modification by any means other than by the audit mechanism, and that deletion of records is impossible. Further, the log needs to be protected in a manner that ensures that it cannot be used as a mechanism for a denial-of-service attack spawned from its contents.

The primary difficulty with auditing in the Grid environment is inherent with the type of applications and connections that go along with the Grid in general, because many normal Grid activities may appear similar to some network attacks.

Access Control

Access control deals with the configuration of users and the actions that each user should be allowed to do. Within the database, it is the creation of uses and the granting of them to those users with roles and privileges, allowing them to do those things that necessary to accomplish their jobs.

Access control technology has evolved from research and development efforts that were originally supported by the Department of Defense (DoD) and resulted in two fundamental types of access control: discretionary access control (DAC) and media access control (MAC). Because of its Defense Department background, the initial research undertaken and the applications that resulted from the research addressed, primarily, the prevention of unauthorized access to classified information; recent applications, however, have begun applying many of these policies and their resulting applications to commercial environments.

DAC

DAC allows individual users to permit or revoke access control to any of the objects that they own or have direct control over. These users are considered to be the owners of the objects that they control if they have the authority to make changes to those objects. In corporations where users are not given this level of authority to objects, the corporation or agency is considered to be the owner of the system and all objects within the system, and the owner of all of the programs and operations that act upon these objects and systems.

Access authority and priorities are controlled by the organization typically through systems administrators and are usually based on employee title, employee description, or employee function, rather than ownership of the data.

MAC

MAC is defined in the Department of Defense's Trusted Computer Security Evaluation Criteria (TCSEC) and is loosely defined as a means of restricting access to objects based not on ownership, but on the sensitivity of the information (on the principle of least privilege) and the formal authorization to those objects (often gained though different levels of clearance).

Policies such as these for access control are not always going to be well suited to the requirements of organizations that process unclassified information, as this is not the purpose for which the methods were designed, but rather information in question that may be sensitive to the industry, rather than to the national interest. In these corporately secure, but not critically secure, environments, the security objectives are often used as a means to help support the higher-level organizational policies. These policies have been derived from existing laws, business rules and practices, ethics, regulations, or generally accepted practices within the organization. Organizations such as this and their resulting environments usually require the ability to control the actions of individuals within the organization beyond simply controlling their ability to access information based on its sensitivity.

In a Grid environment, the data that is involved could be sensitive on a great many levels. Medical information may only be accessible on a true need-to-know basis, and access decisions need to be made on a record-by-record basis. The data may be salary information that only certain levels of employees in payroll and HR are permitted to know. The information may be deemed to be sensitive for any number of reasons. These are all case-by-case decisions that will need to be considered when implementing these security decisions. Business rules will often take precedence over any other kinds of decisions that will be made concerning the security and securability of the information.

Frequently, you may want to have a way to let people access your system based on something other than who they are. Often, this other means is by where they come from. This restriction of access based on something other than identity is known as access control and is a critical piece of Grid access security.

Allow and Deny

There are certain directives, typically used in conjunction with a Web server and its software (for instance, Apache), that allow or deny certain access based on IP or the directory structure that is being accessed. These directives provide you with the means to allow or deny access based on host name or the host IP address of the machine requesting the document.

The usage of these directives is as follows:

- *Allow from <address>* — Address is replaced by an IP address or partial IP address, or by a fully qualified domain name (or partial domain name), or by multiples of any combination of these. You can also replace *address* by the word *all* (if it is a public place) or *none* (if you do not want anyone to have direct access to the places that you are allowing).
- *Deny from <address>* — Again, *address* is replaced by any of the same things that are applicable to allow from *all*. Deny from *none* is equivalent to allow from *all*, and deny from *all* is equivalent to allow from *none*.

Table 4.1 is an example of an allow-and-deny configuration for directory/node access.

Allow and deny can be particularly useful in a Grid environment because this level of security and access can be controlled through the configuration files for the Web server. As long as you lock down access to the servers, you have nearly complete control.

Combining order with these other two directives can give you some certainty that you are restricting access in the way that you think you are. The order "deny, allow" tells the server that you want to apply the deny directive first and then the allow directive. The following example will deny access to everyone, but will then allow access from the host named myhost.mycompany.com.

```
Order Deny, Allow
Deny from all
Allow from myhost.mycompany.com
```

The idea of allow and deny is particularly good if you have a well-segmented network. If the accounting department is segmented to a particular series of IP addresses, and they are the only ones permitted to use one segment of a server, or perform one kind of job on the Grid, limiting access to those IP addresses would be a simple way to do this.

Satisfy

There is also a means by which you can specify that any of several criteria may be taken into account and considered when the server is trying to determine if a particular user's server will be granted admission. The selectivity of satisfy is either "any" or "all." The default is to assume that the entity attempting access is "all", meaning that (if there are several criteria) all of the different criteria need to be met to allow someone access to the given portions. If "any" is the specified selectivity, all anyone has to do is meet one of the criteria to gain access.

Role-Based Access

Access is the ability to do something with a computer resource — use the resource, make changes to either the resource or contents of the resource, or view settings or contents of the resource — and access control is the means by which the ability to do these things is granted or denied. Computer-based access control can allow you a fine grain of control over what user or server processes can access a specific resource, as well as the type of access that is permitted.

Role-based access allows the computers to make these access decisions based on the roles that either individual users have as a part of the organization or a Grid component has within the Grid. The determination of appropriate roles needs to be carefully addressed based on business rules within the organization. Access rights are then grouped together based on who is allowed to perform what action on these resources, and the rights are granted to the role that a group of individuals is given. Any individual can be put into one or more than one role, based on the actual role that that person undertakes within the organization. Again, the premise of least privilege needs to play a part, as well as grouping of groups to allow a person with more organizational authority to have more Grid resource authority.

Usage Control

The freedom that has been gained with the advent of the Internet and the World Wide Web to use and transmit data by any number of unspecified users has allowed a lack of usage control over what information is being transferred via the network. This is becoming a growing problem.

Usage control needs to be aimed at managing the use of software, data, and other resources at the point and place of use, so that no matter how the user or entity arrives at that point, there will be equitable management of those resources.

This idea is not new; it has been around for decades, with pay-per-use software and copy-free software, both concepts that are related to usage-based revenue collection in other industries, such as cable video. In this model, software itself could be freely copied and distributed anywhere without charge, but with revenue collection based solely on usage. A usage control scheme expands on this notion by incorporating a mechanism for assigning usage of rights on a per user basis. By applying usage control programs, a far more flexible and user-friendly system of usage control can be obtained, but using simple revenue collection and password-based user approval.

This idea of usage control can be used not only for software distribution, but also for any race sources scattered in your own network. Temporarily, this means mirror servers, routers, and network circuits. However, in a great environment, this can extend to anything within the Grid usage control that can be brought to the level of the virtualized storage files, databases, CPU resources — anything that can be used can have the usage control mechanism applied to it to more equitably distribute these resources.

The system needs to be designed so that the user cannot tamper with the contents. There are various ways to put this protection into place, including installation in a secure place outside the end user's workstation on which to store the information and the communication media between that place and the workstation. This is usually done via a secure communications protocol, and will most likely be done using the public key–private key digital signature.

Cryptography

Cryptography is defined well by Stallion Support Services (www.stallion.com/html/support/glossary.html) as follows:

> A process associated with scrambling plaintext (ordinary text, or cleartext) into ciphertext (a process called encryption), then

back again (known as decryption). Cryptography concerns itself with four objectives: 1) Confidentiality (the information cannot be understood by anyone for whom it was unintended). 2) Integrity (the information cannot be altered in storage or transit between sender and intended receiver without the alteration being detected). 3) Non-repudiation (the creator/sender of the information cannot deny at a later stage his or her intentions in the creation or transmission of the information). 4) Authentication (the sender and receiver can confirm each other's identity and the origin/destination of the information). Procedures and protocols that meet some or all of the above criteria are known as cryptosystems.

Block Cipher

A block cipher is a method of encrypting text to produce ciphertext, or the cryptographic key is used with the algorithm and both are applied to a block of data (for example, 64 contiguous bits) at once as a single group, rather than one bit at a time. To ensure that identical blocks of text do not get encrypted in exactly the same way in a message, it is common to use the ciphertext from the previously encrypted block as part of the algorithm to apply to the next block in the sequence. This makes it more difficult to decipher the ciphertext should someone happen upon it either inadvertently or deliberately. So that identical messages that are encrypted on the same day do not produce the same ciphertext, an initial vector derived from a random number generator is typically combined with the text in the first block. This initially unique vectored text is combined with the key; this ensures that all subsequent blocks resulting in the ciphertext will not match the first encrypted block.

A block cipher is a symmetric key encryption algorithm that transforms a fixed-length block of plaintext into ciphertext of exactly the same length. That transformation takes place under the action of the user-provided secret key and decryption, and is performed by applying the reverse transformation to the ciphertext using the exact same secret key. The fixed length is called the block size, and for many block ciphers, this is 64 bits. In the near future, the block size will increase to 128 bits as processors become more sophisticated.

It is possible to make block ciphers even more robust by creating an iterative block cipher. This is accomplished by encrypting a plaintext block by processes that have several rounds; each round of the same transformation (also known as a round function) is applied to the data using a subkey. The set of subkeys is derived from the user-provided secret key by special functions. The set of subkeys is called the keys schedule. The number of rounds in any one iterated cipher depends solely on the desired security level; however, it is important to remember that there is a trade-off between security and performance. In most cases, an increased number of rounds will improve the security offered by the block cipher, but for some ciphers, the sheer number of rounds required to achieve adequate security will be entirely too large for the cipher to be practical or desirable.

Stream Ciphers

Another encryption algorithm, an alternative to block ciphers that is less commonly used, is stream ciphers. A stream cipher is a symmetric encryption algorithm (symmetric, where the message is encrypted and decrypted using the same key). They can be exceptionally fast algorithms, even faster than block ciphers, partly because they operate on smaller units of plaintext data, usually at the bit level.

A stream cipher generates a keystream; combining that keystream with the text, typically using a bitwise XOR operation, provides the encryption. Generation of the keystream can be either a synchronous stream cipher, where the keystream is generated independently of either the plaintext original or the ciphertext, or self-synchronizing, where the keystream can be dependent on the data and its encryption. Synchronous stream cipher is the most common type. As of yet, there has been little attempt at standardization on any particular means of deriving a stream cipher, although there are modes of block ciphers that can be effectively transformed into a keystream generation algorithm, making a block cipher double as a stream cipher. This could be used to combine the best points of both means of encryption, although stream ciphers are likely to remain faster.

There are a many different types of stream ciphers that have been proposed in cryptographic literature, and at least as many that appear in implementations and products worldwide. Many are based on the use of linear feedback shift registers, as this type of cipher tends to be more amenable to analysis, and it is easier to assess the security that it offers.

To generate a keystream, an algorithm is required. The following are examples of different keystream-generating algorithms.

Linear Feedback Shift Register

A linear feedback shift register (LFSR) is one of the mechanisms that are used for generating a keystream sequence of bits. The register, whose behavior is regulated by a clock and clocking instances, consists of cells, set by an initialization vector. The vector is typically the secret key. The contents of the register's cells are right shifted on position, and a bitwise XOR of the resulting cell's contents is placed in the leftmost cell.

Linear feedback shift registers are fast and easy to implement at both the hardware and the software level. However, sequences that are generated by a single register are not completely secure, because any reasonably powerful mathematical framework allows for their straightforward analysis and decryption. Linear feedback shift registers are most useful when used as building blocks in even more secure systems.

One-Time Pad

A one-time pad, or its alternative name, the Vernam cipher, uses a string of bits that are generated completely at random. The keystream is exactly the same length as the plaintext message that it is intended to encrypt. The random string is combined with the plaintext using a bitwise XOR and, as a result, produces the ciphertext. Because the entire encryption keystream is random, an opponent with even an infinite amount of computational resources can only guess at the content of the plaintext if he sees the ciphertext. Such a cipher is said to offer perfect secrecy. The analysis of the one-time pad is one of the cornerstones of modern cryptography.

One-time pads saw high use during wartime, when messages over diplomatic channels required exceptionally high security. The primary drawback to the one-time pad is that the secret key, which can only be used once, is exactly as long as the message, and therefore difficult to manage. Although a one-time pad is perfectly secure, it is highly impractical.

Stream ciphers were originally developed as a close approximation to the one-time pad. Although contemporary stream ciphers are unable to provide the satisfying theoretically perfect security of the one-time pad, they are far more practical.

Shift Register Cascades

A shift register cascade is an entire set of linear feedback shift registers that are interconnected together so that the behavior of any given register depends directly on the behavior of the previous register in the cascade. This interconnection is achieved by using one register to control the clock of the following register. Because many different configurations are possible, and many different parameter choices are available, this is one of the methods that take the simple linear feedback shift register to a more secure level.

Shrinking Generators

Shrinking generators, developed originally by Coppersmith, Krawczyk, and Mansour, are stream cipher based on the simple interaction between the outputs from two linear feedback shift registers. The bits from one output are used to determine if the corresponding bits of the second output will be used as a part of the keystream. They are simple and scalable and have good security properties. A drawback of the shrinking generator is that the output rate of the overall keystream will not be consistent or constant unless precautions are taken.

A variation of the shrinking generator is the self-shrinking generator. In a self-shrinking generator, the output of a single LFSR is used to extract bits from the same output, rather than the output of another LFSR. As of yet, there is little in the way of effects and results from tests on the cryptoanalysis of the technique.

Part of the interest in stream ciphers is their commonalities with the one-time pad. One-time pad encryption is touted to be the closest to unbreakable as we have achieved. If (and only if) the key is truly perfectly random, a bitwise XOR-based one-time pad is perfectly secure. This means that an attacker cannot simply compute (or uncompute) the plaintext from the ciphertext without explicit knowledge of the key. This is true even for a brute-force search of all of the keys. Trying every possible key combination does not help, because any possible combination of plaintext is equally as likely from the ciphertext. In this symmetric encryption, random bits of a pad are bitwise XORed with the other bits of your message to produce a cipher that can only be decrypted by re-XORing the message with a copy of the same pad. Although the decryption depends on the safe transmittal of the exact key used for encryption to facilitate decryption, the main drawback to the one-time pad as a security measure is that there are exactly as many bits in the key as there are in the original plaintext message, and no portion of the key sequence is ever to be used (or rather, reused) in another encryption (this how it got its name, one-time).

Accountability

Problems concerning resource allocation arise continuously in computer services, and these issues are usually solved by making users accountable for their use of resources in a Grid environment. This takes planning and discipline. Traditional file systems and communication media use accountability to maintain centralized control over the resources for which they are responsible. Typically, these controls are implemented by way of constructs known, ironically, as user accounts. Administrators use quotas on file systems as a means to help to restrict the amount of data that any user may store on the system. Internet service providers (ISPs) measure the bandwidth their clients are using and that the traffic on their clients' Web sites are using and often charge monetary fees in proportion to the amount of space and bandwidth used.

Even Web hosting is often based on a combination of the amount of bandwidth that is allocated to an account and the amount of space and number of e-mail accounts that are allocated to that hosted site. Without these limits and controls, any user has the incentive to attempt to squeeze all he can out of the resources to maximize his personal gain. However, it is also true that not only does one user have this incentive, but that all users on the system appear to have the same incentive. Without controls, it will soon become impossible for anyone to get anything done on the server. Without strict controls and strict accountability, all resources could soon be used up.

This is no less true in a Grid environment, although it is interesting to note that it would likely take more time to hit the saturation point in a system where you have nearly unlimited resources (at least in theory). In a system with nearly unlimited resources, as the Grid, the potential to exhaust these resources still exists, although reaching that point is more difficult. For this reason, runaway programs may be less detectable than they are in a conventional system. And for this reason, it is even more important for programmers to understand what their programs are doing and what effect those programs have on the system at large. The breaks are put on programs early in a system where there are limited resources, and those breaks need to be in place in a Grid system just the same.

The overloading of a system's bandwidth or processing ability, and the ultimate causing of a loss of service on a particular network service or of all network connectivity, is called denial-of-service attack. A denial-of-service attack, although typically wreaked upon a network by an outside entity bent on deliberate destruction, can also be caused by legitimate internal clients simply by using the available resources on the network. One simple way to maintain data availability is to mirror it. Instead of allowing data to be hosted on just one machine, store it on several distributed places that are all available on several different machines. Because of the inherent underlying architecture of the Grid, this is simple. When one machine becomes congested, when a denial-of-service situation occurs because of resource unavailability or extremely heavy network traffic, or when no one server goes down entirely, all others in the network have access to the data that resides on different servers that are still available for connection.

The exploitation of a system by storing a disproportionately large amount of data, a large number of files, or in any other way overloading the storage capabilities of that resource, thereby disallowing other users the ability to have a proportionally equitable amount of space, is considered a storage flooding attack.

These two attacks are often seen as attacks from the outside, but cannot simply because by lack of accountability structures within a network without a way to protect against these kinds of attacks, whether intentional or accidental, kind of collaborative network that is found in either peer-to-peer or in Grid computing environments built on relatively shaky ground.

Accountability can be enforced in part by restricting access, whereby each computer system tries to limit its users to an assigned set of a certain number of connections, a certain quantity of data storage, or a certain amount of data that can be either uploaded to or downloaded from the system. Favored users are often granted extended resource allowances. The determination of the favored user status is normally done through the maintaining of a reputation for each user that the system communicates with. Those users seen as having lower reputations are typically allowed fewer resources or are mistrusted entirely, and find that their transactions are either rejected or given significantly lower priority. Favored users are granted more access to resources — not only storage and bandwidth, but also CPU and other resources.

In relatively simple distributed systems, rudimentary accountability measures are typically sufficient (access control lists are on or the measures typically employed), particularly if the list of accounts is somewhat static and all of its account members are known to teach host name or address; then any misbehavior on any user's part can lead to that user receiving a permanent bad reputation. What is more is that if all of the operators of the system are known, then preexisting legal methods such as legal contracts for nondisclosure agreements can help to ensure that system administration abides by protocol.

However, by definition, the Grid environment is not that of an inherently simple distributed system. The technology makes it harder to uniquely and permanently identify Grid users, their operations, and their contributed resources. Even if these users have been identified as trusted on the Grid, they have no idea to what resource they are connected or on what resource their jobs are going to run. Therefore, there is not a perfect way to centrally access the history or the authorized users or to predict performance for any single given job. Furthermore, individuals using the Grid environment are rarely bound by any kind of legal contracts and would likely not be charged for breaching those contracts if they were so bound. This is because the cost–benefit analysis of the direct and indirect costs associated with time delays involved in attempting to enforce them would be prohibitively high.

The main goal of accountability is to maximize server utility to the overall system while minimizing the potential threats that either that server or that access to the Grid through that server could pose. There are two primary ways to minimize the threat. The first approach is to limit the risk that the bandwidth used or whatever resources might be improperly used by maintaining an amount roughly equal to the benefit from the transaction. The second approach is to make the risk proportional to the trust that we have in the other parties who are also on the Grid.

Data Integrity

Data integrity refers to the validity of the data resident on or accessible by the Grid. It is a term that often encompasses many other ideas. It often refers to the consistency of the data, its accuracy and correctness, the preservation of the data for its intended use, and its being maintained in an identical condition during any operations (transfer, storage, and retrieval). In data communication, data integrity refers to the condition that exists when data is transferred from the source to the destination and has not been either accidentally or maliciously modified, altered, or destroyed.

Data (either singularly or as a chunk or set) means different things to different people. It is distinct pieces of information, usually formatted in a particular way. Data can exist in a wide variety of forms. It can be numbers or letters and words on a piece of paper. It can be bits and bytes that are stored in electronic memory (working memory or stored to disk, in an electronic system), or it can be individual facts and memories that are stored in a person's brain. What we are talking about, naturally in relation to the Grid, is the binary, machine-readable information that is the storage for human-readable information. Although there are often distinctions made between plaintext ASCII files and what is considered to be data files, both are stored as binary bits and bytes at the machine level, and are therefore both within the conceptual realm of what we are talking about. These distinctions blur even further when database management systems and their files enter the equation and the amount of information and data that has to be maintained with integrity expands.

Data integrity can be compromised in a number of ways.

One of the most common is simply human error when the data is entered. This is the garbage in, garbage out scenario. Controlling this type of integrity can come down to the interfaces that are created through which users can add or alter data. Another alternative is to add constraints to the database and the data tables to ensure that only appropriate data is entered (data types defined at the column level, check constraints to ensure that only valid values are entered if there are a finite number of values that a column can take, or referential integrity). Often, controlling human error is considered to be idiot proofing the data.

Errors occur when data is transmitted from one computer to another. Sometimes these errors are introduced accidentally; other times the error introduction is deliberate. The deliberate introduction of errors can be controlled in the manners that we have already discussed. Accidental introduction can occur during the transmission, through attenuation, impulse noise, cross talk, jitter, and delay distortion. Details of these different error-introducing situations follow.

Attenuation

Attenuation is the weakening of the transmitted signal over increasing distances. Attenuation occurs in both analog (voice over phone lines) and digital (data over whatever transmission media) signals, and the loss of signal is expressed in either units of decibels or voltage loss per unit of distance (this distance is dependent on the media over which the signal travels). The lower the attenuation amount, the greater the efficiency of the media (fiber optics are more efficient than twister pair phone lines). Repeaters can be used to reboost the signal to allow it to travel with less attenuation over far greater distances.

Impulse Noise

Noise, or undesired disturbances within the frequency band of interest (the band through which the signal you are concerned with is traveling), consists of random occurrences of energy spikes caused by a short surge of electrical, magnetic, or electromagnetic energy, each spike having random amplitude and spectral content. Noise in data transmission is considered to be the random variations of one or more of the characteristics of any entity such as voltage, current, or data, amplitude or frequency.

Cross Talk

Cross talk is the disturbance along a circuit, caused by electromagnetic interference. This occurs when one signal disrupts a signal in an adjacent circuit, causing one or both of the signals to become confused and cross over each other. In a telephone circuit, the phenomenon of cross talk can result in your hearing part of a voice conversation from another circuit. It can occur in microcircuits within computers and audio equipment, as well as within network circuits. The term is also applied to optical signals that interfere with each other (a much bigger problem before the advent of cable and satellite TV). Shielding the different circuits from each other and separating them with distance are both effective ways of controlling cross talk.

Jitter

Jitter, at its most basic definition, is distortion or variation in the timing of a signal caused by poor synchronization. The different kinds of jitter are detailed in the following two sections.

Phase Jitter

Phase jitter is the unintended phase modulation of a primary signal by one or more other signals somewhere through the transmission process. Phase jitter is expressed in degrees relating to the peak-to-peak deviation over the specified frequency ranges. When jitter becomes excessive, it can cause errors and result in the need for data recovery. Jitter measurements are typically made in conjunction with noise measurements, because noise and jitter can have a high impact on one another. Phase jitter may be transient or periodic in nature and may be caused by noise in the transmission media.

Amplitude Jitter

Amplitude jitter is the measure of incidental amplitude modulation of the transmitted holding tone. It can be caused by many of the same sources as phase jitter, and can be caused indirectly by attenuation distortion and envelope delay. Amplitude jitter can be caused from phase jitter, and vice versa. Noise can also have a deleterious effect on amplitude jitter measurements. Because there are several possible contributors to this situation, it is often necessary to measure for these parameters as well to determine the true cause of the impairment. Amplitude jitter is evaluated over the same frequency ranges as phase jitter, and is expressed in percentages.

Delay Distortion

Delay distortion describes a condition where various frequency components of a transmitted signal exhibit different propagation delays, with the greatest delays occurring near the upper and lower limits of the circuit band due to reactance. Reactance is the property of resisting or impeding the flow of a current.

Delay distortion is the difference in delay between the frequency that is being tested and a reference frequency near the center of the circuit band, which is the point of minimum delay. When delays between various frequency components of the data transmission become great enough, interference can result and is expressed in microseconds.

Software bugs and viruses are other causes of disruption in data integrity. Software bugs can cause corrupt data or invalid data. A program may not take into account the fact that leap years will occasionally end on a Sunday, causing a month-end closing to not be able to occur on an appropriate schedule. That can cause reports to be incorrect because of the timing of the recognition of revenues.

But the corruption can be far worse. Bugs have been the cause of data becoming invalid and unreadable as well. Viruses are also the cause of data integrity issues. Viruses have become more of a means of flooding servers with mail volume in recent years than being truly destructive, as they have been historically, but this trend may not continue. Destructive and invasive viruses can be the cause of extreme corruption in a good scenario and devastation in others.

Hardware malfunction can be another place where data integrity issues can be seen. Disks crash, controllers go bad, and other hardware components can cause corruption. Hardware redundancy can help with this.

Natural disasters, such as fires, floods, tornadoes, and hurricanes, can also have a devastating effect on data integrity. Not only can disasters cause outages, but they can also affect the power that is available to the network. Floods can cause damage to computer components. Fire can destroy components beyond repair and beyond recovery. Disaster recovery practices, and practices that have been performed and found adequate, can assist in the mitigation of the damages caused by these disasters.

Capability Resource Management

Capability is all about access.

Preventing access means making sure that person A can neither access nor damage person B's data or resources. John should not be able to read Mary's medical records, for example, unless John has both a valid reason to do so and has been given the authority to do so. If John can access those records, he should definitely not be able to alter or delete them because he is not the owner of them.

Limiting access to information means that you are working to ensure that an individual or a program cannot do more than you intend it to do. Limiting infers that authority has been granted to access both the system and the given information. This is something that is often seen as concerning spyware, pop-ups, and viruses, limiting what those programs that have not been authorized to access your computer are able to do. However, a program that is not intended to access all of the records in a database may also be considered to need limited authority and access, and an inadvertent faxing of medical information to the wrong individuals because of a computer restoration glitch may also be considered to need limiting factors assigned.

Granting access means that a user or an administrator wants to allow another user or another group of users the ability to work together on a project, a particular file, or set of files. You may need the ability to be selective in who can work on the given files or what access rights each user has on that resource. Jill can read, Bill can read and write, Armand can read, write, and execute.

Revoking access is undoing the granting of access; when the group is done working on the project, you can take away the access for them to read, alter, and update the files that the group had previously been working on. If someone attempts to overstep his authority, you can revoke that authority from him.

The term *capability* was first introduced in computing by Dennis and Van Horn in 1966 in a paper that entitled "Programming Semantics for Multiprogrammed Computations," wherein they suggested that we can design computer systems in such a way that to access any given object or resource, a program or a user must have a special token. The token is used as a means to designate a particular program or user as being able to have certain rights on a given resource or object. The token gives an accessing program the authority to perform a certain specific set of actions (read or write or update) on that object. This token is known as a capability.

The capabilities of a system can be compared to the keys on a typical person's key ring. The car key has the purpose of providing access to one specific car; the actions that you can perform on that car are the capabilities on that car (opening the doors, opening the trunk, starting the car). However, there are other keys on the ring. The house key's purpose is to open the door on one specific house; the mailbox key is the means by which you can open a single specific mailbox. The keys do not care who has them or their ring. If your neighbor wants you to water his plants while he is out of town, he hands you his key (delegates his authority for you to access his house). Car keys often are either the primary key or the valet key, or a door key and an ignition key. The valet key can start the car and unlock the door, but cannot lock or unlock the glove box, a real-world scenario of how two capabilities can be designated for the same object (in this example a car, but in a computing scenario, particularly the Grid example, two capabilities can be designated for the same computing resource), but allow (authorize) different actions to be taken on that object. Just as with keys, capabilities can be copied. If my neighbor gives me his key to water his plants, there is nothing to stop me from taking that key to the local hardware store and making duplicates. Because my neighbor would not have given me his keys if he did not trust me, the likelihood of my making these copies is small. If I were to prove untrustworthy, he could change all of the locks connected to that key, thus making all of the keys useless (in the case of capabilities, this can be done by revoking or rescinding capabilities). What is more is that you can go further than simply copying the capabilities; you can make variants of the initial capability accomplished through the copy.

Figure 4.2 shows an example of what is becoming known as capability-based resource management. The term *resource* refers to software, servers, network segments, or circuits; a *client* is any human or computer or other component or data packet being sent through the network; *condition* is the specification under which the resource may be used. *Capability* is the rules associated with the client determining that client's prerogatives, the description of the rights that user holds, and under what condition a resource may be used by that client.

In a capability-based computer system, a system that can have significant ramifications on a Grid system, all access to all objects in the system is accomplished through capabilities. Capabilities provide the *only* means a client has of accessing the system's objects. Every program holds a set of capabilities, its set of keys to the system. If program A has been given the capability to talk to program B, then these two programs can grant their capabilities to each other (to water the plants, for example). In most capability systems, a program can (although it may not be practical to do so) have an infinite number of capabilities. Systems that have programs

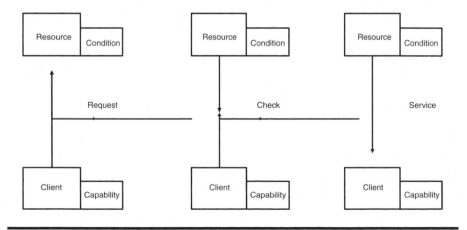

Figure 4.2   Capability system.

with large numbers of capabilities often tend to be slow. A better design idea allows each program to hold only a fixed small number of capabilities (usually less than 50), but allows for there to be a means for storing additional capabilities if they are needed. Capabilities have to be granted. Because the optimum goal is to make the set of capabilities that is held by each program as specific and as small as possible, not only to optimize performance, but also so that a program cannot abuse the authority it does not have, and so that it cannot pass on, unintentionally, this authority to other programs that it can communicate to, the system uses the premise that is known as the principle of least privilege.

Capabilities are often implemented using ACLs, or a special file contains all programs and the users allowed to run those programs. By virtue of the operating system's security mechanisms, the programs running under the authority of the user can access those files to which the user running the program has access, but the programs themselves have the authority to do anything; the user under whom it runs is the limiting factor.

Capability systems have historically not been adopted with widespread acceptance, in part because of the fact that early capability systems were built into the hardware before we knew a lot about hardware architecture, and used capabilities for access to main memory (memory is an object, and any and all access to an object is accomplished through the capabilities). This made them prohibitively slow and often incredibly complex. Even though, with today's more open and flexible operating systems, capability is considerably less complex and more efficient than it used to be, the bad reputation often remains. But in a Grid system, it may be an optimum solution to a new problem.

Database Security

Okay, so we have the different ways to secure a network and the different encryption methods that can be used to implement the security, but what about securing the data and the databases and the files that can be accessed along with the databases. This is particularly relevant because this is a book about databases.

Inference

Databases are typically designed to promote the open and flexible access to data. This design feature is particularly useful for end users who are not usually highly technical people, yet require the ability to access the data, often real-time, with tools that allow them almost direct access to the structures. This is also one of the things that make databases particularly susceptible to less than honorable activity.

One of the design decisions that many database administrators and designers make is to name things so that they are able to be logically accessed by end users through a query tool without the need to map information through an external means, or making the users find their own means to remember what data is stored in what table. This usually means naming a table for the grouping of data that is stored in it, and naming columns within the table logically as well. Ordinarily, this is a design decision that works well, for the end users and the programmers that are accessing the data. Unfortunately, it can also work very well for someone searching through your system for information that he should not have access to.

This problem, from a security perspective, is known as inference. Inference means that someone can piece together, or infer information at one level of security, and use that information to determine a fact that should be protected by a higher security level.

If you look at Table 4.2 to Table 4.4, you can see the contents of a health insurance claim table, the claimant table to go along with the claims, and the diagnosis table to go along with the claims, respectively. It does not take much work to infer that Joe W. Smith has been diagnosed with tuberculosis and that Bill Jones has been diagnosed with hepatitis A.

With current laws governing what information can be freely available, or even less than freely available, the ability to make these kinds of inferences is not a good thing.

Database security can be looked at from four different perspectives: server security, database connections, table access control, and database access control.

Table 4.2   Claim Table

Claim Number	Claimant SSN	Claim Date
12345	111111111	2/29/2004
13456	111111111	3/2/2004
14567	222222222	6/2/2003
15678	333333333	5/5/1998
16789	222222222	4/24/1985
17890	555555555	7/27/2004

Table 4.3 Claimant Table

Claimant SSN	Claimant Last Name	Claimant First Name	Claimant Middle Initial	Claimant Street Address 1	Claimant Street Address 2	Claimant Zip Code	Phone
111111111	Smith	Joe	W	123 Any Street	Apartment 23	79124	8005551212
222222222	Jones	William	J	321 Leftmost Road		16127	8885551212

Table 4.4   Diagnosis Table

Claim Number	Physician Number	Appt. Date	Diagnosis	X-Ray bfile	Test Results bfiles	Physician Notes bfile
12345	123098	3/2/2004	Tuberculosis		Blood work results 12345	Notes 12345
14567	9870654	6/13/2003	Hepatitis A		Test results 14567	Notes 14567

Server Security

Server security deals with physically limiting access to the database server itself. This is one of the most important security issues for both external threats and internal accidents. Therefore, it must be one of the most carefully planned and earliest dealt with aspects of the security setup. Basically, the idea behind server security is that what you cannot see, you cannot access, or you cannot know that you might want to access. This is one of the primary issues with inference. If you can see what might be there, you are more apt to try to see what you can find.

What about internally? Many people in the company know that the financial database resides on the UNIX box and is in Oracle, the HR system resides on a Windows server in the SQL Server, the purchasing system resides partly in the Information Management System (IMS) on the mainframe and partly on DB2 on the mainframe, and the client data resides in several different databases on different platforms and servers, but is all accessed via a Web interface with the Web server sitting on a Linux platform. One person with incorrect access or one person with just enough access and a little too much time and creativity could find information that is inappropriate for that person's position.

One premise of server access is the premise of least privilege. The principle of least privilege has been seen as important for meeting integrity objectives. A person, any person, should be given exactly the amount of privilege that is necessary to perform a job. This means that administrators need to identify exactly what that user's job is, and determine the minimum set of privileges that are required to perform that job. Restriction of the user to a domain with exactly those privileges and nothing more is critical. In this way, denied privileges cannot be used to circumvent organizational security policy, even in boredom or inadvertently.

The principal of least privilege is applicable not only to internal users, but also to people who are permitted to access the server from the outside.

Only trusted IP addresses should be able to access the database server (or any other servers, for that matter). If only trusted IP addresses can access the servers and users access the information through an interface, the least privilege principle is upheld and only servers can access your database server — not end users directly.

Database Connections

Unauthorized database connections are another place where caution needs to be taken. With many of the Grid interfaces taking place via an Internet or intranet site, you need to ensure that you validate all updates to the database to ascertain that they are warranted, and furthermore, you need to make sure that with dynamic SQL you are removing any possible SQL that may get bedded from a user within the interface.

This also extends to allowing everyone to use the same user ID to access the database. Although it is true that this makes for easier administration, it is also true that it is less likely that you will be able to discover what has happened if something should happen to a database or the data within, and it makes it much easier for someone to accidentally come upon the user ID that has the access required to do something if that usage is spread across several different user IDs. What is more important is that you look very carefully at exactly what rights and privileges the user that is connecting needs to have; it is better to have 20 different user IDs over 10 if you can divide the security requirements. Tend to those who have read access and tend to those users who need the ability to update, insert, or delete information.

Table Access Control

Again, following the principle of least privilege, table access needs to be restricted to only that access that is needed to perform the job. If a person needs to update a table, then that is exactly the level of access that he should have. If, however, a user only needs to retrieve data from a table or set of tables, he should have only read access to the information. Although it is much easier to simply grant everything to anyone, or (worse) allow everyone to log in as the same user — the owner of the tables and objects — this poses not only security hazards, but is asking for trouble. Allowing these collections can lead to dropped objects and altered definitions on the objects. Any set of tables or any system should have three different classes of people: the owner of the tables and other objects (this user should be the owner and the only one who is able to alter the physical definitions for the objects, and access to this user should be closely guarded); an update class or role (this class of user is one who can insert information and update information in the tables); and a read-only user who can query the tables and alter nothing. There can be a derivation in the update user. There may be some situations where you have users that should be allowed to update information that is already in the table, and another person who can insert new information into the table. Although it will add another layer of complexity to the user administration in the database, it is better in the long run for security purposes to allow for the added complexity.

Further, columns within the table may contain information that only certain people should be able to see, and others be kept unaware of. If all access to the information is strictly limited through an application interface, the interface can provide a lot of security to this end. Based on log-in or IP or other criteria, certain selective information can be kept from being seen by the wrong people, and in fact, a programmer could keep those users who should not know about the data from even knowing of its existence. However, it is difficult to limit access through an interface, especially when many users may be given a tool like Business Objects or Oracle Discoverer or other graphical user interface (GUI) through which they can select tables and columns and provide limiting criteria to bring back the data that they are looking for. If their access is not limited at either the tool level or the report level within the tool, it has to be limited at the database or schema level by the administrator.

By way of an example, it may be necessary for a user to be able to see all of the employee information except that employee's salary and commission amount. Table 4.5 shows what might exist in a salary table and Table 4.6 the lookup table for the employee information that is associated with that salary information. A simple join on just the employee table with the salary table would yield entirely more information than that user should be able to see. In this case, it becomes necessary, either programmatically or through views or other mechanisms within the database, to limit that particular class of user to the ability to see only the information that is necessary and to not have access or (if possible) to be ignorant of the columns to which they do not have access. They may, for example, see a somewhat less informative salary table (or an aliased version of the salary table so even the table's purpose is hidden), as in Table 4.7.

There is still another consideration when looking at access to tables and the information in the tables. With more and more data being stored, the database and tables are getting bigger and bigger, particularly with the application service provider model. If the data from many different end users and many different user companies is stored together in the same tables, it is important to be able to limit access to the data to only

Table 4.5 Salary Table

Client_ID	Employee_SSN	Employee_Type	Employee_Salary	Employee_Commission	Employee_ID
a74235	777777777	Hourly	18	0.1	434343
a45902	888888888	Salary	29,000		876542
b34562	999999999	Salary	36,000		234567
b74235	999999999	Hourly	9.75	0.25	123456
a43094	111111111	Manager	85,000		989898
a74235	900000000	Hourly	18	0.1	242424
a74235	800000000	Salary	42,000		131313
b34562	700000000	Salary	36,000		111222
b34562	600000000	Hourly	36		222334
b34562	500000000	Consulting	56		444665

Table 4.6   Employee Table

Employee_SSN	Employee_FName	Employee_LName
999999999	Jones	Robert
888888888	Smith	Jane
777777777	Hamilton	David
999999999	Jones	Robert
111111111	Davis	Elizabeth
900000000	Neff	Estella
800000000	Westerfield	Louise
700000000	Roa	Glenda
600000000	Smithfield	William
500000000	Weltland	Michael

Table 4.7   Limited Version of Salary Table

Client_ID	Employee_SSN	Employee_Type	Employee_ID
a43094	111111111	Manager	989898
a45902	888888888	Salary	876542
a74235	777777777	Hourly	434343
a74235	900000000	Hourly	242424
a74235	800000000	Salary	131313
b74235	999999999	Hourly	123456
b34562	999999999	Salary	234567
b34562	700000000	Salary	111222
b34562	600000000	Hourly	222334
b34562	500000000	Consulting	444665

that data that is applicable to the end user. This is true for a read-only user as well as for those able to insert and update and delete information. Different database management systems provide different means to accomplish this.

Again, by way of an example, drawing upon the information Table 4.5, you can see in both Table 4.8 and Table 4.9 that the information in the same table can be seen as if it existed in two different tables based on who is accessing the information. In this way, you can create a virtually

Table 4.8 Salary Table Limited to One Client ID

Client_ID	Employee_SSN	Employee_Type	Employee_Salary	Employee_Commission	Employee_ID
b34562	999999999	Salary	36,000		234567
b34562	700000000	Salary	36,000		111222
b34562	600000000	Hourly	36		222334
b34562	500000000	Consulting	56		444665

Table 4.9 Salary Table as Seen by Another Client

Client_ID	Employee_SSN	Employee_Type	Employee_Salary	Employee_Commission	Employee_ID
a74235	999999999	Hourly	18	0.1	434343
a74235	900000000	Hourly	18	0.1	242424
a74235	800000000	Salary	42,000		131313

private database for each of the users logging on, allowing for ease of maintenance and administration for the hosting company. In this way, a database accessible from the Grid will likely need to be created for ease of access and security at the data level.

Restricting Database Access

Because a database does not exist in a vacuum, and rarely without the supporting access of a network, it is important to look at the network access of the database system. Although this has been primarily looked at through the eyes of being accessed through the Internet or through an intranet, similar ideas need to be looked at for a database that is going to be accessed via a Grid interface.

Because it is usually important to restrict most access to the database to that accomplished through an interface, and to make sure that any access is through verified locations, steps need to be taken to ensure this level of security. There are many ways to prevent open access from the network, regardless of the size and complexity of the network, and every database management system has its own set of unique features, as does each operating system on which each database management system resides. What follows are some of the most common methods:

- *Trusted IP addresses* — UNIX servers are typically configured to answer only those pings that originate from a list of trusted hosts. This is usually accomplished by configuring the contents of the host's file (a file whose purpose is to restrict server access to only a list of specific users).
- *Server account disabling* — Causing a log-in ID to be locked after three failed password attempts, attackers will be thwarted. Without this simple security feature being enabled, anyone could run a password generation program, a program that generates millions of passwords until it guesses the given user ID password combination.
- *Special tools* — Products exist that will alert system administration when they detect what they perceive as an external server attempting to breach the given system's security.
- *Kerberos security* — Kerberos is a network authentication protocol designed to provide strong authentication for client–server applications by using secret key cryptography. Kerberos, named after the three-headed dog, Cerberus, who guarded the passage to the underworld, is available as a free implementation from the Massachusetts Institute of Technology, as well as through many commercial products.

■ *Port access security* — Oracle, as well as other database applications, listens to a specific port number on the server. If someone is attempting to access the database over a port that the database has not been instructed to listen to, no connection will be made.

There are also differences between the ways different database management engines handle their own security. Your database user query stores and analyzes many millions of rows of information, ranging from information that is safely public to data that needs to be kept extremely private. Database administrators (DBAs) grant and restrict access appropriately. However, the database management system (DBMS) must also offer ways to keep unauthorized users from accessing classified data.

DBMS Specific

Every DBMS has its own methods of implementing various levels of security. It is important for the database administrator to work with the rest of a security team in implementing the database-specific features that allow each database to limit within itself what each user can do. It is important that those administrators know what the security features are and how to effectively implement those features in a widespread system.

Chapter 5

The Hardware

If it draws blood, it's hardware.

—Author unknown

Typically, when you think about the Grid, what you most naturally start thinking about is, quite naturally, the hardware. After all, nearly anyone that you ask will assure you that the Grid is all about sharing hardware resources, scavenging for CPU cycles, and making the most efficient use of the hardware resources at an organization's disposal. But exactly what hardware are we talking about?

Computers

One of the most interesting things about computers and the Grid is the fact that nearly any computer, nearly any operating system, can quickly and easily be connected to the Grid and become a Grid server, a Grid member. Because of the nature of the Grid and the fact that as an operating paradigm, it works well with heterogeneous hardware and operating systems, it is flexible enough to adapt easily to having mainframe components along with Intel-based Linux machines, midrange open systems, and Windows servers as components to the environment.

There are systems of supercomputers linked together into an extremely high-performance Grid system; there are computer labs at colleges and universities where the computers in their downtime are linked together through the network and CPU resources are scavenged and used to perform scientific computations. Entire organizations can utilize the same or similar concepts. Every computer in the organization could have their CPUs accessed in off hours to assist in performing the daily batch processing. Think this is stretching it? Think of your own office. How many computers are there in your office? How taxed do you think they are, even when they are at their busiest, 10 percent on average, even 50 percent for the busiest administrator or programmer? Although the hard drives are always getting bigger and faster, it is still surprising how much computing power there is sitting on the typical desktop of an employee today. If you want to give your PC something taxing to do, recalculate the values in the spreadsheet, spell check a word document, or retrieve information from a database. It is unlikely, even if you do all of these at once, that you are going to push the limits of what the common desktop computer is capable of. They basically sit around doing very little, waiting for some important job to come along. Now consider what these computers are doing when you go home at night. I do not know about the regulations at your company, but even the computers that get logged off of at night are left turned on so that software updates can be pushed out over the network. But realistically, how often is the software updated? Once a month? Weekly virus scan updates? Now consider how many companies do batch processing overnight because the network is less busy and online customers are not as active? How many companies base their IT budget on being able to scale their systems so that they can take advantage of the computing power during the day, when online customers are hitting the system hard (but in transactional mode, that is not a heavy CPU hitter, typically), and buy capacity so that they can make sure that the batch processing that occurs overnight can successfully finish during the batch window they have. What would happen if these companies were able to take advantage of the CPU power sitting idle on the desktops of all the employees to assist with the batch processing?

Many companies see CPU loads looking something like Figure 5.1 during a day, or like Figure 5.2 during a month. There is considerably more processing done on the server in Figure 5.2 at the beginning of the month, when the company closes its book in accounting, and the processing load falls off considerably after that. Historically, the company would need to buy enough computing power to meet the needs of 90 plus percent CPU usage. The excess capacity would go unused the majority of the day. But if the company did not have the CPU power at the point where it was needed, batch processing would suffer and the company would probably miss its batch window. Now consider, if this same company were to scavenge the network for CPU power during the hours

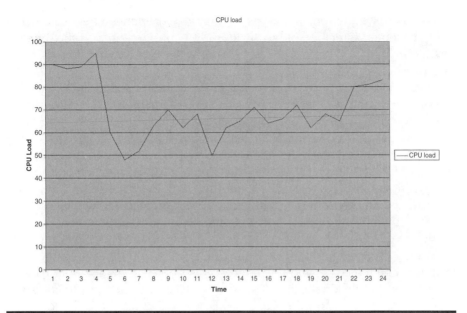

Figure 5.1 **Variation in CPU load over a 24-hour period.**

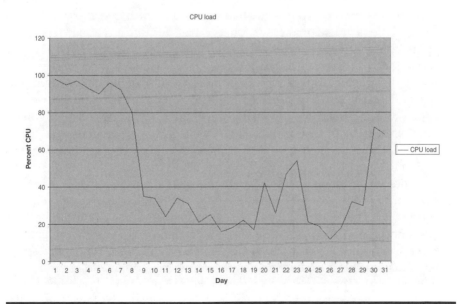

Figure 5.2 **Variation in CPU load over a 31-day period.**

where it was experiencing or expecting to experience the peak batch load, it would better be able to scale its CPU budget back to the average load, roughly just over 70 percent, and make use of the company's other freed resources during off hours.

It gets better. What happens if this picture is not for today's goal, but for processing at month's end? What if this picture is only applicable for one week of the month? Scaling an entire corporation's CPU usage and computing budget for something that happens at most 25 percent of the time and allowing that CPU to go effactually unused for the other 75 percent of the time simply so that the company does not run short during the month-end close is overkill. Think these numbers are out of line? Grid computing can increase the company's computing power while reducing its overall computing costs. Some companies have been able to cut their hardware purchases by nearly 90 percent by accessing existing computing power laying dormant at 10 percent of the cost of building out of a more traditional architecture, and the ability to distribute processing in a parallel processing architecture can also assist with cutting costs by cutting the time it takes to perform the calculations, even cutting times for jobs that once took 18 hours to just over half an hour.

Purchasing computing power so that there are resources available for the times when the company has peaks in CPU usage is what is known as peak provisioning, meaning that the company is forced not only to buy enough computing power to handle its current biggest jobs, but also to buy a little extra to make sure that it has enough, in case these jobs happen to grow. This is true even when the jobs only run occasionally.

In August 2001, the National Science Foundation announced that in the United States, its four computer centers would be linked together into one massive Grid-style virtualized computer. Then a distributed computing system was scheduled to go online in summer 2002. Scientists involved in that project said that the facility would help researchers to better understand the origins of the universe, find cures for cancer, unlock secrets of the brain, and save lives by predicting earthquakes.

A Grid environment is nothing more than several somewhat similar computers clustered loosely together. Internally, individual computers are connected through an ultrafast network and share other devices, like disk drives, printers, storage systems, and memory, with a controlling system that takes care of load balancing and sharing in computing and other processing.

One major difference between supercomputers and a Grid environment is that a Grid is primarily built from a larger number of self-contained computers, often commodity systems or blade servers that have the ability at some level to work independently of the Grid.

Intel introduced a new chipset ideal for Grid servers and workstations in late 2002. The company started shipping the new Intel Xeon processors for two-way servers and workstations with speeds up to 2.8 GHz with a 512-kb integrated cache, support for faster CPUs, and a 533-MHz front-side bus to help speed the rate at which data can get to the processor. Intel also launched an additional three chipsets. The E7501 chipset is designed for two-way servers to help improve system performance and also to be used in embedded computing. The E7505 chipset, formally named Placer, is for two ways, and the Intel E7205 chipset, formerly known as Granite, was designed for single-processor entry-level workstations and is based on the Intel Pentium 4 processor.

The National Center for Supercomputing Applications (NCSA) is using Itanium-based Linux servers to power its scientific computing system, dubbed teraGrid. This system allows researchers to analyze, simulate, and help solve complex scientific problems. The National Science Foundation announced in August 2001 that teraGrid is a computing implementation that will serve as the underpinnings for what has been called the world's first multisite supercomputing system, initially linking the National Center for Super Computing applications, the San Diego Super Computer Center, the Argonne National Laboratory, and the Center for Advanced Computing Research, and later adding the Pittsburgh Super Computer Center, Oak Ridge National Laboratory, Purdue University, Indiana University, and the Texas Advanced Computing Center. The distributed terascale facility (DTF) will provide over 10 teraflops of distributed computing power and nearly 1 petabyte of data via the comprehensive infrastructure. And all of this will be connected together through a network operating at 40 gigabits per second. IBM, Intel, and QWEST Communications add their names to the mix as just a few of the corporate partners in the project.

Coming online in January 2004, teraGrid is now providing researchers with a highly valuable tool for their repertoire.

Although it is true that the Grid that can be, and often is, made up of inexpensive commodity-style hardware, typically running on Intel-based processors, it is also true that mainframes and other large midrange systems are capable candidates for being incorporated into a Grid system. Saying that a mainframe will never be part of Grid computing is somewhat like saying that everyone will be driving Fords in every NASCAR race next year. It simply will not happen. Just like the world would not be the same without a mix of cars, Dodge, Ford, Chrysler, the Grid would not be a true Grid without multiple computing platforms, including the mainframe as a part of the lineup. Because Grid computing allows a wide array of systems to take advantage of untapped resources from across an enterprise, making them available where and when they are needed, eliminating the mainframe as a source (or sink) of data and CPU resources would not be handling corporate resources in an efficient manner. When you sit back and look at mainframes, including the new ZOS series, it only makes good business sense to include the Grid in the data center. A data center typically already has a mainframe anyway, and thinking that it is not going to leverage what it has would be a bad assumption. The center is going to optimize the computing power it has in the mainframes and optimize it to the best of its ability.

IBM is one of the companies at the Grid frontier. It has made announcements that it not only believes in the mainframe and the data center, but also believes that the Zseries servers can bring high availability and business continuity, on-demand processing power for applications, new workloads, backups, reserve capacity, and quicker deployment of Grid-based applications to the Grid infrastructure environment, primarily because the mainframe has always proven to be an ideal platform for development, testing, and application prototyping. Many business partners have also announced products aimed at delivering Grid computing capabilities to the Zseries servers. These products and components are aimed specifically at systems running on Linux as the mainframe, because many believe that mainframes are ideal for the Grid. The mainframe has historically relied on virtualization as a key concept, and as we have seen that this is also one of the key features of the Grid. The Zseries has inherent virtualization capabilities through the ZOS operating system virtualization. Further, this platform allows administrators to move workloads from one platform to another for better utilization, and allows shops to manage spikes and lulls in demand, similar to the way that the Grid automatically switches to commodity hardware of blades servers, allowing for the addition of hardware capacity on demand if the application requirements call for it. These servers along with other external Grid servers would communicate among themselves using an external Transmission Control Protocol/Internet Protocol (TCP/IP) network. The servers would actually be operating as virtual servers within the Zseries mainframe hardware.

Blade Servers

One of the new technologies that will assist more companies in being able to consider implementing a Grid environment is what is known as a blade server. Blade servers are narrow, hot, swappable CPUs, several of which can fit into the space that would have been taken up by a single chassis, all stored in a rack that looks remarkably like a bookshelf. The resulting visual effect is similar to a library. You have several of these racks, each with several blade servers attached, and each blade is an independent server with its own processors, memory, storage network controllers, operating systems, and copies of applications. The servers simply slide into the bay and plug into the backplane. The single unified backplane and chassis bring to the system shared power supplies, fans, floppy drives, CD drives, switches, and ports.

Because the blades share switches and power units, precious space is freed up in each blade. This means that the blades can be placed with a far higher density within the cabinets far more easily than has historically been possible. What is more is that because they will plug into a common backplane, you do not have the issues of hundreds of cables being strung through and around the racks.

Blades come in two varieties: server blades and option blades.

A server blade is an independent server containing one or more processors and associated memory, disk storage, and network controllers. It runs its own copy of both the operating system and all applications.

Several server blades may share a single set of option blades. Option blades provide those server blades with additional features, such as controllers for external input/output (I/O) or disk arrays and additional power supplies. Option blades are mounted inside the same racks with the shared infrastructure features. Historically, option blades would have been externally attached to server arrays. By installing option modules containing Gigabit Ethernet switches, KVM switches, or keyboard, video, mouse, and fiber channel switches, you can save sidewall space within your racks. Because blades are powered by the rack and backplane, the usual cascade of cabling used to connect each server to a power source is not required, again saving sidewall space and money.

Other types of option modules can contain systems management controllers, power supplies, advanced cooling systems, and additional redundancy and efficiency components.

Blade servers are a highly efficient solution for not only Grid, but also for adding scalability in capacity to any data center. Most blade server chassis use capacity that you add directly into a standard rack. These racks currently exist in data centers all around the world today, and can be reused for blade server storage as the more traditional server components are aged out. This means that blades can coexist alongside the existing traditional rack-mounted servers, and there is no need for special rack investments just to add the scalability of blade server chassis.

The quick, easy addition of blade servers to a potential Grid environment, as well as to the physical rack, allows for flexibility, scalability, and the freeing up of the limitations of the type of processor that you can use within the system, and the type and speed of available processors for your environment. With processors becoming faster and faster, and therefore hotter, the ability to add extra fan units by simply plugging in an option's server makes that server even more flexible and customizable.

Because they are hot swappable, if one server should fail, thereby causing processing to have to be redistributed over the other servers in the Grid, the failed server can be swapped out simply by dismounting that server from the blade rack and snapping another into its place. This means that commodity components can more reliably be used to power the availability requirements of mission-critical systems while providing cost-effective solutions for organizations.

Blade servers will allow many organizations to realize cost savings partly due to the purchase price of individual servers being significantly lower, in large part due to the reduction in the duplication of components. You will realize further savings because of the reduction in the need for KVM switches and cabling, because of the architecture's limited need for Ethernet cables, because the data center will need fewer racks to house the higher number of servers. You will save on the cost of rack systems. By far, one of the greatest overall cost savings will be the savings that an organization will see in the reduced need for those hundreds or thousands of cables currently running through and under your data center.

Further, you will not only save the installation costs and man-hour costs of unpacking the components, assembling the server installer rails, installing the servers, and reconfiguring the hierarchy of KVM and power distribution units, but also reduce the footprint and floor space required for the same amount of overall processing. Due to the increased density of blade servers, you may need only half the expensive floor space that would have been required for traditional rack-optimized servers.

You have fewer components to fail, meaning fewer components to replace in case of failure. The reduction in the number of points of potential failure means the ultimate reduction in the cost of servicing the servers should they fail. Because blades servers eliminate the need to purchase excess processors up front to provide for expansion, they enable a company to correctly size purchases, rather than upsizing them. They allow you to buy exactly what you need today for the Grid system to meet your current needs, and as your computing needs expand, you can simply plug another blade (or another dozen blades) into the server rack. This will allow you to spread the cost of capital expenditures over time.

Many companies today are starting to provide blade servers, such as IBM, Sun, and HP. Even Apple is starting to enter the blade server arena. Many companies that are starting to provide Grid solutions to companies (Sun, IBM) are providing blade servers as part of the total solution package.

Storage

Because to a great extent the Grid implies separating the storage from memory, and both from I/O, another component that needs to be addressed in the hardware realm is storage. Because of the component nature of blade servers, often people make the choice to only put an operating system, or only the operating system and the minimal application code, on the blades for emergency purposes. Others may simply opt to buy diskless blades. With diskless blades, you simply point to a blade server at the logical unit number (LUN) on an array and that blade assumes the personality of whatever operating system (OS) is running on that disk array. The operating system boots off of the array and picks up the applications and personality of that array and the application. This not only is true for blades servers, but also can be applicable for traditional servers.

Current storage architecture will need to evolve and adapt to the concept of virtualization. Storage virtualization allows for separation of the on-disk physical storage from the logical view of that storage, just as it would be seen had it actually been the server's physical storage. This virtualized storage could reside anywhere within the company's storage network and could be from any vendor. Although the virtualization layer provides a logical view of all storage connected to it, even individual storage systems would no longer remain separate and distinct, but rather would be pooled into a single reservoir of capacity. This allows the description of storage needs in terms of simple capacity, response time, cost, and backup frequency, as well as allows administrators to make the best possible use of resources by disbursing that storage capacity to only where and when it is needed. One would no longer have to worry about where something is located, only what that something is called. This is true, be it a file or information stored in a local, federated, or distributed database. Consider the fact that, with a Grid, data is ordinarily moved between servers over Ethernet, the date is taken off the disk and sent to the server, and often off to another server or several other servers, and back to yet another disk array. It would be more efficient if a storage area network (SAN) could self-provision itself, creating a zone of specific Grid applications for specific time.

Storage virtualization is not a new concept; it has been around for decades on the mainframe, back when IBM transitioned its mainframes from System/360 to System/370, in the late 1960s, and nearly every storage vendor claims to be able to offer virtualization at least across some of its products. Virtualization creates a single view of multiple storage devices and can simplify (and thus lower the cost of) storage management. What is more is that storage virtualization can reduce the number of new arrays the company needs to buy by combining the data from multiple servers for applications into a single shared poll of storage. It provides an alternative to buying more storage for one overtaxed server while huge amounts of disk space sit empty on servers beside it. However, because of the proprietary nature of the way much of the storage virtualization is created, it is important to remember that in many cases, a vendor's virtualization offerings work only for its hardware. Most organizations own storage hardware from many vendors, and that storage is accessed by hardware servers from many other vendors.

Some virtualization works only at the file level, with the storage and retrieval of information as files, while other servers' virtualization works best at the level of blocks (the smallest form in which data can be stored and retrieved from these devices). It is important to remember that virtualization should not be seen as a product feature of its own, but as an enabling technology that will allow the users, system administrators, and programmers alike to solve business problems.

Because of the heterogeneous nature of the Grid and Grid computing, companies will likely want the flexibility to move data among servers, each server running a different operating system. These companies will likely opt for fabric-based virtualization, in which the intelligence needed to reformat the data as needed is built into switches linking the storage devices.

What is more is that fabric-based virtualization (or the more trendy buzz phrase, fabric-based intelligence) vision is not limited simply to the management of applications, allowing them to find new homes; it also provides different types of administrators with their own views of data and varying levels and different views of storage infrastructure. Database administrators can view and manage the logical structure of the database and its data constructs on the same system that storage administrators view and manage the underlying resources, all through the same portal.

It also may become apparent that storage systems will need to become truly open equipment, much the way that Linux is an open operating system. These open-hardware system standards will be able to be acquired from multiple vendors and not only sit side by side with, but interoperate internally with, one another. There will have to be server and software compatibility and the ability of different server storage arrays to share information, all with centralized management functions. Administrators have been unable to integrate networks into a true heterogeneous patchwork of technology partly because storage devices have been unable to share their information with one another. This has had the effect of a conglomeration of isolated data islands.

It is, in effect, networking as it would be if a network were a supermarket chain that kept its different departments in different stores in different parts of town and each department spoke its own language. If you want bread, you go to the southeast store and speak French. If you want dairy, you go to the northeast store and speak Mandarin. Fresh fruits and vegetables are available at the downtown center, where English is spoken, and meat and poultry in the upper east side, where Hindi is spoken. The ability to centralize components becomes paramount in allowing heterogeneous servers to access required data on equally heterogeneous storage devices.

It all comes down to the Grid requiring its underlying infrastructure to play nicely together and to become one big happy family the way that its software components do.

Again, storage virtualization is not really anything new with the Grid. It has been done for decades on mainframes. Nearly every storage vendor claims that it is offering virtualization across its products, or at least some of its products. By creating a single unified view of multiple storage devices, virtualization can not only simplify, but also lower the cost of storage. Administrators just have to remember to check and double-check that the interoperability is supported on whatever product is ultimately chosen.

Grid is by design a highly I/O-intensive system, typically with inordinately large demands, such as satellite data processing, seismographic data analysis, data warehousing, and data mining. The fact that researchers of many venues are increasingly relying on scalable computing architectures for their requirements means that it is becoming critical that a wide range of scalable computer architectures form an infinite virtual cluster of workstations to provide sufficient support for these I/O-intensive applications

I/O Subsystems

The required communication between different processors has traditionally been a bottleneck for applications and related data elements that are distributed across a network. If we consider how distributed the Grid system could become, this bottleneck could easily become a preventative feature. Scalable computers and CPU sources are becoming more and more available and less and less expensive, meaning that it may well be that in the very near future, the I/O subsystem will become the bottleneck in the equation, moving rather than removing it from the process.

Because of the continuing improvement to high-speed interconnects such as Asynchronous Transfer Mode (ATM), Fiber Channel, and other high-speed technologies, these preventative bottlenecks will become less of an issue.

Underlying Network

There are intelligent switches that utilize externally defined policies to make the decisions of when and how to establish connections between two servers, storage arrays, and other networking resources as they are required by each application. These switches shuffle application images from the storage array to the server, and then link each server with the necessary amount of storage and network bandwidth. By automating the processes involved with resource connection, these switches can help remove many of the more tedious aspects of application provisioning.

Historically, database vendors have often tried to work closely with switch vendors to help them bring their expertise to the table and enable the ability to form scalable database clusters across the network. This cooperation is a good starting place, but it needs to expand and continue to fill the available void of cooperation that has typified open systems and the Grid, as its beginnings have proven.

Operating Systems

Table 5.1 shows a representation of what platform–operating system combinations are supported by the Cactus project's development product. More information on the combinations is available at http://www.cactus-code.org/Documentation/Architectures.html. Although different compilers are suggested as being supported, the number of operating systems and compiler and hardware platforms that are actually supportable are nearly endless, with just a few lines of code changes.

In keeping with the ideals of open systems and open sources, many Grids are operating on versions of the Linux operating system with Globus middleware.

Visualization Environments

Modern visualization environments can allow those users involved to go much farther than simply viewing static data. These environments can allow them to interact with the data in dynamic and flexible user-controlled

Table 5.1   Representation of OS Combinations Supported by Cactus

Compaq Alpha Linux	Intel IA32/IA64 Linux	Cray T3E
Compaq Alpha OSF	Intel IA32 Windows 2000/NT	IBM SP
Mac OS X	Mac Linux	Fujitsu
Sun Sparc	SGI 32/64 bit	OpenBSD
	Hitachi SR8000-F1	

environments, which are becoming a reality in a lot of areas. The days when users were happy with text-based interfaces and lists of data are quickly fading, being forced into history by the requirements of science, research, and business communities. There are now different needs, changing every day it seems, to see different data at different levels by different sets of users. Virtualization is an attempt to meet these needs. Some may prefer to see their information at a broad overview level. Others have the need to filter the data and see more detail. Who knows what the needs will be in the future?

Scientific visualization has had a tremendous impact on how science has been practiced in recent years, concentrating and making the best use of the human power of visual perception to work toward the identification of patterns found in complex data. Research is now being done to find ways to improve how science education is accomplished, in ways similar to how this visualization is being done in research. These environments are currently and will continue to be accessed by many of the high-capacity Grid environments to take advantage of the underlying computing power and provide a deeper and richer environment in which these experiences can be realized.

People

If we consider the quote at the beginning of the chapter, "If it draws blood, it's hardware," then people can easily fall into the category of Grid hardware. Scientists, engineers, researchers, computer programmers, teachers, business leaders, subject matter experts (SMEs), people from many different parts of society are all working together and in parallel toward defining the Grid, its potential infrastructure, and its emerging standards. The interdisciplinary approach is extremely beneficial, because with cross-cultural input, it will become something that everyone will not only be able to take advantage of, but also be comfortable enough with the concepts of to accept more readily the changes that it brings. If we look at how the Internet has impacted the lives of kindergarten students, grandparents, researchers, and game players, and then we consider that the Grid is being looked at as the next great leap in computing, it will likely not only lead to tremendous leaps in research outcomes, but also impact the lives of everyone by providing new ways of doing everything in the coming decades.

Chapter 6

Metadata

I find that a great part of the information I have was acquired by looking up something and finding something else on the way.

—Franklin P. Adams

I'm not dumb. I just have a command of thoroughly useless information.

—Calvin, of Calvin and Hobbes

If we look at the Grid as a loosely coupled set of interfaces (both for humans and for applications), application logic, and resources (databases, devices, computational resources, remote instrumentation, and human capital and knowledge), metadata can be thought of as the glue that holds them all together. The glue is easier to apply if all of the pieces are resident inside of the organization, but if some of them are located outside of the control structure, additional information is needed for the glue to do its work.

Metadata is what is commonly known as data about the data, or information about the data. But this information is intended not necessarily for human consumption, but rather to be used primarily by the machines. Metadata can be used by search engines and can give you a place to record what a document is for and about.

Typically, metadata is considered to be critical in connection with data warehouses. In that context, it provides information relevant to the data as it is used in the system to which it is connected in the industry in question. If we follow through with the insurance industry example, metadata about claim numbers might include any idiosyncrasies that are connected with the assignment of numbers to claims based on claim type, region of the country, status in the process, the claimant, and the number of claims reported by the particular claimant. Any and all of these pieces of information would be data about the data.

A metadata service can provide the means for publishing, replicating, and accessing the metadata.

The Grid, by definition, is computationally and data intensive; therefore, metadata is absolutely necessary not only to the management of the data, but also to the management of the Grid itself. Metadata at the Grid environment level, unlike metadata at either the database or data at a warehouse level, where it's simply information about information, can take many forms and many types. Some of the important pieces of information connected with the Grid will be connected to the computational resources, including computers and storage devices; data to be accessed, such as databases, plain files, semistructured documents, and other structured or unstructured data sources; tools that are available; algorithms that will be used to extract, filter, mine, and manipulate the data, and visualize, store, and manipulate data to a further extent; and knowledge that has been obtained as a result of computing processes, for example, learned models or patterns. Large sets of resources often require complex descriptions to describe the resources, to describe potential relationships, and to provide rich information about all aspects of these resources. Metadata should:

■ Document the features of the application
■ Allow for the effective search of existing resources
■ Provide an efficient way to access these resources
■ Be used by the assisting software tools that support the user in building computational models
■ Be easily accessible and easily updated while still being secure enough to disallow alteration by inappropriate people and processes

Highly specialized Grid services will no doubt evolve for the collection and utilization of these different types of metadata. There are, and will continue to be, mechanisms for storing and accessing the metadata. These mechanisms allow for querying of the metadata constructs based on attributes.

Scientists and business types alike strive to record information about the creation and transformations, as well as the meaning of the data, and they also demand the ability to query the data in the metadata repository based on these and other types of attributes. Historically, many methods have been used to provide this functionality, including descriptive directory names and file names that carry information embedded within the naming conventions, as well as notebooks and note cards. These diverse methods neither scale well to systems containing terabytes or petabytes of data nor necessarily work well together or have applications in heterogeneous environments. What will prove to be critical to this environment will be the extensible, reliable, high-performance services that will be able to support the registration of inquiry of metadata information.

In a data warehouse environment or in any relational database system, the metadata can reside within a separate set of tables in the target database, but would typically reside in a special metadata repository. This repository could be in a database of its own, or in a particular schema within the target database, separated from the data that it explains, but relatively easily accessible to those that need to have such access. For programmers, metadata can explain much about the data that would assist them in better programming based on the data, the meaning of the data, and the business rules that the data portrays.

The metadata in a Grid environment will need to encompass not only the data about the meaning of the data stored within the Grid, but also information about the size of files, their access permissions, ownership, and the location of the files logically within the Grid environment.

If you really consider what kind of information needs to be accessible and distributed across a Grid environment, you will see that there is an awe-inspiring amount of data that needs to be corralled, stored, and distributed between and about the different Grid components. Not only is there the data about the data to be stored, but there is information about work units and results (result sets from the work units and information about the processing and processes that took place in the work units) returning from the jobs, the machines on which jobs run, the availability of machines at any given moment in time, and the state of the system at any given time.

Naturally, there is the typical metadata — data about the data — but there is also information about the activities and jobs, tasks and projects, in fact about any and every piece of work and its associated data as it navigates through the Grid environment. For the Grid resources, there are catalogs, tables designed for looking up and determining the least taxed and most taxed resources in the Grid, and the location of resources that may be available. There needs to be information about the location of the pieces of information resident on any or all of the servers that are available to the Grid.

All this information needs to be stored either directly with the objects that are being distributed (in the form of intelligent file names or other keys directly associated with the physical data) within and through the Grid, or external to the information, independently in files or databases that are available to any and all nodes during the execution of the system. There also needs to be a mechanism for controlling the flow of information into and out of the metadata repository and further mechanisms to make that information reliably available to any requester or updater that needs it.

There is a lot of background information that needs to be stored and distributed within a Grid, and the more extensive the Grid, the more extensive the data that needs to be stored and distributed. The reason we need this information is that all of the machines within our Grid need to know what they are involved in, who they need to contact for different information, and who to talk to when something goes wrong. In short, there needs to be a centralized and distributed configuration repository.

Distributors need to know where to find providers, providers need to have information about any distributor that might be distributing information their way, and both pieces need to have a place to go to get their information for processing their respective jobs.

At the distributor end of the process, you need to be able to have a basis on which to make decisions. These decisions need to be made based on available space, CPU load on any given resource, and which storage node and storage device are available to provide or accept information from the proposed processes.

For servers that do not, or for some reason cannot, report on CPU load, those machines are assumed either unavailable or severely overtaxed and marked as such. This information is also stored for both active retrieval by the users of the Grid, for the purpose of deciding what resources to use, and historic information retrieval, to determine the reliability and predict availability of any given resource going forward.

Looking at storage devices, their available storage capacity and usage is as important a piece of information as their current load status. If there is little or no storage capacity available on a given device, it will not be practical to route a particularly large update or insertion task to that device; however, a retrieval job would be more than applicable on that resource.

What kind of information, in total, that you capture and utilize is (at least in part) dependent on the kind of Grid environment that you are going to be creating? A scavenging Grid needs different kinds of data than a data Grid does, for example.

For a computational Grid, you will need to store and access computational and parametric data that needs to be exchanged internally. A resource Grid will need application-based information, information about what applications are available, running, and have run, and the inputs, outputs, and jobs that have completed or are scheduled. Regardless of what kind you create, you will need to store information about each unit of work's history, the history about each node and component in the Grid, each and every source and destination, locations, and response times, so that the organism can learn from history and be able to funnel jobs to where they are most likely to finish efficiently.

The negotiation between the different components will be critical to the ultimate success of any Grid system. If one component cannot describe what it is looking for, it cannot have it. If an application does not know what it needs to do its processing, nothing is going to walk up and throw itself at that application. If a given resource does not understand how to tell the rest of the system what it has to offer, it will go unnoticed, unused.

If a resource cannot describe what it has to offer, no one is going to be interested in using it. The CPU cycle provider needs to be able to tell the other Grid components that it has cycles at 2.8 gigahertz available for use for the time period starting at 7 P.M. If it cannot make its product known, it will not matter who is shopping for it; they will not know where to look or how to get there.

If a resource or a process or service cannot make its wants and needs known, it will never be able to get what it wants for the price that it is willing to pay.

Information that would likely be necessary, regardless of your environment, would include the following:

- Submitter data: Information about the user submitting the task or job. This information might include, but not be limited to, name, e-mail address, physical location, billing location, phone number, etc.
- Priority data: It might be important in your environment to store different users within the Grid with the ability to schedule their jobs and tasks at different priority levels.
- Date and time information: Historically and for use in tuning and determining optimization features, it is useful to have a searchable record of when a given job was submitted, as well as the time taken to process the job and other timing information that can be attached to individual jobs, tasks, and projects.
- Transformation information: Information coming back from processing will need to either come back in the same format that it was sent or be stored in a different format; that transformation information will need to be stored if it is relevant to processing. Further, if there needs to be a transformation due to heterogeneity

in the database management systems, this information will need to be stored in the repository as well. All of this information will need to be either preprocessed and sent to the providers for further processing or recovered from the providers and then placed into a result queue for postprocessing before sending back to the requesting application.

■ Central catalog (or metadata repository): An index or catalog can be stored on a distributor server or a Grid data server. The index holds information about where data in the Grid system has been stored. The organization of this information is dependent on the type of data that you are storing and the level of heterogeneity and distribution you have existent in the data that is being stored. It is critical to find a balance, even a tenuous balance, between the storage of information for processing purposes and the data that you store simply for cataloging purposes. If you store enough information in the metadata repository that you are defeating the purpose of distributing the data itself, then you are losing many of the advantages that a Grid database environment can bring you.

The metadata that is required in a Grid environment can be broken down into three general types, as seen in Figure 6.1 and described as follows.

Grid Metadata

One of the basic pieces of machinery that is required for the management of information contained in and concerning the Grid is about the Grid itself. This includes information about the file instances, the contents of the file instances, and the various storage systems of the Grid. Grid metadata is data that deals directly with aspects of the Grid and its structure itself — the structure, purpose, components, and resources connected to the Grid, and all of the specifics of those pieces. Is this computer running Linux, Windows, or ZOS? Does that computer have four processors or six? Is that CPU available for processing access now?

Although Grid metadata is not as often thought of as important to processing, it is a vital part of the system in a Grid. It can be determinant in finding proper protocols, proper formatting of queries, and providing quicker, more elegant access to information and resources than might otherwise be possible.

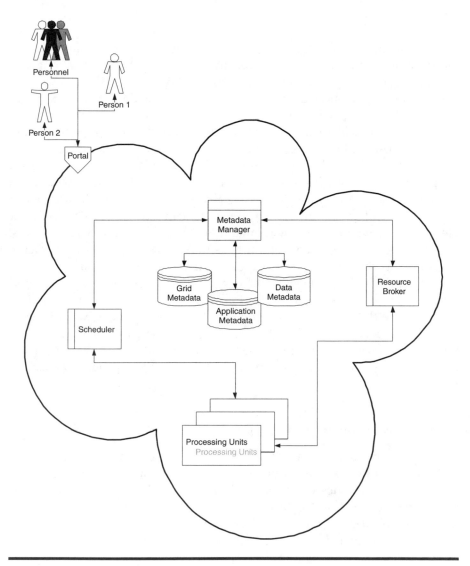

Figure 6.1   Overall view of metadata access in the Grid.

Data Metadata

To a large extent, this is what people typically think of as metadata. It is the data about the data. Data metadata can be further broken down into its own subcomponents of physical metadata, domain-independent metadata, content-dependent metadata, content-independent metadata domain-specific metadata, ontology, and user metadata.

Physical Metadata

Physical metadata encompasses the particulars about the storage of the file or about the data elements saved in a database. Attributes about files and database relations can encompass things like file sizes, file locations, alteration date, creation date, and analysis date, or the particulars about the storage of the given data.

Further, physical metadata will need to include enough information about the data and its format and location to alter any processing, should it be needed to allow the information to be retrieved from a heterogeneous environment. The structure of an Oracle query can differ somewhat from a query against DB2 or MySQL or Informix or SQL Server. The types of processing and joins can be different, as can the form that the data elements take within each environment. For this reason, the data elements' metadata needs to include what form it is in (varchar or varchar2, character, numeric, or other format), the size of the data element, and in what kind of environment that data element can be found. To be truly fluid and flexible, this can also include the information that might be needed to construct the different types of queries in each environment. What is more is that there needs to be enough information not only to make the original transformation to access the required data, but also to retransform the data back into a consolidated response set to the calling program or calling user.

Domain-Independent Metadata

Domain-independent metadata includes the logical names of the file that maps to the physical names of the files. It deals with the structure and physical characteristics of the item to be accessed. Document type definitions would be included in the category at the data metadata level. Is the object in question a flat text file, an image, a sound clip, or a movie? Is the text document a .doc file, .txt file, or .log file?

Content-Dependent Metadata

Content-dependent metadata deals directly with the information about which the information contains. Content-dependent information about data will include attributes like color, size, and species. This can be connected to certain types of information, but is irrelevant to others. Resource information would include file system capacity, CPU speed, and telescope magnification or coordinates.

Content-Independent Metadata

Content-independent metadata will include information like creation date of a piece of information or file, last update ID, the type of sensor involved, or the location of the resource or information.

Domain-Specific Metadata

Domain-specific information would include concept descriptions sourced from the ontology data. Oracle and DB2 are relational database management systems, while flat files are not accessible via the same mechanisms, and IMS is a hierarchical database management system. A Pentium 4 2.8-megahertz PC is a potential CPU source; an electron microscope is a remote data source. Users in accounting have access to financial and certain operational data, but have no need to access low-level data about what job the primary crusher is currently doing.

Ontology

Ontology is the specification of a conceptualization of the description of the concepts and relations that exist for an object, resource, or agent, or a community of things, set of objects, and the describable relationships among and between those objects. It is, in philosophy, the systematic account of existence. Pure logic, and therefore computational logic, is ontologically neutral, making no assumptions about what may or may not exist in any domain. You have to deliberately place information about what may or may not exist in a given Grid domain into the metadata repository; otherwise, it will not be found.

At the ontology layer, metadata deals with general classifications of objects. Classification of data will be domain and topic specific. Classifications of plants and animals would be far different from classifications of accident types or different drug interactions.

Ontological information dealing with the Grid itself would look at the types of resources or devices available to the Grid. Oracle, DB2, or MySQL databases; CPU sources; remote microscopes, telescopes, or other data-collecting device; and storage farms or other resources would be included in the metadata collected at this level.

User Metadata

User metadata includes user-provided annotations to the information about the information, ways that the user uses the information, the way that the information relates to each other, and the significance that is attached to those pieces of information. User metadata gives both the data and the data about the data relevance and perspective, and aids it on its way to becoming knowledge.

Application Metadata

Applications can be thought of as being composed of application components, along with their input and output files (and remember that files refers to any kind of information that the applications work on, files or database information) as identified by their logical names to the users and their physical names to the system, as well as the order of execution in the system. The processes and their components are mapped to the appropriate Grid resources for processing.

This means that the application metadata needs to include the components that each application can be broken into as well as each and every input and output dataset that can be worked on by the application and its pieces, and all of the applicable resources on which each component could run. Permissions of who can run each application can be carried in this location as well as the resources that the applications cannot utilize.

External Metadata

If there are portions of the Grid, components and resources, that are located outside of the organizational boundaries, outside of the control of the organization in which the metadata is being maintained, then extra metadata will be required. Additional relationships need to be defined and determined, particularly if the things that you are connecting are disparate items, and you only have direct or indirect control of your portion of those pieces. This will become one of the primary hurdles when looking at the Grid as a true utility computing type of environment. Because the type, location, and description of all of the components will be nearly infinite in nature, a means by which the Grid can acknowledge the location and existence will become critical.

Not only does location information need to be maintained for the resources located within your organization, but also extended location information needs to be maintained for the information located outside of your organization. IP addresses for servers, access paths for the components, physical location of human resources in the world, and access paths (phone number, address, e-mail address) for those humans will also need to be maintained.

Lifetime information for the data, for the accessibility of the resources (CPU resources and remote instrumentation resources), and for the URL of the portals and the availability of those portals can be classified in this manner.

Access permissions and ownership information and privileges for others to access your resources, as well as your access permissions to their resources, need to be maintained in the system. This will allow you to not only access your portion of the Grid and as well as their portion of the Grid, but also assist in their accessing your information and your resources, and assist in maintaining your security of your Grid environment.

Logical Metadata

Logical metadata describes the contents of a data item that is independent of the location of a specific physical instance of the individual data item. Logical metadata is information about how data items were created or modified, who modified them, when they were modified and the location of the modifications, and what resources created the data items or the analysis software that operated on those pieces of information.

User

It is often not considered that the user is indeed a part of the metadata chain. The users are the ones who use the data or the resources that the metadata is predicated on; they are the ones who ultimately create the data and therefore the metadata, and they are the ones who are most concerned with the correctness of the metadata.

Users bring their own conceptions, or misconceptions, to the system, regardless of what that system is. The only difference between a typical system and Grid environment is the complexity of what is going on behind the scenes and often the interface through which the user interacts with the system.

Users have to be taken into account in the Grid system. From their defined security to their implicit understanding of the underlying data and its meaning, there are data that can be connected directly to the user using the Grid.

Data

The next lowest piece of metadata is the data itself. Although data is not usually considered to be metadata about itself, it can contain relevant information in and of itself to assist in the determination of its internal meaning and importance.

Resources

Finally, the lowest granularity is the resources that are involved in storing, creating, transporting, or analyzing the data.

Metadata Services

Metadata services provide a means to assist with the aggregate sum of metadata mappings into collections and will also allow for the association of aggregation attributes with logical name attributes and the storage related to the province of the information, such as creation transformation. These services should provide both good performance and extreme scalability.

It may be more accurate to think of metadata as the big picture way of thinking about an information system object. It is the sum total of all of the things that you can say about any information object. This total picture is true at any level of aggregation. It is typically considered that an object is any single or aggregate item that can be addressed or manipulated by a system, human, or any other discrete entity. It reflects context, content, and structure.

Context

Context is the *W* words concerning the data (the who, what, where, when, why, and how of the information concerned). It is extrinsic to the information object — what the object contains, what it is about. It is the intrinsic information about an information object.

Structure

This is the formal set of associations within or among individual information objects. Structure can be either intrinsic or extrinsic to the information object.

Although it is possible to store this information anywhere in the Grid environment and in nearly any format, it is also practical to store it in such a manner that it is easily updated, as well as in a format that is accessible to any component that is likely to want access to it within the heterogeneous environment. It can be stored in a database such as Gadfly, MySQL, Oracle, DB2, or SQL Server as what is thought of as typical data, or in eXtensible Markup Language (XML) stored in the database, or in flat files (ASCII text or XML).

However it is stored, there are decisions that have to be made when making that definition.

Define the Data Granularity

The more granular your data becomes, the better defined you must have the metadata. Ironically, the most important pieces of the Grid are typically among the lowest on the radar of most businesses and are perceived to be of little value.

Database

Traditionally, metadata, particularly metadata about data within or accessed through a database, has been stored in a database. Although this has historically meant that the data be stored in a flat-text manner, it does not have to remain so. It is not only possible, but it can be highly efficient to store data in XML in a database (many of which today support the storage of XML in the database itself; others support it by means of external reference to the XML documents).

Access

Again, looking at Figure 6.1, you can see where a client's queries access the metadata service manager with a list of attributes that he or she is looking for. That metadata service manager returns to the user or the user process a list of the logical names from the metadata repository addressing the location of the data to be used in the processes, retrieving the physical name of the data files and the logical names that the user understands. Using this information, the user process knows where to look for the data that is needed to complete its processing.

The user query also accesses the metadata repository to determine where to look for available and applicable resources on which to run the processes that the user seeks to run. This information is routed back to the job scheduler and the resource manager to adequately route the processing to the correct resources.

The application metadata is queried to determine what processes are going to be required for the user process to complete. The security requirements are examined to determine if the user requesting the application has the authority to run the application, if the application has adequate access to the data, and if each of the pieces has adequate access to all of the resources that are required for the processing.

Once the processing is completed, information is sent back to the metadata repository dealing with timing metrics, performance metrics, and updates to the analysis and update/insert/delete information associated with the data.

Metadata Formatting

So we have an idea of what constitutes metadata, but what format should Grid metadata take? What does it take to make it work? It is going to take a standard syntax so that not only can the metadata be recognized as such, but also it can be accessed by anything entering the Grid without the need for extended application programming to facilitate the access. It will mean using a standardized vocabulary to store the information in a central (but again, distributed) location so that any resource or any service can access the information.

The representation and exploitation of centralized, standardized knowledge has always been one of the primary challenges of artificial intelligence (AI), and at its heart, a well-designed Grid system has many of the features of a good AI system. If the Grid can store data and make inferences based on the historic data to make determinations on what to do in the future, then it can almost be considered to be learning. A system that can learn from its history will be able to make better decisions about what to run, where, and when, and how to partition itself, making the overall product a more valuable system. Designing and conceptualizing are easy, but getting those concepts and designs to function and really work in the real world has always been a problem.

Ultimately, what needs to occur is the automatic discovery and acknowledgment of a new resource joining the system, and the registration of that resource with all of its idiosyncrasies and features with the metadata system is what is hoped for. But for that, we have a long way to go. What is more is that it will be, eventually and theoretically, possible to negotiate not only within the enterprise, but also between enterprises to make CPU cycles into truly commodity computing.

The wonderful things about standards, as opposed to Tiggers, are that there are so many to choose from. There are many different options, but one of the most common options is to store the metadata in XML documents, either independently or within a database.

XML

The management of the extremely diverse nature of Grid components with metadata providing the information about the features of the resources and facilitating their effective use is critical. A user will need to know what resources are available, regardless of what that resource is, where these resources can be found, how these resources can be accessed, and when they will become available if they are not currently available. Metadata will be able to provide easy answers to these questions and will therefore represent one key element to effective resource discovery and utilization.

And because of the heterogeneous nature of the Grid, one of the most promising media with which to manage the metadata appears to be XML.

What Is XML?

XML, or eXtensible Markup Language, is a simple, flexible text format that was derived from SGML (Standard General Markup Language) and was originally designed by a committee of the World Wide Web consortium in response to a need for a more generalized form of Hypertext Markup Language (HTML). Where HTML was designed as a presentation language, XML was designed as a means to add consistent structure and to meet the challenges of large-scale electronic publishing. It is, however, also playing an increasingly important role in the platform-independent exchange of a wide variety of data via the Web and elsewhere. It has been enthusiastically embraced in many applications because there are a lot of applications that need to store data that is intended for human use, but in a format that will be useful for manipulation by machine. Ironically, when looking at XML as a metadata storage platform, it has even been referred to as a metalanguage, or a language that is used to define other languages, and has in fact been used to define other languages such as WML (Wireless Markup Language).

With XML you can define data structures, make these structures platform independent, process defined data automatically and quickly, and easily define your own data types and tags. What you cannot do is define how your data is shown; however, XML does provide an easy format that will allow parsers to more elegantly show the data.

Although you can often do the same thing in XML that you can in HTML, HTML tells how the data should appear on a page and XML tells you what the data means. Basically, XML, regardless of how and where it is used, provides metadata about whatever it contains.

The Grid can be designed to have a set of rules governing the contained components in the Grid system. Although all of the components in the Grid have some resemblance to each other, some attributes that are common, they are all different in detail — different operating systems, different CPU speeds, different physical locations. Their commonalities include:

- They have applications.
- They have rules (accounting rules, security rules, and usage rules).
- Each implements its own primary processes.
- In HTML:

```
<p>Sony Vaio Laptop
<br>Best Buy
<br>$1438
```

- In XML:

```
<product>
<model>Sony Vaio Laptop</model>
<dealer>Best Buy</dealer>
<price>$1438</price>
</product>
```

XML has the following characteristics:

- Provides a way to define infrastructure-independent representations of information
- Allows users to define data structures
- Allows the use of powerful query languages, although it does not require them
- Is easily mapped into data structures of object-oriented programming languages
- Is a simple way to start and is easily adaptable and extensible into relational databases that are now being equipped to manipulate and store these kind of documents

XML is much like HTML in that it has standard formatting and has tags that make it look a lot like HTML. But XML is not a markup language; it is used to describe data, any data. This makes XML a prime choice for metadata storage and metadata management, either at the system level or at the Grid level. XML tags, unlike HTML tags, are not predefined, but allow the definition of customized tags that fit the business rules or other requirements (making it a prime choice for something as fluid and flexible as the Grid). XML uses a document type definition (DTD) or XML schema to describe the data (either choice allowing the metadata to be self-descriptive).

Although XML has found much more popularity in recent years, it has been around for several years, long enough to have its support integrated into nearly every commercial database management system on the market today. It has become increasingly popular as a medium for storing data for dynamic content for Web pages, separating the data layer there from the presentation layer, allowing for increased flexibility in coding, allowing for coding a page once, and changing the data for that page any number of times, adding to and taking away, without having to recode the page.

The primary difference between HTML and XML is that XML was designed to carry data and HTML was designed as a presentation layer for data, including the data that is located in an XML document. XML is not a replacement for HTML; they were designed with different goals in mind. XML is concerned with what the data is and in describing the data; HTML is concerned with how the data looks and displaying the information to the user.

It is difficult for some, in particular for those who have an extensive history with HTML, to get their hands around the fact that XML was not really designed to *do* anything; it structures, stores, and sends information in a platform independently. For example, if you look at Table 6.1, you can see what might be presented in XML for a Grid component named hagrid, a Linux server in this case, specifically belonging to accounting, but accessible by the Grid.

Figure 6.2 shows how this information might appear on a Web page. This means that the information on the servers in that document can be monitored (based on additional information maintained in the XML document, like load or availability) from anywhere that the administrator has access to a browser.

In keeping with the ideals of the Grid, XML is both free and extensible, making it a highly flexible medium for storing and accessing Grid metadata. Although many other ways exist that have predefined structures, and the authors and those accessing those documents can work only within the predefined structures, XML does not have these limitations. The tags in XML are not standard; in fact, they are invented, often on the fly, by the

Table 6.1 Grid Component XML Definition

```
<?xml version="1.0" encoding="UTF-8" ?>
- <dataroot xmlns:od="urn:schemas-microsoft-
com:officedata"
xmlns:xsi="http://www.w3.org/2001/XMLSchema-
instance" xsi:noNamespaceSchemaLocation="compo-
nent.xsd" generated="2004-03-13T06:51:04">
- <component>
 <name>hagrid</name>
 <address>123.45.678</address>
 <type>Linux</type>
 <gridinfo>accounting</gridinfo>
 <communication_type>push</communication_type>
 <operation_mode>provider</operation_mode>
 <putmethod>file</putmethod>
 <getmethod>file</getmethod>
 </component>
<component>
 <name>wilbur</name>
 <address>234.56.789</address>
 <type>Windows</type>
 <gridinfo>HR</gridinfo>
 <communication_type>push</communication_type>
 <operation_mode>provider</operation_mode>
 <putmethod>file</putmethod>
 <getmethod>file</getmethod>
 </component>
<component>
 <name>kenny</name>
 <address>393.49.234</address>
 <type>UNIX</type>
 <type>UNIX</type>
```

(continued)

Table 6.1   Grid Component XML Definition (Continued)

```
x <communication_type>push</communication_type>
<operation_mode>provider</operation_mode>
<putmethod>file</putmethod>
<getmethod>file</getmethod>
</component>
<component>
<name>johnny5</name>
<address>678.91.02</address>
<type>linux</type>
<gridinfo>purchasing</gridinfo>
<communication_type>push</communication_type>
<operation_mode>provider</operation_mode>
<putmethod>file</putmethod>
<getmethod>file</getmethod>
</component>
</dataroot>
```

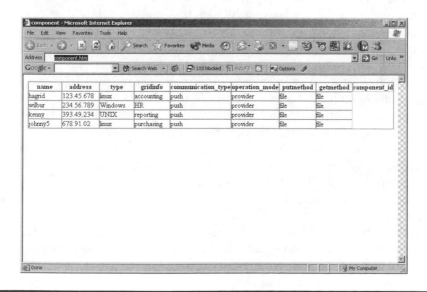

Figure 6.2   Component presentation via browser.

authors of the documents themselves. This means that the metadata for one Grid can be stored in the same kind of format as the metadata for another, and still be as customized as the implementation requires.

XML can store its information in either flat files, as is often the more common case today, or databases (growing in popularity as more and more have added this capability and flexibility, and as it meets more and more of the needs of the organization). But storing the data in a database can add access complexities that might make it prohibitive for a Grid environment. To keep the environment as simple, open, and accessible as possible, it is typically still the case that the XML files are stored as flat files in secure areas of the Grid that allow for interface interaction with the data, but not deliberate human tampering.

Table 6.2 shows how the definition and location of different brands and versions of databases can be stored in an XML file, allowing the Grid to make decisions based on type of database involved in a query. Because databases have different features and different idiosyncrasies in their access methods, this kind of document can be extremely useful to the Grid in allowing it to make the correct decisions on how to format queries and how best to reformat the outputs.

Figure 6.3 shows how this information might appear on a Web page. This means that the information on the servers in that document can be monitored (based on additional information maintained in the XML document, like load or availability) from anywhere that the administrator has access to a browser.

XML, although extremely popular as a Web design tool, is also a very uniform and easily readable form. In the real world of business and economy, as in science and academia, computer systems and databases contain data and are very useful for their owners. But this data is usually stored in formats that may be incompatible from one company to the next. One of the most time consuming functions for developers has historically been to find a means to exchange data between heterogeneous systems in an efficient and elegant manner. Often this data is then exchanged either over a dedicated network link or, more often, over the Internet or an extranet link. Converting that data to XML (with tools readily available in whatever platform you find yourself) can reduce the complexity and create data that can be both read by different applications and accessible and readable on whatever platform the sender and receiver find themselves using.

XML is becoming the language and means of choice for exchanging information, including financial information, between businesses over the Internet. Because, in effect, XML is plaintext format, with tags added for extensibility, it provides hardware- and software-independent ways of sharing data. It is much easier to create data that nearly any application

Table 6.2   Database Definition in XML

```xml
<?xml version="1.0" encoding="UTF-8" ?>
- <dataroot xmlns:od="urn:schemas-microsoft-
com:officedata"
xmlns:xsi="http://www.w3.org/2001/XMLSchema-
instance" xsi:noNamespaceSchemaLocation="data-
base.xsd" generated="2004-05-07T04:01:53">
- <database>
<database_type>Oracle</database_type>
<database_version>9</database_version>
<database_location>Bill's server</database_
location>
<formatting_information>Oracle docs</formatting_
information>
<owner>HR</owner>
</database>
- <database>
<database_type>Oracle</database_type>
<database_version>10</database_version>
<database_location>johnny5</database_location>
<formatting_information>Oracle docs</formatting_
information>
<owner>Stephanie</owner>
</database>
- <database>
<database_type>DB2</database_type>
<database_version>8</database_version>
<database_location>Bill's ZOS</database_location>
<formatting_information>DB2 docs</formatting_
information>
<owner>systems</owner>
</database>
```

(continued)

Table 6.2   Database Definition in XML (Continued)

```
- <database>
  <database_type>MySQL</database_type>
  <database_version>2</database_version>
  <database_location>webserver</database_location>
  <formatting_information>MySQL docs</formatting_
  information>
  <owner>web systems</owner>
  </database>
  </dataroot>
```

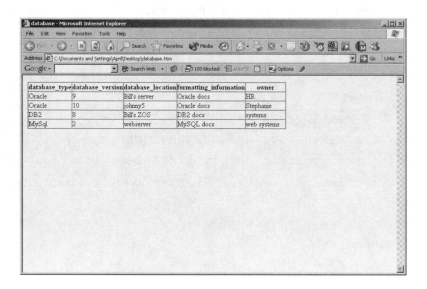

Figure 6.3   Database presentation via browser.

can work with, from Oracle to Access, from Internet Explorer to Netscape, from a single UNIX server to another server, and from one server to another server across the Grid.

Application

Not only does storing metadata in an XML document allow those languages that are specifically built to manipulate the data to access and update the information, but also, because of the nature (platform independence, extensibility, and accessibility) of XML, specialized tools do not necessarily have to be created to work with the documents. Generic metadata services can work on the documents, propagation tools for Grid and peer-to-peer can manipulate the documents for which they have manipulation permissions, and generic metadata registries can be created to allow for extensibility of the document by others for their uses.

Many of today's large databases have the added features of being able to store, access, and manipulate XML data within the DBMS itself.

MCAT

It is often advantageous to find a solution to a metadata situation that is not dependent or reliant on any given RDBMS platform. This will allow you to remove the necessity for relying on knowing the specific access method to get to the data in the repository.

MCAT is a metainformation catalog system that has been implemented at the San Diego Super Computer Center (SDSC) as a critical part of the Data Intensive Computing Environment (DICE) project that is building a national digital library repository to help facilitate the publication of scientific data. MCAT has requirements that are based mainly on the SDSC's Storage Resource Broker (SRB) system — a middleware system that provides a unified interface for connecting users to heterogeneous data sources over a network, and allowing them to simply and elegantly access replicated datasets based on their attributes or on their logical names, as opposed to accessing them via their literal names or physical locations.

Remember that metadata is defined as data about data. MCAT has determined that metainformation can be loosely defined as data about the entities in a system. There were determined to be four different types of elements of interest in a data intensive computing environment:

- *Resources* — Resources include things such as hardware systems, software systems, operating systems, file systems, and application systems. These hardware systems include computing platforms, communications networks, storage systems, and peripherals. Software systems include heterogeneous database management systems, and application systems include digital libraries and search engines, and extend to the logical groupings and extensions of these resources.
- *Methods* — These include access methods for using standardized and nonstandard application programming interfaces (APIs) and system-defined and user-defined functions for manipulating

datasets, data warehousing, data mining, data subsetting, format conversion routines, and composition of methods.

■ *Data objects* — Individual datasets as wells as collections of datasets.

■ *Users and groups* — Users and groups of users who can create, update, or access any of the resources, methods, and datasets, and can access any of the metadata on all four entities.

Conclusion

The unique challenge will be to efficiently determine means by which you can extract and filter relevant information as automatically as possible. One problem, above all, remains. There will be different places that insist on using different terms for different pieces of metadata. This means that mappings need to take place nearly continuously between what one system uses to refer to a piece of given information (for example, the title of a paper) and what another might refer to it as (for example, the name of a paper). There are complexities that exist in simply one language and one organization; if your Grid expands to include other locations, languages, and cultures, these complexities will only multiply.

Chapter 7

Drivers

The great thing about a computer notebook is that no matter how much you stuff into it, it doesn't get bigger or heavier.

—Bill Gates, *Business @ the Speed of Thought*

Why is it drug addicts and computer aficionados are both called users?

—Clifford Stoll

Computer Science is no more about computers than astronomy is about telescopes.

—E.W. Dijkstra

I do not fear computers. I fear the lack of them.

—Isaac Asimov

Any science or technology which is sufficiently advanced is indistinguishable from magic.

—Arthur C. Clarke

Any technology that is distinguishable from magic is not sufficiently advanced.

—Gregory Benford

The Grid, as you might have already noticed, has been more of a matter
of evolution than revolution. Much the way that man is supposed to have
evolved through time, being what we would like to believe is the latest
and most complete evolution, so is the Grid seen to be the most ultimate,
so far, species of computing. Computing has evolved through centralized
computing, the World Wide Web, peer-to-peer computing, and the virtualization of underlying technologies.

Like the Web, and partly because much of the Grid's interface relies
on the underpinning of Web technology, the Grid goes a long way to
keep the complexities hidden and allows every user to enjoy the same
single simplified unified experience. Unlike the Web (whose history and
technological purpose basically are communication enablers), the Grid
extends to full collaboration of all involved parties toward the meeting of
overall common business goals.

Like peer-to-peer, the Grid allows for the free and open sharing of
files across the network. Unlike peer-to-peer, which has as part of its
goals the decentralized sharing of files and information, the Grid allows
for not only the many-to-many sharing of files and information, but also
the nearly unrestrained sharing of computing resources.

Grid computing is a form of a highly distributed system. With a
distributed system that is this extensive, computing resources are shared
across networks, ultimately the Internet. Just as Web standards and the
different Web technologies have more and more enabled the universally
transparent access to documents, so the Grid promises to do this and
much more for computing resources. Grid will help to enable the selection,
extreme aggregation, and sharing of informational resources that may
currently reside on many different servers in many different administrative
domains located in many different geographic areas. These information
resources are shared based upon rules governing their availability, capability, and accounting cost, as well as the user's requirements.

Many commercial products are available today, and more are becoming
available every day that tout that customers can use them to Grid enable
their enterprises.

Grid, like clusters and other distributed computing genres, brings
computing resources together to bear on large problems. Grid, unlike
clusters and distributed computing, which rely on both proximity and
operating homogeneity to accomplish their goals, not only can be widely

geographically distributed, but also can be highly heterogeneous with respect to hardware and operating systems, data sources, and application designs.

Where Grid meets other virtualization technologies (storage area network [SAN], network attached storage [NAS], clusters, and more), there is the virtualization of IT resources. Where Grid goes beyond the others, which tend to virtualize a single system or a single system's view of the components, Grid enables the virtualization of a wide range of disparate IT resources.

Much as Grid appears to be the hot new buzzword in IT today, Grid computing is not a completely new concept, but one that has gained renewed interest and activity for a couple of reasons. One of the main reasons is that IT budgets have been, and continue to be, cut, and Grid computing offers a far less expensive alternative to purchasing larger new servers. Another reason why Grid computing has started gaining more popularity is that there are many problems that involve processing a large, often a very large, volume of data, or that involve performing repetitive computations on the same, or similar, sets of data. These computations, if they have not yet, will soon outstrip the capabilities of the servers to perform the calculations.

The ideal for Grid computing strives to stand as a metaphor for treating computing and computational resources much the same way that the utility grid treats electricity. Jus as utility company consumers do not care where their electrical power comes from, or whether the electrical power that they are using has been generated in a nuclear power plant, a coal-fired generator, a hydroelectric dam, or from a wind farm, so users of Grid computing gain ubiquitous access to computing resources without having to worry about either the configuration or location of the server hardware that is being used to run their applications. This virtualization of computing resources may one day allow organizations' IT departments to make the best use of not only their on-site computing capacity, but also any computing capacity that falls within their sphere of influence. All of this maximization and virtualization occurs while enabling rapid and efficient computationally intensive applications whenever necessary; when the computational capacity is not needed, it is not acknowledged.

Much of the high ideals of the vision have yet to be fully realized or implemented on anything approaching such a grand scale. But just because it has not yet been done does not mean that it cannot or will not be done. And those that are ready by virtue of having a limited implementation in place will have an advantage in making the next larger leap in a more elegant and simple method.

Business

From the business perspective, the Grid brings with it many advantages and features that can help businesses to meet their goals and excel.

Accelerated Time to Results

Because the Grid can run on any hardware and can span not only departments but also entire organizations and interorganizations, it can greatly help with the improvement of productivity and collaboration between parties in the subject matter. This means that not only can projects benefit from the addition of the Grid environment, but also the entire society that is involved in the kind of project can benefit (in the case of a data-based Grid) from the open shared available data. Projects can come to market (regardless of the market) sooner because the resources are available when and where needed to get past the hurdles without the necessity of putting in purchase orders and requests for quotes on significant systems. Ideally, you invest only in the cycles that are necessary to get the job at hand done.

Not only are new projects done faster, but with the Grid and its increased power and flexibility, projects that were previously impractical or unsolvable are now potentially possible. Projects that would have required too much of an investment in hardware can be reevaluated in light of even a departmental or organizational Grid because spare cycles can be reallocated to where they are needed to solve the unsolvable problems. This can mean more core competencies for those companies that choose to take the leap, and a competitive advantage because of solved "unsolvable" problems or innovative new ways of solving problems that were computationally prohibitive, allowing a company to more adequately meet the client's (internal or external) needs.

Operational Flexibility

One of the key features that the Grid brings to the IT mix is flexibility. Where hardware was often siloed because of incompatibility of resources or unwillingness to have all processing entirely centralized, now, with the addition of the Grid-enabled middle layer, mainframes, PCs and super-computers, and midrange systems can all work together toward a common business processing goal. Not enough power at any given time from any given system? Add idle CPU cycles to help out in the tight spot.

With adequate rules set up in the system, you can almost effortlessly and automatically allow these adjustments to make themselves. The system, given an adequate supply of metadata with which to work, can become a sense-and-respond system that notices that a given resource is becoming overtaxed and finds underutilized resources that might be candidates for use to ease the high utilization and spread the processing out.

This flexibility not only allows you to scale the system with respect to different operational loads during the day, or to shift resources from underutilized resources to overutilized ones, but also can allow you to be able to address rapid fluctuations in customer needs and demands. You may have a customer that suddenly runs a query on a database that drags the system to its knees. Because you have a highly flexible system, you can shift resources on the fly for the duration of the demand spike and just as quickly shift them back when the spike is over.

And this ability to shift resources from one area to another in the system not only allows for flexibility in the layout of the system, but also provides the security of having a far more resilient system. Many companies are looking for ways that will allow them to provide a nearly 24/7 system, a system that will provide maximum availability while providing the ability to do maintenance and still have efficiency. Although this is usually a tall order to fill, it is quite possible in a Grid environment.

This virtualization allows the workloads to be untied from the underlying hardware resources and allows resources to be provisioned with far more flexibility than can be found in a traditional environment. Because resources that have been, or are being, virtualized can be allocated precisely and concisely to meet any and all needs of any given workload, administrators (either on the application end or anywhere within the Grid environment) can more efficiently allocate those resources based on rules, accounting demands, or other criteria that are in place for the given system.

Leverage Existing Capital Investments

Capital investments are a big thing in business. They affect the company's bottom line. They are dealt with in accounting and add complexity to everything financial that the company does. The Grid allows you to improve the overall utilization of all existing computing capabilities optimally and effectively. You can then make those capitalized investments later rather than sooner, making the time value of money and the net present value beneficial to your company rather than to the computer company.

What is more is that you can avoid overprovisioning and the excess hardware, software, and licensing costs that are associated with overprovisioning. This can help to free up resources from the burden of administering more and more hardware, while that hardware is underutilized the majority of the time.

Because the Grid is typically maintained through a Web interface, some of the highest costs in a company (the people costs) can be limited as well, because fewer administrators can administer the entire system though the interface. This can allow someone with expertise in UNIX to work on a Windows server at the operating system and middleware levels, where it would have taken two people to do those jobs in a typical architect system.

Better Resource Utilization

Much data that is needed to perform extensive analysis in many companies already exists, in one form or another, in their systems. Traditional processes that access the data and analyze, synthesize, and test the data are typically time consuming and resource intensive. The growing amounts of data in these organizations only tend to exacerbate the problems rather than help eliminate them. Grid computing can manage and distribute resources more efficiently and work toward shortening analysis time, and often time to market for many products.

As it comes time for companies to replace expensive high-end powerful servers because of ends of leases or a system has components wearing out, those servers could be replaced with lower-cost commodity servers, or blade servers, that would meet or exceed the total output of the servers that replaced, if those new servers were added to a Grid system. The combination of these lower-cost commodity servers with the distributed Grid system can result in savings and efficiency.

No longer will an organization buy resources to be dedicated to individual applications or products, but instead it will buy resources that can be shared and distributed across the entire organization. These enterprise resources will be portioned out to individual applications and departments based on need, accounting rules, and policy decisions at the enterprise level.

Management will, in a Grid environment, be able to decide how computing resources will be allocated in the organization, and can alter those decisions more quickly and efficiently than is possible for those companies tied into the traditional purchasing and computing paradigm.

Enhanced Productivity

The Grid allows for extreme gains in productivity because jobs are able to run faster in a parallelized environment, and because with Grid you are able to give users nearly unlimited access to computing, data, and storage resources when and where they want or need them. Because the system has virtualized access to all of the resources it needs, different users with different levels of expertise in a given system and with different abilities and weaknesses can work together, building off of each other's abilities far more easily and in a more ubiquitous environment. If everyone can see the system the same, get to the data in the same way, and experience the same responses at the same time and in the same way, they can all contribute together to provide overall productivity gains; the total is better than the sum of the parts.

Users are often far more productive in a Grid environment because they can concentrate on their jobs and not worry about locating resources and information in different systems and locations. In a non-Grid environment, there is typically no central interface through which the users can access their data, an interface that understands where the information is and how to go about getting it. This centralized interface and ability to centrally locate all information will not only help with productivity, but also add to the acceptance of the system by the end users.

Not only are users more productive because of the unified interface, but because there are virtually unlimited resources at their command (within policy and reason) more jobs can also run faster in shorter time.

Imagine what you could accomplish if you could define your jobs, decide when and how you wanted them to run, and set them off to running. Look at the way that SETI@home works. The Search for Extraterrestrial Intelligence (SETI) with a home computer screen saver. Just a screen saver, right? Just a little program that runs in the background while your computer is just sitting around, right? Do not be so quick to judge. In SETI@home, overall jobs are broken down into manageable chunks and those chucks sent off to be processed on any available CPUs during their otherwise idle time. Since SETI's beginning, 4,992,815 users (including 1100 new users in 24 hours) have dedicated over 1,924,340 years of CPU time so far (over 1100 years in just one 24-hour period). Those CPUs have acted on nearly 62.31 teraflops per second of data in the same 24-hour period. Those users are in over 225 countries; over 150 types of CPUs and over 165 different operating systems donate the cycles to analyze the data.

Think about what this kind of processing and dedication, put to work on your company's tasks, can do.

Okay, your company is not likely to be able to dedicate a million CPUs, even part-time, analyze data, but you are not looking for intelligent extraterrestrial life either.

Let's look at data warehouses. Users expect whatever they define as acceptable performance. They also expect that queries, even the ones designed to mine data (or find those relationships in the data that we don't know), to simply run to completion. These are not unrealistic expectations. With a Grid environment, queries that may have taken days or weeks to finish in a "typical" environment can run in parallel against a Grid-enabled database, will be able to run faster, providing answers faster, with at least as much accuracy as was possible in a typical environment. This means the company is better able to adapt to the market, meet the customer's needs, and answer the questions that need to be answered, giving it a competitive advantage.

Better Collaboration

The Grid allows for collaboration in entirely new ways. Not only can individuals involved in a project or a concept collaborate person to person, but entire companies can collaborate to strive toward common business goals. With worldwide business demand requiring intense problem-solving capabilities for more and more complex problems, the requirement for allowing more and more collaboration of computing resources to come tighter and work together in an attempt to solve the problems facing business adds an additional component to the idea of collaboration in an industry or a company. The Grid allows for this added complexity of collaboration between hardware and other remote resources, making problem solving more simple and elegant and helping facilitate the human collaboration that goes along with it.

Because at its core Grid computing is based on an open set of standards, and open protocols that enable free communication across homogeneous as well as heterogeneous environments that are both centralized and widely geographically dispersed, organizations can optimize computing, data, storage, and other resources, pool those resources for use by large-capacity workloads, share those resources across networks (local area networks [LANs] and wide area networks [WANs] and eventually the Internet), and enable collaboration at entirely new levels than have ever before been contemplated.

A higher level of collaboration can be accomplished through the use of a Grid environment. Users can share data and resources in manageable and consistent fashions across the Grid environment, be it departmental sharing, enterprise sharing, or, in the case of many of the research facilities that have already implemented Grid environments, across the country or around the world.

Scalability

Grid computing enables the company to maintain capacity to grow up thousands of processors while not investing significantly in any more servers. Because you can use blade servers, PCs, or any existing CPUs in the organization, you can utilize cycles that would otherwise go unused, wasted. By harnessing these resources, you can solve your highly computationally intensive problems. And if you find the system getting more and more bogged down, all you have to do is find an existing source that is already in your environment and add it to the system.

If you find that you still have tight spots, computationally, you can invest in commodity hardware, blade servers that are lower cost and built for the adaptability and scalability, and snap them into a rack and go.

ROI

Business types often talk about return on investment (ROI).

Many companies, from some of the biggest to smaller start-ups, claim to already have many corporate Grid computing clients, clients that are trying to make efficient use of their own existing assets and buying extra capacity where necessary, much like an application service provider model. Utility-based computing has far broader intentions than simply being a glorified ASP model. Companies will be able to take advantage of shared infrastructure, resources, storage, databases, Web servers, and other in-demand resources.

This model will likely expand to fill existing and emerging needs. It will take application servers to higher and higher levels, becoming a utility provider, and the utility will compute cycles. This means that companies will be able to buy extra cycles that are needed, allowing them to make better use of their investments.

The academic community has been creating Grids using low-cost commodity computers (often, in fact, the very computers that are making up the university computer labs contribute significantly to the available resources of the Grid) to work together to attack complex and computationally intensive applications that require significant horsepower. Applications that have been successfully run on these Grids include not only what would be considered to be deeply research connected, but also applications that perform risk management computations or financial modeling processing. These are the same applications that many commercial companies who are starting to make inroads to the Grid computing environment are finding run with great efficiency and reliability in their environments as well.

The advantages that are being gained by turning to the Grid in many circumstances are compelling. Major business problems are being parsed and distributed in bite-size datasets and task sets to make efficient use of multiple computers for analysis. In this way, the problems are attacked more rapidly than ever simply by utilizing underused and idle resources. In this way, those resources that were otherwise not contributing to the bottom line can be put to work to help solve the existing problems in organizations. Further, because these resources are now being used, server purchases that may have been on the horizon before the reallocation of cycles can be put off for a significant amount of time, possibly indefinitely.

Reallocation of Resources

Upper management has long recognized that computing cycles of thousands and thousands of machines are being wasted on low-level computationally nonintensive computing tasks such as reading and writing e-mail, word processing, interacting with co-workers on the phone, in meetings, or in impromptu meetings in hallways, and watching the screen savers during breaks or lunch.

Grid's enabling middleware has progressed to allow the lowly desktop computer (that has all of the power of the early computers and more) to cough up those wasted CPUs and contribute to complex tasks from remote locations. Computations that would have once required all of the computing power of supercomputers or mainframes to execute now require an investment in inexpensive middleware that lies in a thin layer between a core set of servers and thousands of clients.

It has meant to those intrepid companies in the financial services market and others with number-crunching massive computational models that with very little new hardware investment, enormous boons to productivity and a highly increased bottom line can be realized.

The financial services sector, insurance companies, TPAs, and those that service claims for those companies, as well as real estate and customer resource management-intensive companies, where data mining plays an important role, are likely to be high investors in the Grid as it adapts and emerges and goes through its metamorphosis over the next few years. Initially, of course, it will not initially be utility computing at its finest. Rather, many of the existing systems will be adapted to use Grid-enabled networks, workstations, servers, and clusters and eventually cause the lowering of demand for high-performance mainframes and supercomputers.

The lower demand for higher-end servers will be replaced by the increased reliance and demand for high-performance Grid-enabled applications to run on these new flexible architectures.

It does not take true global utility computing, however, to make a company able to take advantage of computing on demand. It can be done internally as well as it can be done externally by a CPU utility model company. Internal utility computing services designed to provide CPU cycle for computationally intensive applications can meet the needs of internal clients while allowing the organization to better distribute and track the computing cost to the true users of the cycles and resources.

Rather than dedicating resources to a department or a specific line of business and its applications, the internal CPU utility division can provide all of the lines of business associated with that organization with the processing power that they need for applications that are computationally intensive, while also providing a virtual combined pool of resources from which to draw.

The goal of these CPU utility divisions is to improve the service levels that the internal customers can expect and cut their own costs by charging each business unit for the resources that it uses. The internal CPU utility can even provide peak and off-peak pricing, similar to what a typical utility company can provide.

In this way, many companies could allay their fears of security breeches that they may feel potentially could arise from securing the required CPU cycles from a source outside of the organization and can gain the efficiencies of both scale and scope that can come from each individual department or line of business being able to concentrate on its true core business strengths and allowing those connected to the newly created intraorganizational utility company to do what they will become adept and efficient at doing.

The symbiotic relationship could make for an overall stronger organization and an organization that can grow and flex with changing demands. Change will not be as great an impact if the company can provide the infrastructure on which to change easily and securely.

The concept of charging the cost of CPU usage may be foreign to many organizations, but it will provide information to the overall organization on how and where its resources are being used, and provide more accurate information on what departments are truly more profitable than others, and it can also provide an overview of the fact that information technology departments are not as much of a black hole into which organizations pour money as they may have previously been viewed. What is more is that not only could IT departments be seen as less of a money drain on an organization, but if organizations were to adopt an internal utility company model for the Grid-enabled departments, these departments may even prove to be profitable when looked at from the perspective of the services that they are really providing for the overall organization.

TCO

Total cost of ownership (TCO) takes into account all of the costs and cash flows of a potential or active project and determines what the effect of the project has on the bottom line of the organization. Where many other means of determining profitability take into account obvious costs,

TCO takes into account the costs of redesign, training, and many of the components that would not otherwise make it into the mix. TCO is often applied to the purchase, lease agreement, or outsourcing of large manufacturing purchases to build or buy decisions in a manufacturing organization. It has been applied, with mixed results, to technology decisions for well over a decade.

TCO essentially helps a company make quantitative determinations as to whether it wins or loses from any specific technology implementation. TCO is typically used as a lens through which to look at the overall impact of a hardware or software implementation, or at the decision to change the infrastructure of an organization. Cost is the numerator (usually broken out into categories such as capital costs, technical support, licensing costs, additional software costs, training costs, and the marginal costs that can be associated with one decision over another, administration and end-user operations), and the denominator could be service level, customer satisfaction, quality levels or productivity levels, time to market, relative time to see results from a computation, or the overall success of getting the correct answer back to the requester in a reasonable amount of time, all with quantitative measures assigned, even to the qualitative factors and weights given to each.

Although it is true that there will be some added investment needed for the acquisition of software and training for the Grid middleware that ties all of the disparate components together, the overall cost of ownership for the Grid environment will prove to be lower than that of its traditional counterparts.

And if you look at the effects of the denominator as it applies to Grid and the effects of the Grid environment on the organization, service level, customer satisfaction, quality levels or productivity levels, time to market, relative time to see results from a computation, or the overall success of getting the correct answer back to the requester in a reasonable amount of time, you can see where Grid can lower the overall cost to a fraction of what the alternatives would be.

Because you can more reliably meet service level agreements, with both internal customers and external clients, you can not only lower the costs incurred by penalties levied because of missed timelines, but also increase premiums charged because of the consistent meeting of timelines. Quality levels are met or exceeded by Grid infrastructure, and productivity, as we have already seen, can be improved overall, allowing more jobs to run in a shorter amount of time and more answers to be gained from the same amount of processing power. Because users and customers do not have to wait as long for the answers to important questions, you can see an improvement in the time value of money that is realized because valuable time is not being spent waiting for extended periods of time for answers, and computing time is not being wasted in the wait mode for one process to finish and the next to begin.

What is more, if you adopt a pay-as-you-go model, the cost of ownership becomes completely minimal, as you do not actually own anything and your cost is the utility cost of the CPU capacity that you use as you use it. It becomes, simply, another variable utility cost to the enterprise.

Technology

From the technology perspective, the Grid offers many advantages as well.

Infrastructure Optimization

Because you can consolidate workload management into the scheduler and resource manager, and thereby distribute the workload over multiple servers and CPU sources, you can optimize the utilization of resources and optimize workloads and job scheduling to take best advantage of the resources on hand. Because there is enough capacity in the CPU capacity pool, you can find the necessary supply of resources to throw at high-demand applications as they demand resources. This can reduce the overall cycle time that any single given job takes, and therefore the overall cycle time of a process and the overall time to answer the computationally intensive questions.

Increase Access to Data and Collaboration

In a Grid environment, data is federated and distributed globally, providing extensive access to the data resources at any point in the Grid chain. This distribution and extended access can provide the underlying support for collaboration multidepartmentally, multiorganizationally, multinationally, and globally, depending on the type and security requirements for the data that is involved. This collaboration can lead to overall productivity gains because of the ability of many eyes seeing a problem from different angles and different perspectives, and many minds attacking a problem from different sides, making the problem smaller faster than has ever before been possible.

Resilient, Highly Available Infrastructure

Not only can you distribute workloads, but you can redistribute to balance the workloads on the network and on the individual servers in the system.

Because the organization sees the resources as being shared equitably among the different users, it fosters camaraderie with the users and allows for a more unified overall work environment, where no one feels that he or she is being technologically slighted in favor of another department. That goodwill is one of the things that many organizations strive for, but often fall short on.

Just as important as these is the ability of your system to more quickly, elegantly, and automatically recover from failures of servers, the network, or a given resource in the system. Because there is no single point of failure in the system and jobs can be dynamically redirected in case a component becomes unreachable, the overall reliability of the system is increased, and the comfort level of the users in the system's availability is also increased.

Make Most Efficient Use of Resources

There are many reasons why Grid computing has become such a hot "new" technology. There does not seem to have been any single major breakthrough that made Grid computing more applicable for corporate uses and more capable of meeting not only the widely diverse needs of universities and research organizations, but also the far more complex and controlled needs of corporations and industry. Rather, subtle technical advances over the past decade or more all came together to make the modern Grid an enterprise-capable computing tool.

Grid, amazingly, represents an almost unprecedented case of business and technology goals aligning. That the two have so quickly come to a place where they begin to see eye to eye is encouraging. Standards-based tools that are designed for creating Grid-enabled applications and connecting users to Grids, and Grids to Grids, are appearing on the market just as the need to increase server capacity and optimize utilization grows.

The Globus project and the Open Grid Services Architecture (OGSA) are interrelated efforts that are working together independently to create the tools that are, and will continue to be, necessary to put the Grid to work in the wider corporate world.

Grid has become the technology buzzword of the day much because of the business cases. Before we saw the near crash of the economy, the need for more and more server capacity by all sorts of companies was typically solved by simply buying more and more servers. Although this was exceptionally good for the server manufacturers, it led to corporate technical infrastructures that were segmented, highly dispersed, and running at a mere fraction of what their capabilities were. It has been widely suggested that many Linux, UNIX, and Microsoft-based servers were, and are, running at less than a quarter of their potential capacity.

This is not a great leap. Even with servers that have terabyte databases running and serving hundreds of concurrent users, all running *ad hoc* data mining type queries, it is rare during a typical day to see the CPU on a server spike past 60 percent, and then drop almost immediately back down to 15 to 20 percent. But look at that same server during a daily or weekly bulk load, and you see several CPUs running at 95 to 99 percent and the server not begin able to keep up to the demand.

Beside the server, its brother is sitting with half as many CPUs, because it is a test server that only sees real demand when there are load tests to be performed before a major system move up. Otherwise, that server sits at between 5 and 10 percent at its most taxed.

With Grid, the capacity that sits wasted in the test server could be used by its overtaxed brother to distribute the processing and the load during the load process and allow the jobs to finish faster and give the business side of the house a warmer feeling about not needing to add capacity when most of the time is spent far under capacity.

Many IT departments, particularly in recent years, have been being called upon to provide as much, or more, computing power than they ever had to in the past; however, they are no longer able to simply go out and buy servers on a whim, not without proving to upper management that the job can simply not be done with existing capacity. Making do with less, the solution is to make better use of what already is owned. Grid technology adoption relies on the simple premise that it makes much more sense to provide required capacity without resorting to rushing out and buying a bunch of servers that would sit mostly idle or be underused most of the time.

Although you need to be able to alter the use of processing power on a task-by-task, job-by-job basis, this is what schedulers and resource brokers accomplish. This means that servers and server technology do not have to change because of the Grid coming into its own. How computation is accomplished will change. How applications work will change. The ubiquitous nature of the underlying framework, the soup that is the heterogeneous hardware, will simply run whatever is sent to it.

Lower budgets, smaller staffs, and more demand all work to drive technology to this new paradigm.

Services Oriented

The background of the Grid is a series of interworking services. Together, these services process the jobs that users submit, determine where and when those jobs should run, find interdependencies between these jobs, and return results to the user who called them (and anyone else who has the authority to view those results).

This is one of the interesting differences between the paradigms that typically accompany computing as it has always been and computing as it is in the Grid. The users make suggestions as to how and where their given program, query, or job should run; however, the services that make up the Grid have the ability to override many of these suggestions, with their decisions based on past history and the understanding of what could be right or wrong in reference to the operation. Although, to a great extent, on many operating systems, administrators and often certain services have the ability to override what the user suggests, with the Grid, many of the decisions are made solely by the services.

Batch Oriented

The batch-oriented approach is based on job scheduling paradigms similar to other distributed workload management systems. Through simple interfaces, you can describe parallel workflows, node requirements, prejob and postjob instructions, special conditions, and other job- and environment-specific requirements. Batch-oriented approaches are extremely well suited for precompiled, predefined programs that can be launched many times each with different input parameters. This type of parallelism is called parametric parallelism, meaning that it is parallelized based on parameters that are passed into it, or based on input datasets that it is set to work on. Batch-oriented applications can easily integrate into the Grid with little or no alteration to the underlying source code.

Object Oriented

The Grid makes extensive use of object-oriented concepts and models. Virtually everything in the Grid is an object, or can be expressed in object-oriented terms. A server, CPU, program — everything can be assigned methods and attributes. This feature of the Grid environment makes the Grid extensible and flexible and conceptually far easier for many programmers to deal with. Administration is a major component in the Grid, but programming and building applications, interfaces, and components that take advantage of that underlying structure are just as important, if not more so, as the administration of the services and the maintenance of the hardware and software that make up the infrastructure.

Supply and Demand

Technologists know and understand that the vast majority of the time, the CPU is not one of the overtaxed elements of the existing structure and infrastructure of the environment. They understand that there is spare capacity that exists in nearly every environment and know that the waste is a part of the animal with which they are dealing.

There is an excess capacity, and excess supply, but there is often an excess of demand in other places, demand that means that jobs run slower, need to be paged in and out to share the existing resources (meaning that efficiency is lowered even more due to the paging).

If 10 percent of the time there is insufficient capacity, then there are two different tracks that can be taken. You can ignore it and deal with the slowdowns. This would be the solution if you can deal with the slowdown and the processing window for these processes is big enough to contain them. The other option, historically, would be to buy more capacity, adding to the supply and to the overcapacity.

Now, however, Grid can allow you to divert capacity from other computers to assist with keeping the processing within the available window. No more having to answer the questions on why a process did not finish on time, no more missed SLAs (service level agreements), no more difficult upper management justifications and explanations.

And what technologist would not avoid having to justify to upper management, if at all possible?

Open Standards

The siren call of many technologists is the call to open standards and open systems. The broad adoption of open standards by industry and corporations is an essential key to the utility computing model for E-business on demand, regardless of the size or distribution of the model. Without the open standards all working together, the enabling of all kinds of different computing platforms to communicate and work effectively and efficiently with one another would be much more difficult. Without open standards, the integration of a company's internal systems, applications, and processes would remain a difficult, impractical, and expensive task. Without open standards, the Grid would be not only impractical, but also nearly impossible.

The broad-based acceptance of open standards, rather than the typical adoptions of historic, closed, proprietary architectures, allows the computing infrastructure and the departments surrounding that infrastructure to more easily absorb and adapt to new technical innovations.

Corporate IT Spending Budgets

How many IT organizations today have made the blanket statement that it does not matter the cost or the justification, go ahead and buy whatever resources you think might be necessary to meet the goals? I do not know about yours, but in any organization where I have been, there is a long and rigorous justification process for any additional capacity, and that was the case when the economy was booming, before the dot.com crash. Today such purchase requests are scrutinized even more closely, and the decisions are even more difficult.

Having to make do with what they have has driven many organizations, starting naturally with universities and research institutions; technologists have come up with the creative solution, the Grid. This solution now provides the opportunity for other companies to adopt those creative solutions as solutions of their own.

Cost, Complexity, and Opportunity

Cost is a tremendous driver in today's market. Many companies find it challenging to keep revenues up and costs down. Companies are looking far more closely at expenditures, and typically, today, technology expenditures are among the first to be cut. Prior to 2000, these technology type expenditures were rising at amazing rates. We have often gone from one extreme to the other. Now there is great deal of scrutinizing at the level of expenditures and, because many software and application purchases are tied very closely with the underlying hardware (operating systems, storage infrastructure, CPU source), at the applications that are purchased by the organization.

However, because utilization does increase, and there is required overhead for the utilization of resources, the incremental cost of scaling existing applications to work on existing large computers can tend to escalate, particularly as the cost of adding components to these boxes increases, often nonproportionally to the increased number of CPUs in the box. Licensing fees are often calculated by the number of CPUs on the box, regardless of their dedication to one specific application, and the costs of making the newly scaled applications function efficiently on the scaled-up boxes can add even more cost to the venture.

For this reason, many organizations are feeling the need to move away from mainframes and large-scale UNIX or virtual memory system (VMS) cluster machines to lower-cost Intel processor-based clusters that can be scaled up incrementally, instead of relying on the need to add more and more expensive nodes to existing clusters or upgrading an entire mainframe when the number of available CPU slots gets exhausted.

The Grid and its underlying technologies promise the ability to keep existing infrastructure, limiting the cost of migration or redesign of existing systems, and at the same time linking the other, often less expensive and often widely disparate technologies and Intel- and UNIX-based clusters together. This means that the existing technology can be reevaluated and put to work on problems that it was not likely to have been able to work on before. This will also mean that because the Grid-adopting companies can simply add to existing infrastructure, they can therefore reduce the overall purchase of hardware to only adding the necessary additional capacity, instead of having to completely replace their existing capacity based on current operation decisions. Not only will this limit the cost of hardware, but it will also increase the scalability of existing applications without having to radically redesign everything to take advantage of the new hardware.

The increasing complexity of many firms' technology infrastructure, partly because of changing needs and partly because of changing software decisions that affect the hardware decisions that have to be made, is another solid argument for the drive toward implementing a Grid environment that will allow the existing heterogeneity to work effectively and efficiently together to meet the common goals. Not only will this allow applications to take advantage of the underlying infrastructure through a virtual portal interface, but it will also, through similar virtual portals, allow the infrastructure to be managed with a smaller set of tools (limiting the learning curve and often the siloed maintenance and administrative capacity that exist in many organizations). Lower training costs, lower time to efficiency, and lower frequency of mistakes due to the user (or the administrator) having to remember commands as he or she switches between tools are all additional reasons that a Grid environment is making inroads into some unlikely organizations.

Further, there are more and more firms that have discovered tasks that they have determined to be advantageous to their own business, but that they have also determined to be too computationally impractical to perform without the addition of massive computational infrastructure, with limited IT budgets, or without a better way to leverage the component-based, Web-enabled services and architectures that would be necessary to extend their current technology as a means of meeting these new needs and answering these new questions.

Without funds to acquire additional resources, these firms determine their new needs to be unreachable and therefore forgo the ability to make inroads into these computations that will lead them to a better market position or to adapt new core competencies to their existing business model.

Again, the Grid enables these firms the ability to better utilize their current resources and expedite the desired, computationally intensive analytics they desire, along with the already complex and time- and resource-intensive analysis that they perform on a regular basis, alongside those that are run by users and analysts on an *ad hoc* basis. Faster, more efficient, and cheaper means that the companies that are using a Grid computing environment can take advantage of the opportunity to make advantageous leaps ahead of many of their competitors.

Better, Stronger, Faster

Users and technologists naturally want bigger and better computers, computers that meet their computing needs fast enough to allow them to keep up with what they believe to be their abilities, computers that can keep a dozen or more applications open at one time, and computers that are the latest and greatest, just because they are the latest and greatest. In some cases, for computer programmers, developers, and administrators, these high-end computers are a necessity. However, for most users, the latest and greatest, while nice, faster, and more efficient, is for the most part a waste.

How much is necessary to run PowerPoint, Word, or e-mail or browse the Internet? Most of these applications have a far greater need for memory than they will ever have for CPU cycles. Even in the financial markets, it takes limited capacity to actually enter a trade or update a customer file or send an IM message. It is often necessary to get bigger and better computers to meet the minimum required amounts of memory or CPU speed to run many of the applications in the market today. But many of these same applications could be Web enabled and, by extension, Grid enabled and run on a server, allowing the Grid to manage the load rather than having to scale the PCs to manage the load.

Companies often look at these increased requirements at the end-user level as a waste of money and resources. They look long and hard at who wants a bigger, better workstation, what that user will ultimately do with that workstation, and to what extent is the newer and greater capacity going to be utilized.

If you look at it from the Grid perspective, those investments in user desktop computing can be viewed more as an enterprise investment in capacity than as an end-user cost of work.

Grid can help a company utilize all of the existing excess capacity without ever running short on cycles, even during 100 billion days of share trading, or when a risk management company tries to analyze enterprise risk on a global basis. It can take a company's existing heterogeneous hardware, multiple operating systems, and applications written for and optimized to run on a particular platform and make them perform more elegantly together. Fortunately, many applications and application suites, similar to the Oracle E-Business suite, are becoming more component based and Internet (or intranet) enabled. The programming languages and protocols that these more flexible applications run efficiently (Java,

Simple Object Access Protocol [SOAP], eXtensible Markup Language [XML]) mean that the applications are more robust and more able to be hosted on nearly any server in the network. Although they are capable, with the Grid, they have the ability to prove that they have the staying power to run effectively as well as to deploy themselves in active locations, access the appropriate data, execute the proper programs and protocols on that data, and return the results back to the requesting location in an efficient and dependable manner. For those processes that are bound to a particular operating system, the Grid will be able to determine that operating system and direct the processing necessary to that operating system. This all is the promise and challenge for Grid technology and for the companies that are willing to cut their operating costs while allowing the network and the infrastructure to do the job that they were designed to do.

Efficiency Initiatives

Coupled with the requirement to make due with as much of the existing resources as possible, the necessity to these organizations is to increase efficiency of resource utilization.

There was a time when it did not matter how efficient a process was; as long as it ran and finished in the allotted window of time, it was deemed to be well enough for the task at hand. This is no longer necessarily true.

Now programs and applications are having more efficiency demands put on them and are being required to do the same work in a smaller window, and often more work in a smaller window than they have ever had before.

These new demands mean that programmers, administrators, and developers have to find ways to do more with less, and the Grid is one of the most optimum ways to do that. Jobs that are deemed to be independent, not reliant on the output of one application as the input to the next, can be broken out and run in parallel, allowing for faster execution on existing resources. However, those resources have to have the ability to be totally and completely independent while being orchestrated to work in such a way that all results come back to the user both correct and timely.

The programming paradigm needs to change slightly to take advantage of potential efficiencies and to enable the jobs that can to run in parallel. The Grid will then take these more efficient versions and launch them independently together to achieve the total desired outcome for the end user.

DATABASES IN THE GRID

Computers are magnificent tools for the realization of our dreams, but no machine can replace the human spark of spirit, compassion, love, and understanding.

—Louis Gerstner, CEO, IBM

Now we go onward and upward into the meat of the matter: databases and the Grid.

Data and databases in existing Grid projects and Grid environments have traditionally been simply an extension, an enlargement, of what had been in place before the Grid was introduced. This typically means that the database is centralized, with the software and data residing and accessible through that one server. This means that location becomes a bottleneck, and often a single point of failure. This will not be able to support the Grid environment and access patterns for the duration. We will look at means by which we can adapt existing database management styles that are prevalent today to the new conceptual model of the Grid.

Section 3 gets into the meat of what databases will look like in a Grid environment and what considerations need to be taken into account when determining how to place data into the new environment. To start, let us look at what it means to be a relational database, because these are the databases that will be primarily impacted in the Grid environment.

This introduction to databases will present you with vocabulary that will help you through the last section of the book.

In these chapters, I will tend to focus on Relational Database Management Systems (RDBMS) because they are the most prevalent today and because they are what most companies are either on or moving toward for most of their data storage. Hierarchical systems still exist and thrive, but for the purpose of simplicity, I will target one model. Relational systems have become popular, at least in part, due to their simple data model and flexibility. In a relational database, data is represented as a collection of relations, with each relation being depicted as a table structure. The columns in the tables are considered to be the relation's attributes, and rows (or tuples) represent entities, instances of the relation, or records for those who have their backgrounds in flat-file processing. Every row in the table (every record) has a set of attributes (at the RDBMS level, and hidden even if at the logical level they are allowed to be duplicated).

Chapter 8

Introducing Databases

Where is all the knowledge we lost with information?

—**T.S. Eliot**

Those parts of the system that you can hit with a hammer are called hardware; those program instructions that you can only curse at are called software.

—**Anonymous**

Databases

A database is a collection of related files. How those files relate together and to each other depends almost entirely on the model that is used. One early database model includes the hierarchical model (as in Information Management System [IMS] databases), where all files and all records are and have to be related in a parent–child manner, similar to a single-parent household where each child has at most one parent at any given time, but where each parent can have multiple children. Another early model is the network model, with its files related as owners and members. This model resembles blended and extended families, where each owner (or each parent) can have multiple children (members) and each child can have multiple parents.

Then there is the relational database model with its huge step forward. Relational databases allow files (tables) to be related by means of a common field or fields, and to relate any two tables, we simply join the tables on the common field. This makes the relational model extremely flexible and very adaptable to use in the Grid environment.

Relational Database

Although entire books have been written on relational theory, and careers are made on the design and optimization of relational databases, this book is not designed to do that. I would highly recommend a deeper understanding of relational theory and databases than I intend to touch on in these few pages, and a good textbook is a wonderful addition to your library if you do not already have one. This chapter will serve as a review of the terminology that I will use in the following chapters to get the most out of this book.

An understanding of relational databases requires an understanding of some of the most basic terms:

- Data refers to the values that are stored in the database. On its own, data means very little; 16127 is an example.
- Information is data that is processed to have a meaning. Deriving information (in this case, that 16127 is the zip code for Grove City, PA) requires more than simply data.
- A relational database is a collection of tables. If you do not have a good grasp of relational databases and how their tables interact, think of an Excel spreadsheet workbook as the database and each worksheet in the workbook as a table.
- Each table contains records, or the horizontal rows in the table.
- Each record contains a given set of fields, which map to the vertical columns of the table (or the lettered columns in the spreadsheet).
- Fields can be of many different types. There are many standard types (character, number, date), and each DBMS (database management system), such as Oracle, DB2, SQL Server, or MySQL, can also add its own specific data types to the mix (for example, Oracle adds Varchar2, varray, and nested tables).
- The domain of the data refers to all of the possible values that each field can contain. Marital_status may be limited to the values married, unmarried, and widowed.
- A field is said to contain a null value when it contains absolutely nothing at all.

■ Null fields can create complexities in calculations because they do not equate to anything that is real and can therefore have adverse consequences for data accuracy. For this reason, many numeric fields are specifically set not to contain null values. There are many other reasons to not allow nulls in a column, and many of these tie back to specific business rules for a given company or line of business.

■ A relationship is the way that the data in one table relates to the data in another table. These are often verbs or verb phrases (like *has a* or *is a*).

   ■ A one-to-one (1:1) relationship occurs when, for each row in Table a, there exists only one row in Table b, and vice versa.

   ■ A one-to-many (1:m) relationship occurs where, for each row in Table x, there exist many rows in Table y, but for each row in Table y, only one row in Table x exists.

   ■ A many-to-many (m:n) relationship occurs where, for each row in Table x, there can be many rows in Table y, and for every row in Table y, there can be many rows in Table x.

   ■ A mandatory relationship exists when, for every row in Table y, there must exist a row in Table x (although multiple rows in Table y may correspond to each row in Table x). This type of relationship is often enforced with primary and foreign keys and is considered to be a part of referential integrity.

Tuples

One of the most common words used in relation to a relational database is *tuple*. Many people use it, but we need to have a handle on what it really means. Tuples equate to what people understand as rows or records, but are literally the row, not the data that makes up the row. A tuple is an ordered set of values, commonly separated by commas, that is used for passing a string of parameters from one program to another, for representing a set of attribute values in a relational database (a storage unit or a row in a relational database), and is analogous to a record in a nonrelational database. It is also frequently used in abstract math to denote a multidimensional coordinate system. The number of tuples in a relation is known as the cardinality of the relation. Tuples in a table are unique and can be arranged in any order.

Attributes

An attribute is the property of an entity; it is what the tuple is made up of. Webopedia (www.webopedia.com) says that an attribute is a characteristic; relative to file processing, it is synonymous with a field. Attributes are considered to be the set of values that make up the tuple or the row.

Entities

An entity refers to a real-world object. It is (again from Webopedia) a piece of data, an object or concept about which data is stored. Entities are the columns of the table, the LNAME, FNAME, and SSN to which the attributes can be mapped.

Relationship

The way that the entities relate to each other, how the data is shared between entities, typically these include a verb (*is a*, *has a*, *works for*).

Relational Algebra

E.F. Codd's work that was the basic inspiration of the Relational Database Management System (RDBMS) was based on mathematical concepts. It is no surprise that the theory of database operations is based on set theory.

Relational algebra provides a collection of operations to manipulate relations. It supports the notion of a request to retrieve information from a database, or a query. It provides the following set operations.

Union

Given two relations having similar types of tuples, a union returns a new and unique relation that consists of the set of the unioned tuples. A union is typically signified by the "or" operator, as in all of the people hired in January or all of the people hired in February or all of the people hired in March, providing a unique unioned set of all of the people hired in the first calendar quarter.

Intersection

An intersection creates a new relation by taking the intersection of two relationships and returning the unique set of tuples that answers that description. Intersections are typically created using the "and" operator. "I want to know all of the fruits that are citrus and yellow" would yield grapefruit and lemons.

Difference

A difference returns the set of the difference between two relations. This is often noted by an "and not" operator. "I want to know all of the plant accidents that affected hands and that are not pinch point accidents."

Cartesian Product

So far, I have not been able to come up with a really good reason to deliberately create a Cartesian product. A Cartesian product usually occurs when someone does an implicit join operation that creates tuples with the combined attributes, whether or not they relate correctly to each other. It is often created by not understanding exactly what you really want the database to give you and by not providing a limiting factor on the statement (a where clause). Give me all of the employees and departments in the company.

```
Select employee_name, department_number from
employee, department;
```

This would provide a list of employees and, for each employee, a list of all of the departments in the company, although it is likely that the required information is a list of all of the employees and the departments that they work for, possibly a list of all employees and a list of all of the departments that each employee has ever worked for.

Select

Not to be confused with the select as in a select statement, in the case of relational algebra, *select* is a restriction operator. Where a select in a typical select SQL statement can select anything from all of the attributes in a tuple to a single value from a dummy table to provide for calculation or date verification, select in this case refers to the restriction of the result set to a subset of the rows or tuples of the input table that are returned to satisfy a given condition. Although an SQL select will also accomplish this, the reference in relational algebra is more restrictive. Select in this case is closer to the where clause in an SQL statement.

Project

Project is an operator that limits the columns or attributes that are retrieved from the specific table or tables. Project can also be used in such a way as to determine if there are duplicate values in the target table that will be returned and eliminate those duplicates from the result set. This is typically not the default behavior, and a project operator (in the case of SQL, it would be the select list that is the project operator) simply returns a list of all of the values, regardless of duplication, that appear in a column of a table.

Ordinarily, restriction and projection operators are used together to refine the search criteria and provide the user with exactly those columns with which the user is concerned and only those rows that fit the criteria that interests the user.

Join

This is probably one of the most complex operations to deal with both computationally and logically. It consists, mathematically, of the creation a Cartesian product (usually stored in a temporary table either on disk or in memory), followed by a selection based on some formula. Again, this maps roughly to a where clause and the determinant is typically a comparison operator such as equal (or an inverse comparison operator such as not equal).

- *Equijoin* — An equijoin provides all of the result tuples where one column's value is equal to the value found in a similar column in a different table.
- *Outer join* — In an outer join, you are looking for all of the rows from one table where there is an equal value in the second table, and all of the rows in one table for which there are no corresponding values in the second table. This can be a right or left outer join, denoting which table you want the information on (the left side of the equality operator or the right), that has no matching information from the other table.
- *Full outer join* — Similar to the simple outer join, this provides all of the matching information and all of the information in each table for which there is no matching information in the other table.

Relational Calculus

Relational calculus is the basis for a formal query language that is used to retrieve information from the tables in a relational database. Instead of having to write a sequence of relational algebra operations any time that we want to retrieve information, we write a comparatively simple single declarative expression that describes the result set that we are after, in terms that the end user can understand. This is conceptually similar to writing a program in a programming language, such as C, COBOL, or Java, instead of having to write it in assembler or machine language — closer still to telling your son and daughter to call you if they need help, rather than providing them with information on how to find a phone, dial the phone, and retrieve the phone number at which to contact you if they have trouble (calling would at that point likely be as much trouble as the trouble that they are having). The expressive power of the relational calculus-based language is identical to what would be available if the user actually used relational algebra to access the information.

The query language that nearly any relational database supports is SQL (Structured Query Language).

Tuple relational calculus is a nonprocedural language wherein we provide a formal description of the information required. It is a subset of classical first-order predicate logic. Queries in tuple relational calculus typically take the following form:

```
{Query Target | Query Condition}
```

The query target is a tuple variable whose range is across tuples of values. The query condition is a logical expression such that it is used on the query target and possibly some other variables as well, and that if a concrete tuple of values is substituted for each occurrence of the query target in the query condition, the condition evaluates to a Boolean value of either true or false.

The result of a tuple relational calculus query, with respect to any given database instance, is the unique set of all choices of values for which the query variables make the query condition a true statement about the database instance. The relation between the tuple relational calculus and logic is in that the query condition is a logical expression of classical first-order logic.

In a domain relational calculus, the variables range over domain values of the attributes rather than on a set of tuples. This tends to be more complex, and variables are required for each distinct attribute. It takes the following form:

```
{A, B, C, D … Z | Query Condition}
```

where A, B, C, and so forth are the domain variables over which the condition is applicable.

Object Database

Although there is no official standard for object databases, they have begun to become a popular alternative to simple relational database management systems, and are typically not an either/or proposition, but are an extension of relational databases.

In an object database, the objects and object relationships, as well as the storage of those constructs within the database and within an application, are written in object-oriented language.

An object databases employs a data model that has object-oriented aspects like class, along with attributes and methods and integrity constraints. It provides object identifiers for any persistent instance of a class, supports encapsulation of data and methods, allows for multiple inheritances, and fully supports abstract data types.

Object databases combine the elements of object orientation and object-oriented programming languages with database disciplines and capabilities, providing more than simply persistent storage of programming language objects. Object databases extend the functionality of object-oriented programming languages (C#, C++, Smalltalk, Java) to provide full-featured database programming capabilities, resulting in a high level of congruence between the data model from the application's perspective and the data model of the database. This capability results in less code, more intuitive data structures, and better maintainability, as well as reusability of code (code once, one of the distinct advantages of modular programming). Object-oriented programmers can write complete database applications with a modest amount of additional effort.

An object-oriented language is the data retrieval language for both the application and the database. It provides a very direct relationship between the application objects and the stored objects. The correlation is distinct. Data definition, data manipulation, and data retrieval queries reflect this relationship.

Declarative languages have been suggested, such as Object Query Language (OQL), to allow for database queries, but have not traditionally been completely SQL compliant. The result of an OQL query can be an atomic piece of data, a structure, a literal, one object, or a collection of objects. Most object databases support SQL, primarily for the added context of open database connectivity (ODBC).

In the RDBMS, SQL is the means by which someone creates, accesses, and updates objects. In an Object Database Management Systems (ODBMS), although declarative queries are still possible via SQL, the primary interface for creating and modifying objects is directly through an object language using the native language syntax. What is more, every object in the system is automatically given an identifier that is unique and immutable for the duration of that object's life. One object can contain an object identifier that logically references another object, proving a valuable feature when associating objects with real-world entities, such as products or customers or business processes. The object identifiers also form the basis of features such as bidirectional relationships, versioning, composite objects, and distribution. In most Object Database Management Systems, the object identifier becomes physical when the logical identifier is converted to physical pointers to specific memory addresses once the data is loaded into memory for use by the application. This conversion of references to memory pointers allows access to cached objects at RAM speeds (hundredths of microseconds), instead of the traditional approach of sending messages to and from the server, which can take milliseconds or more.

Architecture Differences between Relational and Object Databases

Relational databases have been historically built around central server architectures, which are much the same as mainframe architectures. Object databases often consume resources on a network of computers, with processing on the back or front end, as well as on intermediate tiers, and with caching on each level and clustering capabilities that are completely independent of type. Although relational databases typically confine their processing to SQL and its operations (SELECT/PROJECT/JOIN and INSERT/UPDATE/DELETE), adding procedural support as needed by their own language or by extending capabilities of other languages through differing means, object databases allow the use of host object languages directly on the objects. Instead of translating back and forth between application language structures (COBOL, C, etc.) and database structures, application programmers can simply use the object language to create and access objects through their methods. The database system maintains the persistence, integrity, recoverability, and concurrency of those same objects.

Object Relational Database

Extended relational database and *object relational database* are synonyms for database management products that try to unify the best aspects of both the relational and object databases, although there is no official definition or standard for what an object relational database really is, and the definition can therefore be vendor interpreted.

The vendors that have products in this space include IBM, Informix (now IBM), and Oracle. Until very recently, extended relational database was probably the more appropriate term. Adherence to SQL standards is a given. Object Relational Database Management Systems (ORDBMS) will be specified by the extensions to the SQL standard and through proprietary vendor implementations. This category of database products has been an amorphous gray area between object and relational databases.

The Object Relational Database Management System employs a data model that attempts to bring object orientation to tables. All persistent information is still in tables, in tuples with attributes, but some table entries can have richer, more diverse and complex data structures, or abstract data types. An abstract data type is constructed by combining basic alphanumeric data types, much the same as a type definition in C. The support for abstract data types is an attractive extension because the operations and functions associated with the new data type can then be used to index, store, and retrieve the abstracted records based on the content of the new data type (graphics, audio, and video). Therefore, you can see that an ORDBMS should be a superset of a traditional RDBMS, and would default to using at least SQL2, or later none of the object capabilities are used. Although simple approaches have provided more structures for modeling more complex data and freestanding functions, they typically lacked the fundamental object requirement of encapsulation of operations with data. With newer releases of databases, this is not always the case, and the concept of encapsulation and object overloading is beginning to be seen in the richer releases. They have also frequently had limited support for abstracted relationships, inheritance, and polymorphism, or for allowing the creation of user-defined persistent classes, and integration with host object languages like Java. Again, with the later releases of database management systems, support for these richer functions and abilities is becoming more prevalent.

An ORDBMS supports an extended form of SQL, sometimes referred to as an ObjectSQL. The extensions are created to support the object model (for example, queries involving object attributes) and typically include support for queries involving nested or abstract objects, set-valued attributes, and inclusion of methods or functions in search predicates. The ORDBMS is still relational because the data is stored in tables of rows and columns, and SQL, with the extensions mentioned, is the language for data definition, manipulation, and query. The object relational database simply extends the concept of relational database. The target and result of a query are still tables or tuples. The key in the object relational access is searchable content.

Vendors supplying Object Relational Database Management Systems would like us to believe that they have unified the two different conceptual data models into single products that integrate the different kinds of processing in a highly efficient way. If the unification is at the interface level, a unifying interface could be elegantly placed over different storage managers, allowing one manager to manage the relational data model and another to manage the object data model. This is similar to the means by which virtualized federated databases (in the following paragraph) handle the access and virtualization. A more comprehensive unification solution extends the integration farther down into the database storage engine itself. This is no mean feat and affects many important aspects of the DBMS. Affected areas include query optimization, performance, and scalability. The major RDBMS vendors know a great deal about how to optimize a traditional RDBMS, and are extending their ability to allow ease of access and manipulation to drawn-in objects, but their investment into these areas has historically been confined to table-based data structures, and much less is expertise is available concerning how to optimize when a data blade is added, for image processing, for example. We have come far in recent years, and people are beginning to take advantage of systems that allow for the deeper integration.

Enterprise data rarely resides in only one database or one type of database; in the Grid, this is particularly true. Therefore, most vendors provide means by which you can integrate processing against multiple, heterogeneous databases. Although this process may involve multiple vendors of one data model (relational, for example) or mixed data models (relational, object, and object relational), the primary support is to be the foundation of the data model that is supported by the vendor's own database product. If a vendor can provide a fairly transparent view of the integrated, virtualized databases, then the integration is often referred to as a multidatabase system or a federated database (this is not to be confused with distributed or replicated databases). This is particularly true for transaction processing systems. If the support for the heterogeneous system is less than transparent, the connectivity is more in the line of a gateway, and these products fall in the category of middleware.

There are currently dozens of terabyte online databases, and they are becoming more common as the price of online storage decreases. With single tables now being measured in the hundreds of gigabytes, with billions of rows, it becomes difficult to scale even mainframes to be powerful enough to meet the input/output (I/O) demands of a large relational database.

SQL

SQL is a nonprocedural programming language; it is a functional programming language, describing the answer set as a means to access the data. The database's optimizer picks the best execution plan, the best data flow web, the degree of parallelism, and other execution parameters (process placement, memory, monitoring).

SQL functions both as a Data Definition Language (DDL) and as a Data Manipulation Language (DML). As a DDL, it allows a database programmer, a database administrator, or database designer to define tables, create views, etc. As a DML, it allows any end user (programmer, database administrator, or functional business type) to fairly easily and elegantly retrieve, insert, update, or delete information from tables. The intent of SQL is to create a structured English-like query language to interface to the early relational database systems, and it was one of the first high-level declarative database languages.

SQL provides several standard operators to allow users to perform the actions that will let them access or manipulate the data as their jobs require.

Select

Select, in the case of SQL, provides similar functionality to the project operator in relational algebra. Tell me what information you want to operate on and what table that information resides in. Select has to be accompanied by a "from" clause to allow the database to know from where you want the information to be retrieved. As of now, no database is intelligent enough to know where the exact data that the user wants resides without some mechanism (programmatic or deliberate) telling it that information. The addition of the keyword *distinct* tells the database that the user wants only the distinct information, no duplicates.

Where

To restrict the information returned to a set of tuples that meet a certain set of criteria (restrict in relational algebra), the user uses the where clause.

And/Or

If there is more than one criteria on which a user wants to limit the result set returned, the "and" and/or the "or" operator can be added to a multiconditional where clause to more precisely define the union or intersection of the individual result sets returned. "And" is evaluated first. "Or" is evaluated after all of the "ands" are evaluated. The only exception to this rule is when a parenthesis is involved. The order of evaluation is similar to the order of operation in math operators.

In

Another means by which we can limit the information returned in a where clause is with the "in" conditional. Typically, when a user wants to limit the information, equality or inequality is used as the limiting mechanism (where state = TX, where city = Houston, where population > 100,000,000), but what happens when there is a list of things to which you want to be able to compare a column value? The "in" conditional allows for a list of values to be included in the comparison mechanism.

Where State IN (TX, AX, NM, OK, LA, CO)

Not only can you tell it what list you want it to be in, you can take the negative approach to similar logic and tell it what list you do not want to have retrieved.

Where State Not In (AK, TN, KY)

Between

Okay, so we are now getting a better feel for what limiting factors we can accomplish in a where clause, but what happens if you want information about a range of values, and any value in that range. An "in" list might be too big to be efficient or elegant. In that case, you can use a "between" operator.

Where salary between 500,000 and 1,000,000

Like

So you know part of a string that you want to find in the result set, and you only want those results that have this string as part of the results. You can take a part of the string and, with the use of a wildcard character, find just those tuples that have attributes that have that string as a part of their value set.

Where Last_name like '*ones' or last_name like '*mith'

Insert

Okay, so we now know how to get data information out of a database, but how do you get information into a database? The insert statement is the means by which you get information into a database via an SQL statement. You can insert a single row or multiple rows. You can insert only specific values for specific columns (insert into employee (last_name, first_name, SSN) values ('SMITH,' 'BILL,' 1234567890), or you can insert values into the columns in the order that the columns appear in the table (insert into employee select * from new_employee).

Update

Once data is in the database, you have to have a way to alter the information in case it changes. The update statement is the means by which you accomplish this. You can update a single column's value or multiple columns in the same statement. It is *very important* when you update to make sure that the where clause is exactly what you mean and that you are updating exactly those records that you mean to be updating.

Update salary set salary = salary * 1.25

would give everyone in the company a 25 percent raise.

Update salary set salary = salary * 1.25 where department = 123

would give only those in one department a 25 percent raise. There may be big difference between these two statements. If you want to update several columns with the same limiting criteria, you would compose the following update statement:

Update salary, department set salary = salary * 1.25, department = 234 where department = 123.

Delete

You may need to make information go away once it is in the database. Delete is the means by which you can accomplish this. As in the update statement, it is important that care be taken to be certain that what is deleted is what is meant to be deleted.

Delete from employee

will delete all of the rows from the employee table, effectively removing all of the employees from the company.

Delete from employee where department = 123

would delete only those employees who belong to department 123.

Database

In the framework of this book, a database is a collection of data records that are tied together with a database managment system of software. Most directly, we will be dealing with relational database management systems.

Data Model

A data model is a collection of concepts for describing data.

Schema

A schema is a description of a particular collection of data, using the given data model.

Relational Model

A relation is a table with rows and columns (tuples and attributes).

Every relation belongs to a schema, which describes the columns and fields.

Users typically have many views of a single conceptual (or logical) structure of the data. The logical layout is an extraction from the physical schema and how the files and indexes are used.

Typically, a database management system, particularly a relational database management system, has a layered architecture.

Anomalies

Anomalies, errors in data or errors in the logic of the data, can cause garbage in, garbage out in your database environment. Although anomalies are typically taken care of with normalization of the data and the database, the additional complexities of the Grid environment can introduce the option for allowing them into the database.

Anomalies are only truly anomalous if they defy business rules of the organization.

Insert Anomaly

An insertion anomaly is a failure to be able to place new information into all the places in the database where information needs to be stored. If a database is properly normalized, there is a minimal number of places where the information needs to be inserted. If any of the places that need to contain the information are missed, due to a failure in either the design of the database or the design of an application, then your data will be inconsistent at best, and completely wrong at worst.

Can you insert an employee if that employee does not have a department assigned to him or her yet? Can there be a department if there is not a manager for that department and there are no employees of that department? Can you have a sale if you have no line items and no customer associated with that sale?

Deletion Anomaly

A deletion anomaly is the failure to be able to remove information from an existing entry. Because it is often the case that either information needs to be removed from more than one place, or relationships exist between data in different tables and associated data needs to be removed at the same time (or should not be removed at the same time and is), then deletion either causes a loss of data that is auxiliary to the data being removed and is associated with other data, or strands data without any association.

If you delete a customer from your database, should all of the purchases that that customer made be removed? If a department is dissolved, should all of the employees of that department be removed from the company, or have they been reassigned?

Update Anomaly

Because an update involves modifications that may be additions, deletions, simple updates of an attribute, or a combination, update anomalies can be either of the anomalies discussed above.

If an employee changes his or her name, does that employee get inserted a second time, for the altered name? If a manager changes departments, does the original department get left with no manager? If there is no manager, is there a department, and if that department goes away, what happens to the employees?

Chapter 9

Parallel Database

> Good Communication is as stimulating as black coffee, and just as hard to sleep after.

> **—Ann Morrow Lindberg**

With the Grid, hardware is becoming modularized; each module can be many little devices. As a consequence, servers are now arrays of commodity parts and automation is becoming a necessity. Parallelism, in the Grid, is simply a way of life. The programs are necessarily becoming parallel as bigger jobs are being split and the pieces that are not interdependent are running concurrently across the system. Software is becoming parallel via data flow, and data is becoming parallel via partitioning.

Parallelism means that many smaller jobs are running concurrently and the result sets are being merged together to provide the end user with the requested information. Further, it means that you can maintain a higher level of data independence at the application layer than in many other circumstances.

Data Independence

Data independence infers that applications are insulated from the need to know or understand how the data is structured and how and where the data is stored. Although the format that the data takes is relevant (Is it numeric, date data type, or character data?), how it is stored should not be.

Logical data independence means protection from changes occurring in the logical structure of the data and allowing for the sliding in of parallel systems under traditional applications.

Physical data independence includes protection from changes in the physical structure of data, as well as the minimization of constraints on processing, thus enabling clean parallelism.

Parallel Databases

Databases housing a large volume of data use a great deal of disk space and large amounts of memory. I/O (input/output) becomes a bottleneck, and often memory access becomes one as well. Disk speed is slower than RAM speed, and ram speed is slower than the speed of the processors. If you consider the situation in the light of Moore's law, where CPU speed and network bandwidth double roughly every 18 months, but disk access speeds have not kept up with that average, I/O bottlenecks will likely continue to worsen if we simply throw more CPU and RAM at problems, which is likely the solution that many companies employ. This said, it would appear that the ideal database machine would have a single, infinitely fast processor and an infinitely large amount of memory with an infinite amount of bandwidth. Because this single machine does not exist, it is possible, and even more possible now in the Grid environment, to somewhat build such a machine. You can build an infinitely fast processor out of an infinite number of processors, each with finite speed. It is also possible to build an infinitely large amount of memory with an infinite number of storage units, each with finite speed. By increasing the I/O bandwidth, by data partitioning and parallel data access, you can increase the throughput from disk. Combining the throughput of many processors and using many nodes, each with good cost performance communicating through the network (with good cost via high-volume components and bandwidth), many of the challenges can be addressed. Because the Grid does this with conventional commodity processors, memory, and disks, it allows a Grid database to be in an excellent position to exploit the massive numbers of CPU cycles and bandwidth and provide extreme performance gains. The challenge is to parallelize the applications and the data to run a well load-balanced system.

A parallel database management system is typically a homogeneous system, with tightly coupled processors using a fast interconnection network with a far larger degree of parallelism than is accomplished with typical distributed database systems. The processors in this system are not always autonomous computers, although there are several configurations with different levels of autonomy, but they are typically controlled by a single operating system and database management system. Parallelism is an unanticipated benefit of the relational model and is accomplished when relational operators are applied to data by one of three techniques: data partitioning of the relations across multiple disks, pipelining of tuples between operators, and partitioned execution of operators across nodes.

With a Grid implementation, you have the potential to be able to truly parallelize the database as well as parallelize or partition the application code. Loosely defined, a parallel database management system (DBMS) is simply a DBMS that is implemented on a tightly coupled (shared memory) multiprocessor system. A parallel database system achieves high performance through parallelism, with both high throughput of interquery parallelism and low response time in intraoperation parallelism. With the additional benefit of high availability and reliability through data replication, the resulting system is even more robust.

There are two different types of parallelism: intraquery parallelism and interquery parallelism.

Intraquery parallelism can be further subdivided into intraoperation parallelism, where multiple nodes are working to compute a given operation, and interoperational parallelism, with each operator runs concurrently on a different site, exploiting pipelining (detailed later in the chapter). Interquery parallelism provides that nodes are divided across different queries.

Ideally, a parallel system has two theoretically demonstrable characteristics. The first of these is linear speedup. Speedup holds the problem size constant and grows the system. Given a fixed-size job, run on a small system, the premise is that twice as much hardware can perform a task in half of the elapsed time. Although a one-to-one correlation of speed to the number of processors may not be likely to be completely achievable, with an infinite supply of processors, anywhere but in theory, we can see the speedup as the ratio of the amount of elapsed time seen on a small system to the amount of elapsed time of the same process seen on a small system.

The second characteristic is linear scale-up. Scale-up measures the ability to grow both the system and the problem. The premise of linear scale-up is that twice as much hardware can perform twice as large a task in the same elapsed time. If resources increase in proportion to the data size on which the processes are working, then time is constant. Again, mathematically (with an infinite supply of hardware), this is probably only truly achievable in theory, but the ratio, in practice, of the amount of scale-up is equal to the ratio of a small system's elapsed time on a small problem to a big system's elapsed time working on a big problem. The elapsed time of one processor on a small problem's elapsed time in relation to the elapsed time of n processors on a problem and associated data that is n times the size of the original is the measurement of both the system's and the problem's ability to grow. If that ratio is exactly 1, then linear scale-up has been achieved. This type of scale-up is typically seen in transaction processing systems and time-sharing systems. Scale-up can be further subdivided into two different views: transaction scale-up and batch scale-up. Transaction scale-up is ideally suited to parallel systems because each transaction is typically not large and the transactions are ordinarily independent from each other. Each independent job can be run on a separate processor. Transaction scale-up says that although you can add more clients and more servers to the network, as the additional servers are added to the configuration, similar response time is desirable.

The second form of scale-up is batch scale-up. Batch scale-up arises when a task is presented to the system as a single large job. This type of job is typically of large database queries (complex reports run against the database, data warehouse and decision support systems) and scientific simulations. Ordinarily, batch scale-up consists of using an increasingly larger computer to solve an increasing larger problem. In the case of a database, batch scale-up translates to being able to run the same query on an increasingly larger database; in scientific problems, it means performing the same calculation on an increasingly finer grain or on an increasing longer simulation.

There are several barriers to linear scale-up and speedup.

Start-Up

Start-up is the time that is needed to start a parallel operation. If thousands of processes must be started, the start-up time can easily dominate the actual computation time. Start-up includes the creation of a process or a thread, opening files, and optimization. It takes time to start a parallel operation. Time is needed for thread creation and connection overhead. Depending on the speed of the resulting operations, this start-up process may take more time than the actual computational time for the process.

Interference

Interference is the slowdown of the system that each new process imposes on all of the other processes when accessing shared resources. When accessing shared resources, there can be interference from the other things accessing these same resources, causing each new process to slow down the others to one degree or another. Interference can occur at the device level (at the CPU, disk, or bus), at the logical level (with contention for locks or logs), or at the server level for other resources. This creates what is known as a hot spot, or a bottleneck.

Skew

As the number of parallel steps increases, the average size of each step decreases. The variance in the speed can exceed the mean. Skew occurs often when a task gets to be very small and the variance of the execution time of that task is greater than the service time. This is an example of the law of diminishing returns. The response time of a set of parallelized processes is only as fast as the time of the slowest process in the set.

There are several different kinds of skew, all of which can cause problems for intraoperator parallelism, the solution to which is sophisticated parallel algorithms that deal with skew and dynamic processor allocation at execution time.

Attribute Data Skew

In parallel database systems, data is generally partitioned and stored on secondary storage devices of different processors. The occurrence of a value in an attribute column in the partitions can be very different from those that are located in another value of the same attribute.

Tuple Placement Skew

When tuples of a relation are initially partitioned and stored in different processing systems, the number of tuples in one system can be different from those in other systems.

Selectivity Skew

If the same selection operation is performed on two different partitions of a relation, the number of tuples produced from one data partition can be different from the number produced from another partition.

Redistribution Skew

This is when data produced in a parallel processor for one operation causes other operations to be off balance. The data needs to be redistributed to accomplish load balancing in the next operation, and the redistribution may not accomplish balanced data loads. Examples of this are the use of indexing or hashing to accomplish redistribution.

Join Product Skew

The results of a parallel join operation may not produce the same number of tuples in different processors.

The parallel database system employs a session manager that performs transaction monitoring and a host interface that initiates and closes the user sessions. There is a request manager that is in charge of compilation and optimization. It manages the data directory and provides semantic data control and recovery and query and transaction execution control. There is also a data manager that is responsible for the database operations, management of supporting transactions, and management of the data.

Multiprocessor Architecture Alternatives

Shared Everything

Figure 9.1 is a graphic example of a shared memory/shared everything architecture.

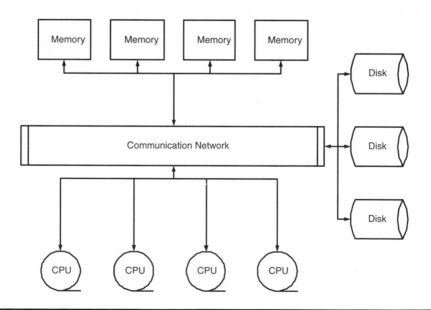

Figure 9.1   Shared memory (shared everything).

In a shared memory system, all of the processors share direct access to common global memory and to all of the disks. The advantages of a shared memory, shared everything system are its simplicity and load balancing ability. Programming in a shared memory, shared everything architecture is easy, but building the system is expensive and scale-up is difficult. Other disadvantages are its overall cost, limited extensibility, low availability, conflicting access to memory, and memory fault.

In a share everything system, the communication consists of a high-speed bus. Examples of hardware that typically contribute in a shared everything architecture are IBM mainframes, SGI Challenge, or Pentium-based SMP (symmetric multiprocessor). In a shared everything architecture, typically databases involved have been Informix's earlier releases: Oracle back in Oracle 7 and Oracle 8 and IBM DB2 for MVS (multiple virtual system).

Shared Disk

Figure 9.2 is a representation of a shared disk architecture. Primary advantages of shared disk architecture are the cost, extensibility, load balancing, availability, and easy migration. Disadvantages are the complexity, performance problems, distributed locking, two-phase commit requirements, and access to shared disk in potential bottlenecks.

In a shared disk architecture, the typical hardware involved is similar to Intel Paragon. Typical databases making use of this architecture are

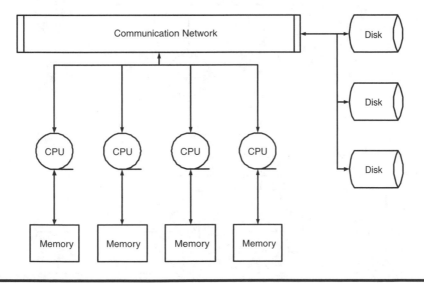

Figure 9.2   Shared disk.

IBM IMS database, DEC (Digital Equipment Corporation) VAX database management systems, or Oracle on DEC's VAX clusters or nCube computers.

Shared Nothing (Message Passing)

Figure 9.3 shows a graphic example of a shared nothing architecture. In a shared nothing architecture, processors communicate with each other only by sending messages via interconnect networks. Tuples of each relation in the database are partitioned, or declustered, across disk storage units attached either directly to each processor or through a storage area network (SAN) or network attached storage (NAS) system. Partitioning allows multiple processors to scan large relations in parallel without requiring specially designed or specially built I/O devices.

In a shared nothing architecture, each memory unit and portion of the disk are owned by some processor, and that processor acts as a server for the data. Mass storage in this architecture is distributed among the processors by connecting one or more disks.

Shared nothing architectures minimize interference by minimizing resource sharing-exploiting commodity processors and memory without

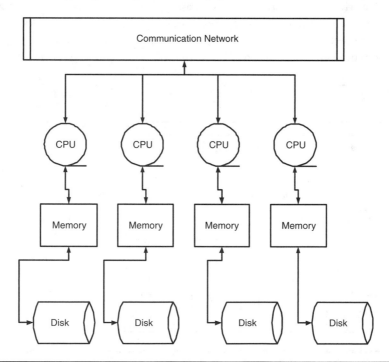

Figure 9.3 Shared nothing.

the need for an incredibly powerful interconnection network (although with enough speed and bandwidth to support the processing).

Where the other architectures move large quantities of data through the interconnection network, the shared nothing design moves only the questions and answers through the network. Memory access and disk access are performed locally in a processor, and the filtered data is passed back to the calling client program. This allows for a far more scalable design by minimizing the traffic on the interconnection network.

The main advantage of a shared nothing architecture multiprocessor system is that it can scale-up to hundreds or thousands of processors that do not interfere with each other, where the largest shared memory, multiprocessor machines available are limited to far fewer processors.

Advantages of shared nothing architectures are lower cost, higher extensibility and scale-up, and availability. However, programming for a shared nothing network is hard. Other disadvantages include complexity of implementation of distributed database functions and difficulty in load balancing.

Hardware that has taken part in shared nothing architecture is similar to the IBM 6000 SP, and databases used on this type of system are similar to Tereadata, or the IBM DB2 parallel edition.

Hybrid Architecture

Hybrid architectures, as seen in Figure 9.4, attempt to maximize the benefits of different kinds of architectures and minimize the disadvantages. Examples of systems that have taken this approach are Sequent computers and Bull PowerCluster.

Hierarchical Cluster

In a hierarchical cluster, as depicted in Figure 9.5, several share everything clusters are interconnected through a communications network to form a shared nothing structure at the interconnect level. This approach attempts to minimize the communications overhead associated with a simple shared nothing structure while allowing each cluster to be kept small and within the limitations of the local memory and I/O bandwidth. There are databases designed to take advantage of this type of architecture. Tereadata database systems for the NCR WorldMark 5100 computer and the Sybase MP system took advantage of this system. The Informix online extended parallel server was also built to allow the database to take advantage of this architecture. The flexibility and performance of the shared everything architecture are coupled with the high extensibility of the shared nothing architecture.

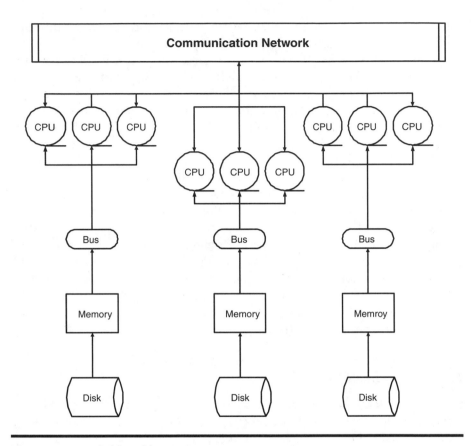

Figure 9.4   Hybrid architecture.

NUMA

The Nonuniform Memory Architecture (NUMA) employs a single address space on a distributed physical memory. This eases not only application portability, but also extensibility issues. In a cache-coherent NUMB system, the main memory ID is statically divided across all of the nodes. In a cache-only memory architecture, the per node memory is pooled into a large cache of the shared address space.

Disadvantages of Parallelism

It has been said that no good deed goes unpunished. Parallelism is no exception. Parallelism in a database adds architectural complexity, as the parallelism has to be maintained, and it is critical that the overall

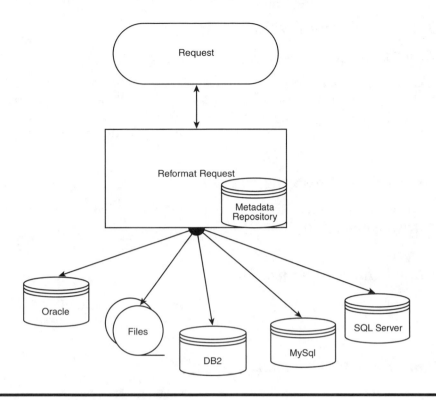

Figure 9.5   Hierarchical architecture.

administration is in place to be able to maintain all of the different pieces. This complexity leads to added cost for the maintenance and programming of applications that can take advantage of the altered paradigm.

As in much of the Grid environment, parallelism in the database and in the programming leads to altered needs for security and additional places where that security can be breached.

It is more difficult to unconditionally ensure that the integrity of the system and of the data and database is maintained.

But the biggest disadvantages are the lack of standards and the lack of applicable experience in the marketplace today. Those who have successfully implemented parallelism and made it work efficiently and effectively are few and far between and are typically ensconced in their own organizations. Because the Grid, and with it parallelism, is so new, the fully robust standards that exist in many other areas (for example, Web programming) are lacking. The standards are beginning to emerge, but they are not quite as robust yet as they could be.

Database Parallelization Techniques

Data Placement

Data placement refers to the physical placement of the database onto multiple nodes in the system. This placement can be static (prescribed and deliberate) or dynamic (as in a Grid environment, where the degree of parallelism is fluid, changing with every node added to the system).

Parallel Data Processing

Selects are easy in such a configuration, but joins and all other nonselect operations are more difficult.

Parallel Query Optimization

This option makes the choice of the best parallel execution plans, automatically parallelizing the queries and atomically load balancing.

Transaction Management

This is similar to distributed transaction management.

Parallelism Versus Fragmentation

Parallelism and fragmentation are similar, and can even be used in conjunction, with fragmentation increasing parallelism. This typically is designed to occur when the data is much larger than the programs. Programs should be, as much as is attainable, executed where the data resides. However, with parallelism, there is no need to attempt to maximize local processing, because users are not associated with any particular node and load balancing is often difficult with fragmentation when you start dealing with a large number of nodes. Maximizing response time or interquery parallelism leads logically to portioning. Maximizing the total amount of work throughput typically leads to clustering. Fully partitioning versus clustering often leads to variable partitioning.

Data partitioning of a relation involves the distribution of its tuples across several disks, regardless of architecture, and provides high I/O bandwidth access without the necessity of relying on specialized hardware. Partitioning is typically accomplished by several methods: round-robin partitioning, range partitioning, and hash partitioning. These partitioning methods are used in conjunction with any database-specific partitioning

methods that are implemented by different vendors. They are comple-
mentary, but often not the same kind of application.

Round-Robin

Round-robin partitioning maps the i-th tuple to disk I mod n. It places
the tuples equally among the disks, regardless of the given partitioning
attribute's uniformity. It is the most simple of the partitioning strategies;
however, it does not typically lend itself to support of an associated search.
This type of partitioning is excellent for sequential scans of full relations
(either for a point query, returning a single value or a single set of data,
or for a range query, returning all data fitting into a given range), but is
poor for associative access. One of the primary reasons why people adopt
this partitioning methodology is that load is fairly evenly distributed.
Round-robin is particularly good for spreading the load.

Hash Partitioning

Hash partitioning maps each tuple to a disk location based on a hash
function. Placing the tuples uniformly if the partition attribute is uniform,
hash partition's distribution may or may not be uniform if the partition
attribute is not uniform. It offers the associative access to the data tuples,
with a specific attribute value accomplished through directing the access
to a single disk. The algorithm is excellent for exact matches. However,
it does tend to randomize the data rather than cluster it for logical
accessibility.

Range Partitioning

Range partitioning maps contiguous attribute ranges of a relation to the
same sets of disks. Placing the tuples uniformly if the partition attribute
is uniform, range partition's distribution may or may not be uniform if
the partition attribute is not uniform. Range has the added feature of being
able to keep the tuples in some sorted order. It has the advantage of
being very good for an associative search and for clustering data for logical
accessibility, but it risks execution skew by directing all the execution to
a single partition. If, for example, we assume a relation that has client_ID
as a partitioning key, and all client_IDs less than 1000 are found in one
partition, all client_IDs greater than or equal to 2000 and less than 3000
are located on another partition, and all client_IDs greater than or equal
to 3000 are located on a third partition (and so forth). If a query attempts
to find client_IDs between 2100 and 2500, the query would be sent

exclusively to the third partition, leaving the others to run other queries independently. Range partitioning is particularly good for equijoins, range queries, and "group by" statements.

Horizontal Data Partitioning

As with fragmentation, you have the option of partitioning data horizontally. The rows or tuples are fragmented across devices in such a way that the tuples all stay together and are distributed by value across the devices.

Keep in mind that data allocation strategy is really simply an optimal usage strategy with respect to any given query type if the execution of those queries can always use all of the processing nodes available to the system. It is an optimal balance strategy with respect to any given query type if the execution of the queries always results in a balanced workload for all of the processing nodes involved. The strategy is optimal with respect to a query type if it is both optimally balanced and usage optimal with respect to any particular given query type.

Primarily, it remains important to not only understand storage strategies, but also understand what the data is and how the users typically access the data. An allocation scheme that is very good for row and column queries is often not optimal for all queries. Equijoins perform especially well on hash partitions.

Replicated Data Partitioning

A high availability requirement means that data replication is required. Simple hardware replication can be accomplished with RAID (redundant array of inexpensive disks) solutions that allow for mirrored disks or mirroring with parity. There are load balancing impacts on the system, however, when one node fails. More elaborate solutions can achieve load balancing. Interleaved partitioning or chained partitioning can accomplish this without having to rely on hardware replication.

Interleaved partitioning allocates a primary copy of a relation on each node. It then provides a backup copy of a part of a different relation to that same node.

For instance, if we look at Table 9.1, we can see that node 1 has a primary copy of relation 1; node 2, relation 2; and so forth. Node 1 also holds a quarter of relation 2, a quarter of relation 3, a quarter of relation 4, and a quarter of relation 5, staggered across the nodes so that the portions are allocated in a somewhat round-robin fashion. Each node has

Table 9.1 Interleaved Partitioning

Node	1	2	3	4	5
Primary copy	1	2	3	4	5
Backup copy piece		1.1	1.2	1.3	1.4
	2.1		2.2	2.3	2.4
	3.3	3.4		3.1	3.2
	4.2	4.3	4.4		4.1
	5.1	5.2	5.3	5.4	

the same number of primary copies and backup pieces, but the distribution of data access allows for accessing the data in a more distributed fashion.

Chained Partitioning

In chained partitioning, there exists a primary copy of the partition on each node, and the backup of that partition resides on the next node in the network. For instance, if we look at Table 9.2 we can see that node 1 has a primary copy of relation 1; node 2, relation 2; and so forth. Node 1 also holds a quarter of relation 2, a quarter of relation 3, a quarter of relation 4, and a quarter of relation 5, staggered across the nodes so that the portions are allocated in a somewhat round-robin fashion. Each node has the same number of primary copies and backup pieces, but the distribution of data access allows for accessing the data in a more distributed fashion.

Placement Directory

A placement directory performs two functions. It allows the relation name and the placement attribute to be associated with a logical node. It then allows the logical node to be associated with a physical node. It also requires that the data structures in either case should be available whenever they are needed at each node.

Table 9.2 Chained Partitioning

Node	1	2	3	4	5
Primary copy	1	2	3	4	5
Backup copy	5	1	2	3	4

Index Partitioning

Index partitioning uses the index as the means to determine how to partition the data. Hash indexes would be partitioned by hash, and b-tree indexes would be partitioned as a forest of tress, with one tree per range.

Partitioning Data

So, these are the different partitioning types, but how is the data distributed?

Disk Partitioning

For range partitioning, a sample of the load on the disks is taken. Hot disks are cooled by making the range smaller. For hash partitioning, you would cool hot disks by mapping some of the buckets to other disks.

River Partitioning

In river partitioning, you use hashing algorithms and assume a uniform distribution of data. If you are using range partitioning with this data distribution method, the data would be sampled and use a histogram to level the bulk.

Data-Based Parallelism

Database management systems typically hide parallelism. They automate system management via tools that assist with data placement, data organization (usually through indexing), and periodic maintenance tasks (such as data dumping, recovery, and reorganization). Database management systems also provide venues for fault tolerance, with duplex and fault failover for data and transactions. What is more is that they provide an avenue for automatic parallelism, with maintenance among transactions accomplished through locking, and within a transaction through parallel execution.

Interoperation

In interpretational parallelism, a set of P operations, all pieces of the same query run in parallel.

Intraoperation

The same operation runs in parallel on different data partitions.

There are three ways of exploiting high-performance multiprocessor systems:

- Automatically detect parallelism in sequential programs, as in Fortran.
- Augment an existing language with parallel constructs, as in Fortran90 or C.
- Offer a new language in which the parallelism can be expressed or automatically inferred.

Pipeline Parallelism

In pipeline parallelism, shown graphically in Figure 9.6, one operator sends its output to another in a pipeline fashion; the output of one operator is consumed as the input of the following operator. However, different upstream processes can run in parallel.

```
Insert into claim_history
Select * from claim, payment
Where claim.claim_number = payment.claim_number;
```

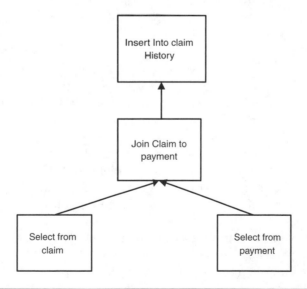

Figure 9.6   Pipeline parallelism.

Although the insert into a single table will run by itself, and the merge into a format that can be inserted will run by itself, immediately before the insert, serially as in a pipe, the selects that feed the merge can run in parallel against the two tables.

There are limited returns on attempting to run SQL queries and attempting to reap the benefits of a pipeline parallelism because (1) relational pipelines are rarely very long, with a pipe of chain length 10 being highly unusual; (2) relational operators do not always emit their outputs until they have consumed all of their inputs (aggregation and sorting are two such operators) and can therefore not be pipelined; and (3) often the execution cost of one operator is far greater than any of the others (a prime example of skew), and the speedup obtained by pipelining will be extremely limited.

Partitioned Parallelism

By taking large relational operators and partitioning their inputs and outputs, it is possible to use a divide-and-conquer approach, turning one big job into many smaller independent ones, allowing partitioned execution to offer much better speedup and scale-up. Partitioned parallelism proceeds with input data partitioned among different multiple processors and memories with operators split into many independent operators, each working on its own part of the data.

Partitioning a relation involves the distribution of its rows over several disks. At its roots, this type of distribution was originally created because files were simply too large for a single disk, or for a single file in some cases, and because file access pages could not be supported by single disks. Distributed databases use data partitioning (or fragmenting) when they place their relation fragments at different network sites. Data partitioning allows parallel database systems to exploit the I/O subsystem and bandwidth of multiple disks by reading and writing them in parallel, proving bandwidth utilization that is far superior to typical RAID systems without the need to resort to specialized hardware. Figure 9.7 shows an example of what partitioned parallelism might look like.

By taking the large relational operators and partitioning their inputs and outputs, it becomes possible to turn one big job into many independent little ones.

Most database programs today are written making use of SQL, making it possible to take standard applications written for single-processor systems and execute them in parallel on the shared-processor systems.

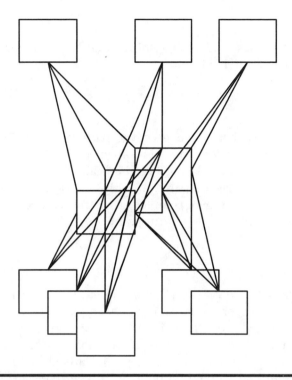

Figure 9.7   Partitioned parallelism.

Parallel Data Flow Approach

A scan's output stream can become another relational operator, be returned to the calling application, be displayed on a terminal screen, or be sent to be printed out to a report. The uniformity of the data and other operators allows them to be arbitrarily composed into data flow diagrams. If the other operators are sort operators, the tuples will be reordered in parallel based on the attribute specified in the sort criteria, either allowing for duplications or eliminating them. Because standard SQL defines several aggregate operators that are used to summarize the attributes into a single value (minimum, sum, maximum), the insert operator adds tuples from a stream into a value, and the update or delete operators alter and delete tuples in a relation matching a scan stream; the inputs to these operators can be parallelized and then the flow can take on a pipeline flow, or further operators can take this single input and parallelize further operations.

Retrieval

There are three types of dataset retrieval that are particularly optimized in a parallel database environment.

Point Query

A single point query that is issued on the partitioning attribute causes all disks to be searched under a round-robin method. Whether or not there is an index on the column being searched, all of the disks will need to be searched. Under a hashed partition, only one of the disks needs to be searched, whether or not there is an index on the searched column. Under range portioning, only one of the disks needs to be searched.

Range Query

A range query is issued on the partitioning attribute to return a range of values. Following the previous client_ID example, if you want to find all of the client_IDs that are between 2100 and 2500, you would perform a range query. If you want to find this information, a range partition would be the optimum partitioning scheme, particularly if all of the retrieved tuples are located on a single partition or disk. If they are spread across disks, all of the partitioning schemes perform roughly equally in the query return time.

The same is true for strongly correlated information. If you have the data partitioned by age, and you want to retrieve all employees who have a salary over $80,000, you are likely to find that there is a strong correlation between age and salary. Although there will be outliers in the data, where someone relatively young has a higher salary or someone who is relatively older has a salary that is lower than would be expected, the query will very likely be able to take advantage of parallelism to retrieve the sought information.

Inverse Range Query

An inverse range query is issued excluding a range partitioning attribute. The same metrics that are true of range partitioning are true of inverse range partitioning. Depending on the correlated data, and the information sought by the user, if all of the nonexcluded information is located in one or two partitions, and therefore one or two disks, this query would do well in either a range or hash partitioning scheme and would perform no worse than a round-robin partitioning scheme.

Parallelizing Relational Operators

The objective of parallelizing relational operators is to be able to use existing operator implementations without need of any further modification. Three mechanisms are needed to facilitate this parallelizing and, as a result, provide a RDBMS that is capable of both linear speedup and linear scale-up. These operators are operation replication, merge operators, and split operators.

Operator Replication

Operator replication assumes that a relation is partitioned on a partition key. If we partition by client_ID, and you are executing a query that is only as restrictive as where account_balance > $1,000,000, then the query will be executed in parallel across all partitions. If you select the client_name, client_ID, and account_balance, where client_ID = 1010 and account_balance > $100,000, the query will go directly to the required information and do a partition scan on a single partition. The operator replication mechanism scales arbitrarily, subject to the cost of starting an operator on each partitioning processor.

Merge Operators

Merge operators combine output streams from two or more producers (two or more scans) into a single-input stream for a subsequent relation. Select all client_IDs where account_balance > $500,000 and the due_date is older than 60 days, and insert that information into an overdue table. The select would be parallelized, merged into a single-input stream, and that information inserted into the specified location.

Split operators split a single-tuple stream into two or more streams by applying a function to each tuple in the stream. In this way, a pipeline stream can be parallelized and then later re-pipelined. A split operator can assist with the redistribution of a result set or with the partitioned execution of complex operators, such as joins.

Parallel Sorting

The ideal of parallel sorting is that a scan is done in parallel, range partitioning as you proceed. As the tuples arrive, the system begins to sort locally on each node. The resulting data is in sorted order, and can easily be range partitioned (although this may result in skew). To speed this up as much as possible, it would be important to sample the data before the beginning of the execution of the task to determine the beginning partition points.

Parallel Aggregation

For each aggregate function, first perform a decomposition, and for each group, subaggregate the groups so that they are closest to the source. You would then pass each of the subaggregations to its group's site, chosen via the hash function that is used to distribute the data.

Parallel Joins

A parallel join comprises three phases. First, there is decomposition of joining into a number of n tasks, with each task being a join of a subrelation of the base relations. The tasks are then assigned to a number p of processors, and finally the results are reassembled, and the ultimate join results. Consider the join of all tuples such that a.r = b.q and these tuples are distributed over potentially all disks in the system. All of the a.r information would be scavenged in p degrees of parallelism from the system and joined to create the ultimate a.r set, and the same would happen for the set of all b.q, and those two result sets could then be joined together in parallel.

For nested loop joins, each node would broadcast m its personal fragments of q to all of the processors, and each node would join its local a.r portion to the entire b.q fragment sets, all of the a.r occurring in parallel.

A sort merge join would redistribute all of the tuples with the attribute a.r to all of the nodes in the system, finding all of the p-1 values from the tuple set and distributing them to the processors p equally. The same distribution would occur with the b.q tuples, and the results would be merging joined in parallel, with each node merge joining its portion of both a.r and b.q, and those results joined back together to arrive at the ultimate result set.

A hash-based join is the most typical and has many variations. Each node would split its portion of a.r into a number m of buckets, and the buckets would then be distributed to the respective nodes. The same is repeated with the b.q tuples using the same functions, and upon receiving the records of its a.r and b.q, the node would then perform the join locally and the joined data would be joined together to acquire the ultimate result set.

Based on existing solutions, there are three logical phases to the taxonomy of join algorithms. Each task requires task generation, task allocation (or load balancing), and task execution.

Task Generation

A join is split into a set of independent tasks. With each task, another set of joins of subrelations of the base relations, and the union of these subrelations' tasks, should be identical to the original join relation if that relation were to be run without being parallelized. This task generation can be broken down into four subtasks: decomposition, task number, task formation, and statistics maintenance.

Decomposition — The basic criterion for decomposition is that the union of results of the subtasks needed to reassemble into the result of the original join. There are three methods to decomposition: full fragmentation of the original task into a number n of subtasks, fragmentation and replication into a number n of subtasks, or full replication into a number n*m of subtasks.

Task Numbers — Task generation needs to determine what the optimum number of tasks is and evaluate what the balance is between too many tasks and too few tasks. Given a number of processors p, the four methods of task number determination are:

1. Generate p tasks, one task to node.
2. Generate more than p tasks and allocate those tasks in such a way to balance the load based on a criterion.
3. Generate more than p tasks and split the larger tasks into smaller ones, and allocate those total tasks to balance the load based on some criterion.
4. Generate more than p tasks and merge the smaller ones, and then allocate those tasks and balance the load based on some criterion.

Task Formation — Task formation is done regardless of whether the tasks are physical or logical. Physical tasks exist before execution, and logical tasks are formed during the execution phase. Logical tasks are typically more useful for load balancing and are lower cost in terms of transmission and input/output.

Statistics Maintenance — What statistics do you want to maintain during task generation, and what statistics do you want to maintain over time in the Grid metadata repository to assist in the task generation going forward? These statistics are used by task allocation and the load balancing phase to determine how the tasks should be allocated. Perfect information would be in regard to relation size and result size. These statistics are used as a basis on which records are grouped into equivalence classes to maintain a given number of distinct classes — for each class, the number of distinct attributes and the number of records from the relation. The maintained statistics can be used as a basis on which to estimate the result size and expected execution time.

Task Allocation

In a Grid environment, when a job of tasks or a task comes into the system to be processed, there are two strategies on task allocation that can occur: allocation without load balancing and allocation with load balancing. Data access task allocation on the Grid is no different from other task allocation on the Grid. Allocation without load balancing occurs when tasks are generated and sent to appropriate nodes. This allocation method is bad for skewed data. Allocation with load balancing allocates tasks so that the load across all nodes is approximately the same. Tasks are sorted according to some criteria or weight on each task, allocated in descending order, and then are allocated to nodes in such a way that the next task to be allocated is sent to the node that expected to finish first.

But what is the criterion under which the allocation occurs? Typically, there are two metrics used to determine load allocation: cardinality and estimated time. Tasks are allocated either adaptively or statistically.

Adaptively — Adaptive task allocation is demand driven, with each node assigned and one task processed at a time. When the current task is completed (and only when the current task is completed), the node acquires its next task.

Statistically — In statistical task allocation, allocation is done prior to the execution of any of the tasks. Each node knows ahead of time exactly how many and which tasks it is expected to finish. This method has historically been the method used. In a Grid environment, with more nodes being added as they are needed, it would be difficult to most efficiently allocate tasks in a statistical method, as it does not allow for the flexibility that can be gained by adding or removing nodes dynamically.

Task Execution

Each node independently performs the join tasks that have been allocated to it. Based on workload and execution rules in place ahead of time, this can mean that no redistribution occurs once execution begins, or that redistribution can occur if the system becomes unbalanced. If the system allows for redistribution, there needs to be a task redistribution phase that runs to move the tasks or subtasks from an overloaded node to an underloaded one. The system must be able to figure out what server is overtaxed and which is underutilized and the optimum redistribution of the information over the nodes.

Data Skew

No only is there skew to be considered at the partitioned server level, but there is also data.

Attribute value skew suggests that there is an attribute value that appears more often than others. Tuple placement skew says that the initial distribution of records varies between partitions. Selectivity skew is the selectivity of selection predicates and varies between nodes. Redistribution skew expresses the mismatch between the distribution of join key values in a relation and the distribution that is expected to be existent based on the hash function. Finally, join product skew is the join selectivity at each node and it also differs.

Load Balancing Algorithm

Statistic load balancing balances the load of the nodes when the tasks are allocated. There is no worry about the redistribution of the load when new nodes are added to the Grid system. Once the task is initiated for execution, no migration of the tasks or subtasks from one node to another occurs. One of the requirements for optimum statistic load balancing, as in optimum execution plans for a database query, is the maintenance of adequate statistics.

During partitioning, each node collects its statistics on the size of the partitions assigned to it. A node is designated as the coordinator that is responsible for collecting all of the information. The estimation of the result size and execution time and the estimate of the average completion time are required from the coordinator server, and those estimates are broadcast to all of the participating nodes. Each node finds the smallest number of tasks such that the completion time of the tasks allocated will not exceed the average completion time. A node is considered to be overloaded if it still has tasks remaining when other nodes' tasks are completed. Each node is responsible for reporting to the coordinator the differences between its load and the average load, and its excess tasks. The coordinator is responsible for reallocation of the excess tasks to the underloaded nodes. After this redistribution, each processor then independently processes its tasks.

There are extra communication and I/O costs associated with this technique for load balancing. The granularity of the load balancing is an entire task, typically not a subtask, and this manner of load balancing is not good for highly skewed data. Solutions to these problems include forming logical tasks out of as many of the tasks as possible and the splitting of expensive tasks into smaller, less expensive subtasks. This allows for a more equitable redistribution of tasks.

Dynamic Load Balancing

Dynamic load balancing is useful when statistical estimation is wrong. The redistributed tasks may be partially executed from one node to another. Tasks are generated and allocated during their respective phases (the same as for statistic load balancing), but the task execution phase is different. In the task execution phase, each node maintains additional information about the tasks that are being processed. This information deals with the size of the data remaining and the size of the result generated so far. When a node finishes all of the tasks that have been allocated to it, it will steal tasks from other nodes in the system. This is an optimum configuration for a Grid environment. The overloaded nodes and the amount of load to be transferred are determined, and the transfer is realized by shipping the data from the donor to the idle nodes.

Idle nodes send a load request message to the coordinator to ask for more work. The coordinator, where requests are queued and processed in a first-in, first-out, or first-come, first-served, basis, broadcasts load information messages to all of the nodes, suggesting that there are remaining jobs to be completed on the system. Each node computes its current load and informs the coordinator of its status. The coordinator then determines which is the least taxed server and sends a transfer load message to the donor. After the load transfer message, processing precedes to serve the next "more work" request. A donor determines the load that it needs to transfer and sends the load to the idle node. Once a load is determined, the donor can then proceed to compute its new load for another request. The process of transferring loads between a busy and an idle node is repeated until the minimum time has been achieved or there are no more jobs to transmit.

Any busy node can be a donor; the one with the heaviest load is preferred. The load on the node is determined by using the estimated completion time of a node or the estimated time of the unprocessed task plus the estimated completion time of the current task.

Heuristics are used to determine the amount of task to transfer unprocessed. The amount of load transferred should be large enough to provide a gain in the completion time of the operation. The completion time of the donor should be larger than the estimated completion time of the idle nodes after the transfer.

Chapter 10

Distributing Databases

How would a car function if it were designed like a computer? Occasionally, executing a maneuver would cause your car to stop and fail and you would have to re-install the engine, and the airbag system would say, "Are you sure?" before going off.

—Katie Hafner

If parallelism is taken to its ultimate conclusion, it becomes a distributed database, adopting either a fragmentation schema or a fully replicated schema to implement the distribution.

Grid environments distribute processing over a flexible number of computers to take advantage of the added horsepower to meet the peak computing needs. This means that several processes are running in parallel on the different systems. Programming logic gets distributed across systems, control gets distributed across systems, and the data required for processing gets distributed across systems.

Distributed computing deals with a number of autonomous processes (heterogeneous or homogenous) that are connected to each other by a computer network and that each cooperate in the performance of their assigned tasks. Distributed computing has been known by other names as well. It is synonymous with distributed data processing, backend processing, time-shared computing systems, functionally modular systems, and many other equivalent phrases. Processing logic is distributed, as are functions, control, and (as is the primary dealing of this book) the data.

A distributed database system is a collection of logically interrelated shared databases, which are physically distributed across separate nodes in a network managed by a database management system that allows the distribution to appear transparent to the end users. They share no physical components and run on sites that are completely independent of each other. Transactions can access the data at one or more sites. This should not be confused with a database that is centrally located on a single node in a network and accessed by multiple other network machines. But you also have to take into account the placement of the applications that run against the database and the database management system software across the nodes in the network. A distributed database system is the combination of a distributed database (DDB) and the distributed database management system (the software that manages the DDB, providing an access mechanism that makes the literal distribution virtually transparent to the users). What is a distributed database system not? It is not a network database management system. It is not a time-sharing computer system. It is not a loosely coupled or a tightly coupled multiprocessor system. It is not a database system that simply resides on one of the nodes of the network of interconnected computers. It can reside on several computers; it can reside on a time-sharing computer system, and it can also reside on loosely coupled or tightly coupled clusters.

The distribution of data is difficult and interesting enough if you are dealing simply with flat files; it becomes increasingly difficult if you are dealing with databases, and the complexity is even greater when you start dynamically adding nodes to the equation, over which you may need to dynamically distribute the data and the database management system (DBMS).

In a homogeneous distributed database, all sites in the system have identical DBMS software. Each site is aware of every other site and agrees to cooperate in processing user requests, yet also agrees to give up part of its autonomy in terms of its right to change schemas within the system. Primarily, it appears to the user as a single unified system.

In a heterogeneous distributed database, different sites may use not only different software or software versions, but also different schemas. Differences in schemas cause difficulties for query processing. Differences in software and software versions can cause difficulties in transaction processing. Further, although sites may be made aware of each other, they also may not be aware of each other, and therefore may have limited facilities for cooperation in processing transactions. Different versions of the same vendor's product will provide more of a chance for the different sites to be more aware of each other, but this still does not ensure that they are aware of or will cooperate with each other.

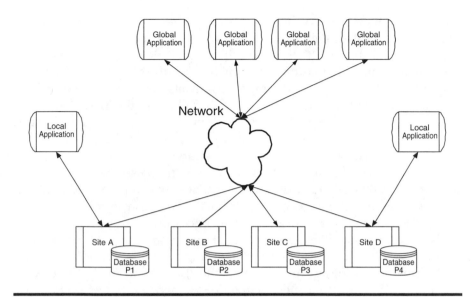

Figure 10.1   Distributed database system.

Figure 10.1 shows what a typical distributed system with a distributed database might look like. The user (human, program, or computer) would connect to the global applications, which would in turn connect across the network to the sites on which the fragments are located, process the pieces of the application applicable to those sites and their data, and return the result set to the calling application. At the same time, in a normal distributed system, local applications, local to the individual site and its data, can process on only that server or site. In a Grid, this will be more along the lines of a global application that requires information across several sites, distributing its processes across the different sites. An application that requires only a portion of the data, for example, the data located on site A, will run its processes on only that server as long as all of the data that is required for that process resides on that site.

The database management software needs to have a transaction manager, scheduler, recovery manager, and buffer manager. Additionally, it should have a facility to allow it to manage and coordinate both global and local transactions, as well as a facility through which it can perform intersite communication through a data communication interface.

One of a distributed database's major advantages is scalability. Growth in the database can be more elegantly controlled in a distributed environment than in a centralized model. It also can assist in placing data as close to where it is needed for processing as possible, while allowing for central access to all data at the same time. Not only is it more scalable, but it is also more sharable. Users at different locations, depending on the manner in which you choose to distribute, can expect far quicker access times for their data if it is stored where it is used than if it is stored in a central location with all of the other similar data, but not what those users need. There is improved reliability, again depending on how the distribution is accomplished, improved availability over a centralized design (particularly if the single point of failure is the node on which your primary database is located), and improved performance (taking advantage of parallel execution of jobs and accessing the data locally to where the primary point of processing occurs).

A Grid allows for more extensive parallel processing than could be gained in a centralized database, where parallelism can be gained at a table level, but there will always be bottlenecks. If you can distribute the data over multiple servers, and distribute the processing of the data along with it, there will be many advantages over simply distributing the processing.

Keep in mind, however, that with anything that you can find advantages for, there are also disadvantages. With the distribution of databases over a number of nodes in a network, there is more complexity than in a centralized database, where you have all components in a central location. There is added cost for the additional network resources and maintenance. Controlling the integrity of the data is more difficult, and the tendency for anomalies to occur has to be taken into account. Database design is more complex, and there is a lack of experience, tools, and crystal-clear methodologies to assist in the process. And again, one of the biggest concerns in distributed databases is one of the biggest concerns in the Grid systems in general: security. The network must be made as secure as possible to support the distributed database.

How to distribute the data, and the ramifications of the distributions, requires the designer to make careful decisions. There are two primary ways that data becomes distributed across systems. The data within the database can be distributed by fragmentation or by replication. These two concepts are different in their implementation and ramifications, and bring with them their own issues.

There are two conceptual approaches to design strategies that are employed when designing any system, and distributed databases are no different. A top-down approach to design is typically used when designing a new system, and most typically when looking at a homogeneous system from scratch. A top-down approach typically starts with the objectives, business rules, requirements gathering, and analysis. It continues down through the conceptual to the logical design of the database, and then through the distribution design and decisions, and finally ends up with a physical design of the database file layout. Naturally, because you are designing new and from scratch, this is the optimum type of design that you can do in any system.

More typically, you are dealing with a system that is already in place, a system that you have to deal with and live with during the process, and a system that very often is not only heterogeneous across operating systems and hardware platforms, but also heterogeneous in database management systems, often across heterogeneous database paradigms. In this situation, you will end up doing a bottom-up design. Bottom-up, almost opposite to top-down, starts with the underlying existing structure, the physically existing layout, and a set of user requirements (optimally there will be user requirements). You will then have to determine how best to distribute the data up through the distribution design to the conceptual to meet the user requirements.

Advantages

Advantages of a typical distributed database system include the fact that it can be constructed in such a way that it can easily reflect the organizational structure. This can be extended into a Grid system as it grows and evolves from a departmental Grid to an enterprise Grid. Because many departments have their own databases, or their own portions of databases, this could lend itself to a natural extension of what is considered to be a normal distributed database system.

Adding to the list of advantages, there is improved sharing while allowing for local autonomy, improved availability (single-site failure does not make the system entirely inoperable), economy (many small computers cost less than a single big one), and modular growth (new modules are easily added to the existing system). These are attributes that make a Grid system desirable in an organization. There are the added advantages of improved reliability and performance.

Disadvantages

There are naturally also disadvantages to distributed systems. They are complex. There are added costs of system management and a learning curve that needs to be overcome to efficiently administer such a system. Security is an added concern in a distributed system. This adds even more concern to the Grid system, in which there are increased security concerns because of its configuration and multiple points of interception.

Integrity control is more difficult in a distributed system. There is still, in a distributed database system, a considerable lack of standards and a considerable lack of experience in distributed database creation and administration.

The most difficult disadvantage to overcome is the added complexity of design. This is due, in large part, to the allocation of fragments to different specific locations. This will be an increasing concern in a Grid environment where, by virtue of its very nature, the distribution will need to become more and more fluid and nondeterministic. With the addition of each blade or each server to the configuration, the available locations for distributions also increase.

Rules for Distributed Databases

There are several general rules for distributed databases. Although they are not hard and fast things that have to be done, doing them will allow for a more elegant and consistent database, and overall system performance will benefit.

- *Local autonomy* — Local autonomy of the database means that administrators retain control over their local databases while the distributed fragments remain consistent. In this way, local users can have immediate access to the data that they need, and remote users can be assured that their data integrity is not compromised simply because of the location from which they are accessing that data.
- *No reliance on a central site* — All processing is decentralized. There is no single point of failure, no single point at which total loss of data can occur.
- *Continuous operation* — The entire system need not be shut down to perform standard maintenance or for any minor emergency that does not require the immediate declaration of disaster (and often even if there is a declaration of disaster, the system could remain available and functional).
- *Location independence* — Users can retrieve, insert, and update data regardless of the site where that data happens to be located and be assured that their information is current and accurate.
- *Fragmentation independence* — Parts of a table can be stored at different locations and there is no impact to the user or the user's queries. Fragmentation independence allows for both horizontal and vertical partitioning.
- *Replication independence* — Stored copies of data can be located at multiple sites. Read-only replicas and updatable replicas provide for full functionality on the distributed database. Multimaster replication allows for the updating of any of the replicas and for the pushing out of those updates to any and all of the others.

- *Distributed query processing* — Users can query the database regardless of what node they are connected to and regardless of where the data is residing at any given time. The query is directed to the node where the data can be located.
- *Distributed transaction management* — Transactions can update, insert, or delete any data regardless of where it is located, even if it is sourced from multiple databases. The two-phase commit mechanism in many distributed relational databases ensures the integrity of distributed transactions. Different levels of locking ensure a high level of data concurrency.
- *Hardware independence* — One distributed database can include different hardware platforms and often different database platforms.
- *Operating system* independence — One distributed database can include different operating systems; no specific operating system is required, and multiple operating systems can coexist.
- *Network independence* — One distributed database can span local area networks (LANs) and wide area networks (WANs) with different network topologies and protocols. Network independence allows communication across not only homogeneous, but also heterogeneous networks. Consider the Internet and the wide variety, from UNIX to Windows to wireless, that coexist elegantly. Network independence in distributed databases enables applications to communicate with databases across multiple network protocols.
- *DBMS independence* — One distributed database can include database management systems from different vendors. Only the interface through which interaction with the database is accomplished needs to be central and transparent.

This layout can support multiple database transparencies.

These 12 rules imply complete and nonselective distributed transparency, although many applications do not require this, and a partial solution may be enough. If it is possible to fully achieve complete distributed transparency, performance may be unacceptable, but it is unlikely to be fully achievable anyway.

There is an implicit assumption that all of the databases are relational. Although these assumptions would be unrealistic — at least 80 percent of a typical organization's data is nonrelational — there is a need to consider integration with emerging data persistence technologies in postrelational and object databases, and non-database-distributed object stores.

Database middleware typically aim at heterogeneous remote data access, gateways to mainframe databases, and database-to-database extraction, but not ordinarily at distributed systems. Products supporting query access only, but not updates, provide reasonable performance and stability.

The Open Database Connectivity (ODBC) 1.0 specification that was issued in 1991 tackles the problems of heterogeneous remote data access. It supports widespread support from nearly all database vendors and from application vendors. ODBC supports nonrelational as well as relational data.

The view of distributed database from the perspective of distributed systems is tainted with the complexity of any application partitioning. Remote procedure call (RPC) is not necessarily designed for small-scale client–server systems, and is not necessary for them either. RPC is useful across a broad range of applications and RPC/application server development products are unproven and immature. Vendors must provide evidence that their products enable rapid development of a large-scale heterogeneous client–server system.

Transactions need to have atomicity (all or nothing), consistency (transactions must be self-contained logical units of work), isolation (concurrent transactions must not affect each other), and durability (what is done must not be undone). But in a distributed system, the transactions involving multiple distributed databases are coordinated as are the transactions involving operations other than database update.

There has been a great deal of research and development effort sunk into distributed databases, but no vendor has yet delivered a fully distributed database solution. However, practical partial solutions do exist.

Fragmentation

Fragmentation is the mathematical determination of a way to separate the data into smaller chunks to take advantage of the distributions and the parallel processing. It is the division of relation (r) into subrelations (r1, r2, r3 ..., rn) that contain enough information to allow for the reconstruction of the original relation r.

- *Horizontal fragmentation* — Each tuple of r is assigned to one or more fragments.
- *Vertical fragmentation* — The schema for relation r is split into several smaller schemas. In vertical fragmentation, all schemas must contain a common candidate key (or superkey) to ensure lossless join property. Further, a special attribute, the tuple ID attribute, may also be added to each schema to serve as a candidate key.

Typically, an application does not act upon the total set of data in a database, but uses views of the data that are applicable to that application; therefore, fragmentation is often appropriate because it provides logical subsets of the information. It is often more efficient to store data with the application that is going to act upon that subset of the data.

A well-designed fragmentation scheme is said to be correct if it is complete, reconstructable, and disjointed.

Completeness

A relation is considered to be complete if, when it is decomposed into fragments, each data item in the original relation can be found in at least one fragment. When you are looking at vertical fragmentation, this means that each and every attribute that was found in the original relation can be found in at least one fragment. In horizontal fragmentation, completeness refers to being able to find each and every tuple from the original relation in exactly one fragment.

Reconstruction

It must be possible to define at least one relational operation that will reconstruct the original relation from the information in the individual fragments. Reconstruction is achieved if there is such a relation that when fragmented, it is possible to reconstruct the original relation. This has to include the ability to ensure that the constraints and dependencies that were defined on the original relation are preserved in the reconstructed version of the original.

Disjointedness

Any single data item that is *not* a part of the primary key in vertical fragmentation (covered later in the chapter) can appear in exactly one fragment. In horizontal fragmentation, this means that every tuple appears in exactly one fragment.

Transparency

Furthermore, it is important that the distributed database be transparent in several ways, and the fragmentation has to be designed in such a way that these transparencies are in place and well supported. Because the Grid is a virtualized environment where the user (regardless of what user is using the environment — human, computer, program) needs to be presented with a logical model of the entire overall system so that it appears to be one application running on one system running against a single centralized database with all files stored on a single conceptual disk, these transparencies take on even greater importance.

Distribution Transparency

Distribution transparency allows any user the see the database and the data that he is permitted to access as a single logical entity.

Fragmentation Transparency

Fragmentation transparency is the highest level of distribution transparency, and the one that should be strived for in a Grid environment, as location and fragmentation levels are likely to change within the Grid as the demand fluctuates. Database access is based on a global schema and the user (either human user directly accessing the data or computer-generated user program accessing the data in batch or other manner) does not have to be able to supply a fragment name or location to access that data. A query by a user needs to be able to access the fragments or the distribution means in the same manner that it would access a centralized database, without having to be rewritten.

Location Transparency

Location transparency is somewhat less transparent to the user (again, user can be either human or computer). Any user can know that the data is fragmented, but he does not need to know the location of any given piece of data or to worry about the means to get to the location of the data. Also, the user does not have to supply a union operation to allow the data to be reconstructed within the query. The union in any reconstruction needs to be handled without any awareness at the user level.

Replication Transparency

In replication transparency, the application does not need to know or care how many copies there are of the data or where those copies are located. The application sees only the single unified interface that it is presented with.

Local Mapping Transparency

Local mapping transparency is the lowest level of transparency, and the user (regardless of user type) needs to specify the specific fragment name and location of the data items to be accessed to access them. Metadata will be relied upon to a great extent in this scenario.

Naming Transparency

Naming transparency typically comes when you have accomplished distribution transparency. In naming transparency, each distributed database needs to have its own unique name within the given domain. This is usually true of nondistributed (centralized) databases as well. This needs to be ensured either by creation of a central names server, prefixing an attribute with site identification, or with alias use. A central names server will cause a loss of local autonomy and create site bottleneck at the central site (causing low availability and a single point of failure). Prefixing an attribute with a site identifier can cause partial or total loss of distribution transparency. The best option would be to allow the distributed database management software to perform the task of mapping by creating internal aliases (transparent to the user) for the database objects.

Transaction Transparency

The distributed database management software (DDBMS) needs to be able to ensure the atomicity of the transactions to ensure both concurrency and consistency. The transaction is subdivided into subtransactions until there is one transaction allocation for each site or node in the Grid. The DDBMS must be then able to synchronize the subtransactions, ensuring concurrency transparency and failure transparency. Concurrency transparency is accomplished when the DDBMS ensures that local as well as global transactions can coexist without interference with each other. Failure transparency means that there are in place recovery procedures that will take over and handle the loss of a message or failure of a communication channel or link or the failure of a distribution site or node. Not only does it have to be able to handle the loss of a link, but it also has to adapt to the loss by taking a synch point and redistributing itself, and picking back up at the point of failure.

Performance Transparency

Performance transparency is accomplished when the DDBMS allows the database to perform as if it were a centralized database. The query processing mechanism of the DDBMS has to map a query to the data that is being requested by it, break the query down into a series of steps that are able to be parallelized, and send those operations off to work on the distributed data. This brings with it some added complexity, as there needs to be remapping to the fragment to be accessed and the location of the fragment to complete the process. The overall performance is then not just the combination of access time and CPU processing, as is the case with a simple centralized database, but there needs to be added in the time that is required to have both the request and the resulting data transmitted across the network. In a LAN environment, the majority of the time will likely be in the access and CPU portion of the equation, as the network is not likely to be the bottleneck. In a WAN environment, input/output (I/O) access and CPU are likely to be less of an impact than in a LAN, and the network latency will play a bigger part.

Vertical Fragmentation

Vertical fragmentation splits tables vertically across the nodes in the system. It thereby allows tuples to be split so that each part of the tuple is stored in a location where it is most frequently accessed. Adding to each tuple and each tuple fragment, a tuple ID attribute will allow for the efficient rejoining of vertical fragments. There should be some decisions, based largely on historic metadata, on where and how fragmentation will occur in the Grid environment if it is to follow a vertically fragmented model. It would be highly impractical for the continuous redistribution of fragments.

Table 10.1 to Table 10.3 show a base table with several of its tuples. The original table with its tuples could be stored as is in a centralized database, but it could also be fragmented vertically into smaller relations that could be stored on different servers on the network. The fragmentation algorithm, in a Grid system, would need to update the metadata repository with information on where in the Grid each fragment could be located so that the different transparencies could allow for the seamless coexistence of the data in the distributed system. Or if it were a homogeneous conglomeration of information, the Relational Database Management System (RDBMS) could be allowed to maintain, internally, the information on where in the system the information is located.

Each of the fragments carries with it the primary key information that causes this relation to be unique. Because you have to be able to reconstruct these original tuples from the fragments to maintain the

Table 10.1 Original Table with Several Tuples

Claim Number	Claimant First Name	Claimant Last Name	Insured First Name	Insured Last Name	Claimant SSN	Insured SSN
123456	John	Smith	Mary	Smith	123456789	234567890
234567	Bill	Jones	William	Jones	098765432	304958678
890678	Mary	Johnson	John	Johnson	294384757	949494949
99900	Fred	Mcpherson	Fred	Mcpherson	102030405	102030405
454545	Winifred	Mcmasters	Alfonse	Mcmasters	888992222	999223344

Table 10.2 Vertical Fragment 1 Stored on Site A

Claim Number	Claimant First Name	Claimant Last Name	Claimant SSN
123456	John	Smith	123456789
234567	Bill	Jones	098765432
890678	Mary	Johnson	294384757
99900	Fred	Mcpherson	102030405
454545	Winifred	Mcmasters	888992222

Table 10.3 Vertical Fragment 2 Stored on Site C

Claim Number	Insured First Name	Insured Last Name	Insured SSN
123456	Mary	Smith	234567890
234567	William	Jones	304958678
890678	John	Johnson	949494949
99900	Fred	Mcpherson	102030405
454545	Alfonse	Mcmasters	999223344

consistency of the information, this added storage is necessary, although it may appear to defy normalization constraints.

Vertical fragmentation could be carried out at a higher level as well, with different schemas or different tables from a single schema being distributed onto a different node in the Grid cluster. Although this is not inherently as simple to achieve with just the RDMBS being in charge of the maintenance, it would limit internal inconsistencies in the data.

Horizontal Fragmentation

Horizontal fragmentation splits the database tables on the row boundaries across the nodes on the system. This solution will allow for the parallel processing on different fragments of a relation much more elegantly than vertically fragmenting could achieve, as well as allow the relation to be split in such a way that not only are all tuples located in a place where they are more likely to be accessed, but also the redistribution of fragments is more efficient with the addition of more and more nodes to the system. Overtaxed nodes could be permitted to offload entire tuples to new nodes entering the Grid system rather than attempting to find ways to create new vertical fragments of the underlying tables.

If we look at the same base table in Table 10.1 and determine a means by which the table could be horizontally fragmented, we can see that, as shown in Table 10.4 and Table 10.5, the table can be easily split (similar to the idea of internal partitioning in a RDBMS) into horizontal fragments and that the extension of fragmenting could be even further implemented in a much more simple fashion.

Table 10.4   Horizontal Fragment 1

Claim Number	Claimant First Name	Claimant Last Name	Insured First Name	Insured Last Name	Claimant SSN	Insured SSN
123456	John	Smith	Mary	Smith	123456789	234567890
234567	Bill	Jones	William	Jones	098765432	304958678
890678	Mary	Johnson	John	Johnson	294384757	949494949

Table 10.5   Horizontal Fragment 2

Claim Number	Claimant First Name	Claimant Last Name	Insured First Name	Insured Last Name	Claimant SSN	Insured SSN
99900	Fred	Mcpherson	Fred	Mcpherson	102030405	102030405
454545	Winifred	Mcmasters	Alfonse	Mcmasters	888992222	999223344

Hybrid

Vertical and horizontal fragmentation can be mixed together to create a more efficient vertical fragmentation plan. Each vertical fragment can be successively fragmented further and further (exceptionally effective for tables with hundreds of millions, billions, or more rows) to any arbitrary depth based simply on need and on the availability of resources to act upon those fragments.

If we look at Table 10.2, we can see the vertically fragmented table. Adding the horizontal fragmentation to this table, we can arrive at the results seen in Table 10.6 and Table 10.7 with each slice of the fragments on its own node.

Replication

Replication is the copying of all of the data from one node to another node in the system. A relation or fragment of a relation is considered to be replicated if it is stored redundantly in two or more sites. Full replication of a relation is considered to be achieved when the relation is stored at all sites. A fully replicated and redundant database is one in which every

Table 10.6   Vertically Fragmented Table with Its First Horizontal Fragment

Claim Number	Claimant First Name	Claimant Last Name	Claimant SSN
123456	John	Smith	123456789
234567	Bill	Jones	098765432

Table 10.7   Vertically Fragmented Table with Its Second Horizontal Fragment

Claim Number	Claimant First Name	Claimant Last Name	Claimant SSN
890678	Mary	Johnson	294384757
99900	Fred	Mcpherson	102030405
454545	Winifred	Mcmasters	888992222

site contains a copy of the entire database. This may have storage disadvantages and come with extra overhead, with having to maintain consistency with inserts, updates, and deletes (as each replicated copy of the relation has to update at each replicated site) and with maintenance as administration has to orchestrate based on the consistency rules that are in place for the updating of the different pieces.

Despite these drawbacks, there are some very important advantages to replicating all of the data to all applicable sites. One of the primary advantages is availability. Failure of one site in the Grid, regardless of the relation that that node contains, does not result in the unavailability of the relation because its replicas exist.

Parallelism is not only possible, but highly efficient, because each fragment of the program, running parallel, has the ability to access exactly the data that is required of it. Every node can be processed in parallel, allowing for the seamless representation of the use of the result set without the overhead of the initial run having to locate the data and the node on which that data is located.

Further, there is a reduced need for data transfer to occur. Because a relation is available locally to each site in the Grid, if it happens that a process running on any given blade in the configuration requires access to every piece of data, it has access by virtue of that relation existing on every node available. Although this would also mean that there is the added cost of re-replicating should another node be added to the Grid, the replication can be ongoing as the processing is occurring, without necessarily interrupting the process.

Metadata

Here again, metadata will prove a critical player in the process. With the distribution of the databases across nodes, and the active redistribution occurring along with the access, it will become critical to find a way to track what is where and what the ramifications would be to any redistribution. Allowing the system, either the underlying structure or the peopleware, to become a learning system, aware system, and using the history of what has worked best in the past to color the decisions that are made going forward will allow the system to become even more efficient.

If you know what data a given application acts upon, it can be predetermined how to partition the data, how to fragment the data, so that the data that the application is going to be acting upon is stored in the same location as that given piece of the processing. This will allow the application to process most efficiently as it is acting on a local copy of the data that it needs, and network traffic and lag time can be limited.

Distributed Database Failures

There are failures that are unique to distributed databases and other distributed systems. Those failures and their descriptions follow.

Failure of a Site

Depending on how the distribution is constructed, the failure of one site in a Grid would not necessarily mean that the entire fragment and its information would be unavailable for processing. This is one of the reasons that careful consideration needs to be given to the manner in which the fragmentation or replication is accomplished in the Grid environment. Care must be taken that there is no single point of failure in a system where the processing and data are distributed variably through the system.

Loss of Messages

Losses of messages are typically handled by network transmission control protocols like TCP/IP (Transmission Control Protocol/Internet Protocol). Because the ACK and NAK messages (acknowledge and not acknowledge messages) will cause a resend of the information to its ultimate destination, this is less of an issue than it appears.

Failure of a Communication Link

Failure of a communication link is also usually handled by the network protocols rerouting the messages through alternative, nonaffected links.

Network Partition

A network is considered to be partitioned when it has been split into two or more subsystems, with the subsystems lacking a physical connection between them. A subsystem does not have to consist of multiple sites or nodes, but can have a single node per subsystem. Because of the way that the networks are architected, it is often the case that network partitioning failures and site failures are indistinguishable from each other. If the coordinator and all of the participants remain in one partition, the resulting failure has no effect on the commit protocol or access to the information needed by applications. If the coordinator and its participants belong in several different partitions, sites that are not in the partition with the coordinator believe that it has failed and execute predefined protocols that deal with the failure of a coordinator. Although no real harm results from this situation, many sites would likely have to wait for decisions, or lack of decisions, from the coordinator. Those sites that are in the same partition as the coordinator believe that the sites in the other partitions have failed and follow the usual protocols. Again, no harm actually results from these beliefs, but inefficient processing can result.

Data Access

There are two predominant approaches for distributed systems. Remote data access (RDA) is typically used for databases, and remote procedure calls are used for distributed computing. Remote data access is based on Structured Query Language (SQL) and is used to access relational databases or a derivation of the relational model. Remote procedure calls are based on interface definition languages (IDLs) and access the application server. In a Grid system, where both the database and the processing are distributed, a combination of these two processes would be employed.

Historically, both have been client–server approaches to the situation, and each brings with it its own unique advantages. The question is, How can you take advantage of both?

RDA interacts with the databases using SQL statements that retrieve, insert, update, or delete records either individually, as in an online transactional processing system; in a set all at once, as in a batch update into a reporting instance; or in a set one record at a time, as you would in a data warehouse, updating a previous present record with a historic flag at the same time that the insertion of the new record is made. Statements can be grouped into transactions, and those transactions would fail or succeed as a whole rather than individually. The location of the remote database remains transparent.

One computer, acting as the client, could be made responsible for the remote calls to the individual pieces of the distributed database, to each of the fragments, with the SQL transparently accessing the data and proving the information to the user. The SQL can be either dynamic or static, and it can have the added extensions of distributed transaction processing, distributed query processing, and stored procedures that would store the static SQL within the database. RDA provides flexibility for clients, enabling them to define application-specific views of the higher-level operations. These are typically possible through a vendor-supported interface and application development tools. These tools include but are not limited to data browsers, report writers, fourth-generation languages, spreadsheets, graphing packages, and so forth.

SQL defines the logic and can be executed. There is single standard SQL syntax.

A remote procedure call (RPC) provides a means by which the application interacts with the objects in the IDL. Individual statements invoke individual operations, allowing a remote procedure call to do anything that any ordinary procedure call would do. Transaction servers can also be employed if they are available.

A transaction server can be defined as follows:

> A component-based transaction processing system for developing, deploying, and managing high performance, scalable, and robust enterprise, Internet, and intranet server applications. Transaction Server defines an application programming model for developing distributed, component-based applications. It also provides a runtime infrastructure for deploying and managing these applications. (http://www.host-web.fr/iishelp/adc/docs/adcdef01_21.htm)

RPC features transparent remote procedures and static procedures. This functionality can be extended for transactional RPC, truly distributed transaction processing, and dynamic procedure definitions.

With RPC, there is a high level of abstraction, with the application programmer being able to easily code without having to be as concerned with how the application will be distributed; there is semantic integrity protection, and a far lower amount of communications traffic. With static compilation, RPC becomes highly efficient and allows for automated type checking.

RPC is particularly applicable for non-database-dependent services, such as device control or file processing.

With RPC, and as an extension because of IDL, the IDL defines only the interface; the program logic can be created and written in the programming language. There are several different IDL syntaxes, including CORBA and DCE.

Chapter 11

Data Synchronization

1. When computing, whatever happens, behave as though you meant it to happen.
2. When you get to the point where you really understand your computer, it's probably obsolete.
3. The first place to look for information is in the section of the manual where you least expect to find it.
4. When the going gets tough, upgrade.
5. For every action, there is an equal and opposite malfunction.
6. To err is human ... to blame your computer for your mistakes is even more human, it is downright natural.
7. He who laughs last probably made a back-up.
8. If at first you do not succeed, blame your computer.
9. A complex system that does not work is invariably found to have evolved from a simpler system that worked just fine.
10. The number one cause of computer problems is computer solutions.
11. A computer program will always do what you tell it to do, but rarely what you want to do.

—Murphy's Laws of Computing

Concurrency Control

A lost update, a discrepancy, or an anomaly caused by an uncommitted dependency and inconsistent analysis problems will not only exist in a Grid database (and because of their existence, have to be handled), but their occurrence will have even farther reaching ramifications and will have even more places where these problems will potentially occur.

For this reason, data synchronization and data concurrency need to be addressed when considering how best to design and implement a database across a Grid environment.

Distributed Deadlock

In a deadlock situation, a group of processes are in a circular wait situation, with each process waiting on every other process for the release of a resource or a reply to a request that will never happen, for whatever reason. Figure 11.1 shows how a deadlock condition can occur in any system. If you follow the arrows, you can see that because every process is waiting on a resource that is in turn waiting on a resource, and something is waiting on the original process (regardless of where you start), the waiting cycle could be infinite.

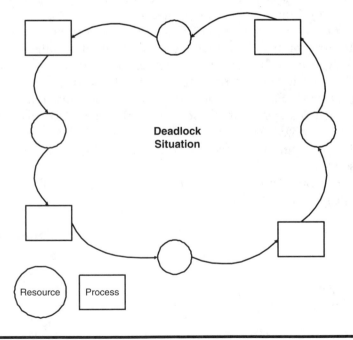

Figure 11.1   Deadlock.

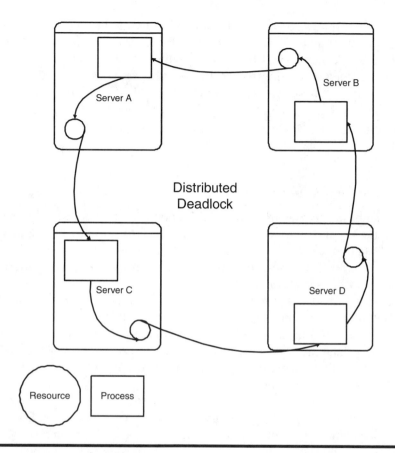

Figure 11.2   Distributed deadlock.

In distributed deadlocks, different sites (or different machines) own different resources (databases, files, instruments), and different processes (either from the same site or from a different one) request a resource, either in an acquisition of all required resources or as an incremental acquisition of each piece as it is needed. Figure 11.2 shows a distributed deadlock where processes are waiting on different processes and resources on different servers (nodes or sites). The situation of a typical deadlock is only amplified when you look at sites that are distributed over a network and relying on even more components than a regular deadlock situation.

In an acquisition of all required resources situation, one means of avoiding a distributed deadlock is to assign the requestor of the resource or set of resources a time stamp when the request is received. Any given request can be preempted by a request with an older time stamp or with a higher priority. After the work is accomplished, all of the resources are released as a set. Because any request can be preempted by a request with an older time stamp, a deadlock can be avoided because the blocking process or resource will be assigned to the process with the oldest time stamp, and the newer will have to be paged out to wait.

An even better solution would be to have requests occur as resources are needed and have processes time stamped. If your rules are set up such that an older process can never wait on a younger process to complete or compete, you will not have any circular references, and therefore deadlocks are not expected.

Database Deadlocks

In a database, particularly in a Grid database distributed over several dozen nodes and with very large databases, the volume of data raises several challenges. As the volume of data increases, the time required to run the queries increases, and as the duration of the queries increases, so do the occurrences of database deadlocks.

Database deadlocks are similar to other deadlocks (both typical and distributed ones), except they occur internal to the database. One update statement can find itself waiting on another update statement on another part of the database, and that in turn can be trying to get a lock on the table that the first has already gotten an exclusive lock on, and they can wait for each other to end.

Most databases have mechanisms that assist with deadlock detection and prevention; however, programmatic errors can cause deadlocks that the database management system (DBMS) cannot remove. To resolve these issues, you will likely need to visit those processes that are locking and blocking the others, as well as the processes that are being blocked. Once you have determined why deadlocks are occurring, you may be able to modify the processes involved and allow for more concurrent execution, or limit the degree to which the processes can acquire locks (row level locks as opposed to table level locks, where this is possible, or even shared locks as opposed to exclusive locks).

When a database deadlock happens, the Relational Database Management System (RDBMS) typically ends the deadlock situation by automatically choosing one of the processes to continue and aborting the other process. The aborted transaction is rolled back and an error message is usually sent to the user of the aborted process (be it a Structured Query Language [SQL] interface or an application program). Generally, either the transaction that requires the least amount of overhead to roll back is the transaction that is aborted, or the one that first detects the deadlock is the one rolled back. Most well-designed applications will resubmit the aborted transaction after receiving a deadlock message, and will at this time most likely complete successfully.

There are some basic tips that can be very helpful in avoiding deadlock situations.

- Ensure the database design is properly normalized.
- Have the application access server objects in the same order each time they run.
- During long-running transactions, do not allow any user input. Collect all required inputs for a transaction before the transaction begins.
- Keep transactions as short as possible.
- Reduce the number of round-trips between your application and the database server by using stored procedures or keeping transactions with a single batch.
- Do not perform the same reads over and over again. If you need to read the same data more than once, cache it.
- Reduce lock time. Develop applications so that they grab locks at the latest possible time, and release them as soon as you can.
- Reduce lock escalation, lock the lowest possible granularity, and do not lock a table when you can lock a row.

Multiple-Copy Consistency

Replicated data must be kept in a consistent state. This is one of the primary reasons to limit the number of locations replicated to or, if possible, the frequency of updates in a fully replicated environment.

However, because of the highly distributed nature of the Grid, with each distribution comes increased performance gains.

In any system, creating multiple copies of an object introduces the problem of consistency between the copies. This is particularly true in a Grid environment, because you can find that you have multiple copies being updated concurrently, and those changes need to be merged back together to form a logical and accurate whole in the end.

To complicate matters further, consistency needs can differ significantly across different applications and different data. Changes to documents may not have to be made visible to other users as soon as those changes take place; at other times, changes in the states of any shared objects have to be made available to everyone as soon as the changes are made. For this reason, it is often desirable to allow the database to allow for multiple consistency levels to coexist. This can be less difficult than it appears, particularly when changes to objects can be integrated without thought or reason going into their changes, by allowing those changes to occur automatically with the assistance of the DBMS. This can add performance benefits in that you can choose whether it is necessary to fully replicate changes back to the all of the other locations, and it can be more efficiently implemented than can stronger levels of consistency.

One of the times that strong consistency cannot be ensured is in situations where clients are temporarily disconnected, either voluntarily or involuntarily, from the central site, as in mobile communications. These nodes can still be considered members of the Grid and can be providing computations (as in SETI@home) when the computers are not physically connected. It is a matter of allowing for the adjustments in any data that may result from these disconnections to be integrated into the whole, and any adjustment to the whole to be integrated to them when the reconnection takes place.

Allowing multiple levels of consistency also helps with performance overall and provides an added level of functionality that would not be possible in a strongly consistent environment. As an informal definition, different copies of objects are mutually consistent if they can exist together in an application's view. If caching is not employed, it is possible only for mutually consistent copies of the objects to be accessed by applications.

Dr. Qin Ding, now assistant professor of computer science at the Pennsylvania State University in Harrisburg, in a presentation written while she was at North Dakota State University's Computer Science Department, compares the pessimistic concurrency control with optimistic concurrency control and poses the suggestion that there is also a third option (http://midas.cs.ndsu.nodak.edu/~ding/occ-pcc.ppt).

She explains that the primary difference between the different concurrency control algorithms is in the time that they detect the conflicts and the way that they resolve the conflicts once they are detected.

Pessimistic Concurrency Control

Dr. Ding explains that pessimistic concurrency control algorithms detect conflicts as soon as they occur and resolve them by blocking one or more. Locking mechanisms in a database can be considered to be pessimistic in orientation because database resources are locked against transactions that may cause conflict with executing transactions. For this reason, pessimistic concurrency control is often referred to as locking-oriented concurrency control.

The transactions are controlled, in a locking approach, by having them wait at certain points in their processing. The determination of which transactions to block is accomplished through ordering transactions by their first access time for each object. There is the danger, inherent with locking in databases, of deadlocks occurring in pessimistic concurrency control.

Two-Phase Commit Protocol

The Two-Phase Commit Protocol, or two-phase locking, is a pessimistic concurrency control algorithm. A Two-Phase Commit Protocol is typically used in multidatabase transactions, but is also applicable in a distributed environment like a Grid environment, depending on how the distribution is accomplished.

When all participating databases signal the global recovery manager that any part of the transaction involving each has concluded, the manager sends a prepare-for-commit signal out to the databases involved. Each participating database will then force the writing of all of the log records to disk and send a ready-to-commit message back to the manager. If the force writing fails, or if the local transactions cannot, for any reason, commit, then that participating database sends back a cannot-commit message. If the manager receives no messages, neither ready to commit or cannot commit, then a cannot commit is assumed.

If all of the participating databases reply that they are indeed ready to commit, then the manager sends a commit message to all of the participating databases and each database writes a commit entry for the transaction in the logs and updates the database structures permanently. If there is even a single cannot commit, the manager sends a rollback message to all of the participating databases and the entire transaction is rolled back.

Because all local effects of the transaction in question have been recorded in the logs of the database, recovery from such a failure is possible.

Time Stamp Ordering

Another pessimistic concurrency control device is time stamp ordering. Time stamp ordering helps to eliminate deadlocks that can be caused by other locking mechanisms by ordering transactions based on order of access, aborting those transactions that attempt to access data out of order. It increases the concurrency in a system by never allowing a read access to block a writer operation of another.

Time stamp ordering assigns time stamps to transactions whenever they are started. These time stamps are used to order the database transactions. A time-stamped version of the data is created whenever a transaction writes a new value to the data item. The data has the same time stamp as the writing transaction.

The following steps then occur whenever a transaction accesses data in the database:

■ Read operations are allowed and the version that is read is the version with the largest time stamp that is still less than the time stamp of the reading transaction. This allows the read to access the most concurrent data as of read time. The time stamp of the read transaction is added to the data items read as a read time stamp.

■ If the accessing operation is a write operation, then a new version of the data item is created, and that data time is associated with the time stamp of the writing transaction. This occurs as long as there is no transaction with a more recent time stamp that is currently reading a version of the data item that has an older time stamp than the time stamp of the writing transaction. If there is a transaction that holds a data item with a read operation, then the writing transaction is temporarily aborted and will be restarted.

Optimistic Concurrency Control

In pessimistic locking schemes, incremental synchronization checks are performed on each read or write operation, either by using explicit locks or through the use of time stamps, as seen above. These incremental checks can be expensive, particularly if they involve disk access to perform their transactions. Further, there is often unnecessary overhead associated with transactions when there are no conflicts (this is particularly true in read-only queries). They can often cause unnecessary aborts because of locks that are kept longer than necessary to accomplish the transactions.

Optimistic concurrency control divides every transaction into a read phase, a validation phase, and a write phase. Reads are performed on local buffers with no lock checking taking place. During validation, the system performs synchronization checking to ensure that writes will occur on the correct version of any data accessed. In the write phase, local writes are pushed to the distributed data, making those writes global. Each transaction is assigned a unique time stamp, which gets assigned at the end of the read phase. The transaction (T1) is validated if it completes its write phase before another transaction (T2) begins its read phase, as shown in Figure 11.3. It is validated if the T2 transaction does not read any of the data that the T1 transaction is writing, and if T1 can finish its writes before the T2 transaction begins its writes, or if the T2 transaction neither reads nor writes any items that are read or written by the T1 transaction, as seen in Figure 11.4.

Subsequent transactions (the T2 transactions) are aborted when validation cannot be accomplished. This approach is highly efficient when there are no conflicts, but wastes time when there are conflicts. Aborting transactions becomes a severe problem, particularly in a Grid environment,

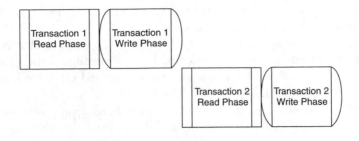

Figure 11.3   Validation of complete read after write.

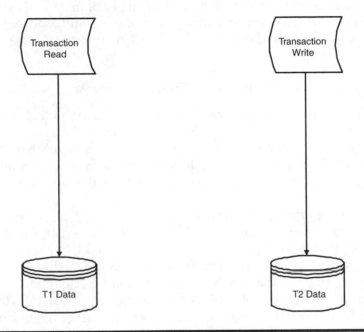

Figure 11.4   Validation of complete independent data.

when the transactions have been long and computationally intensive and the reapplication of the aborted transaction will be equally as computationally intensive.

Dr. Ding suggests that optimistic concurrency control algorithms detect the conflict at the time of transaction commit and resolve it by rolling back the transactions. In an optimistic approach, database resources would not be locked, but left available in hopes that the currently active transaction's data will not be modified by other transactions. Because optimistic concurrency control only deals with concurrency when conflicts actually occur, they are also often referred to as conflict-oriented concurrency control and are based on validation.

Optimistic control is efficient only if the amount of work that is caused by an aborted transaction is insufficient in relationship to the amount of work performed in the database, and is therefore cost effective if the level of conflict remains relatively low.

Optimistic approaches do not stop transactions from processing and nearly completing, but rather allow for the control by backing up the transactions as the process. Transactions are assigned a transaction number to assist in determining their order of access.

Most database management systems opt for the pessimistic approach because the relative cost of locking and rolling back in case of occasional deadlocks is typically less expensive than the restart-based method of conflict resolution associated with the optimistic approach.

Heterogeneous Concurrency Control

As heterogeneity seems to be the core of a Grid environment, it appears as if there is a middle ground in concurrency control as well. In a heterogeneous concurrency control environment, active database transactions are partitioned into a set of clusters, with the partitioning algorithm ensuring the lack of conflict between transactions that are distinct within a cluster.

Because optimistic concurrency control techniques perform more cheaply and efficiently than pessimistic concurrency control when there is low contention for data resources, the transactions within the newly formed clusters could be handled by an optimistic scheduler.

Dr. Ding suggests that this heterogeneity can be referred to as speculative concurrency control. Speculative concurrency control combines pessimistic and optimistic concurrency control by using redundant computations for the same set of transactions. One copy of the transaction runs under optimistic control, the other under pessimistic control. The optimistic version runs until a potential conflict threatens the consistency of the database. At that time, the pessimistic computation is started as early as possible after the potential conflict is detected, allowing for the alternative schedule to process to the point where the conflict was detected. The pessimistic alternative is adopted if the suspected inconsistency materializes; otherwise, it is abandoned, with minimal waste to processing cost. Although there will be wasted computations, redundant processes will be started for every transaction where a potential conflict is detected, helping to ensure that the processes will complete.

Distributed Serializability

The global schedule and the union of all of the local schedules are serializable provided that the local serialization order is the same as the global order. This means that all subtransactions must be in the same order or in an equivalent schedule at all times.

All actions of a transaction occur consecutively, with no interleaving of transaction operations. If each transaction is consistent (that is, it obeys the integrity rules), then the database is guaranteed to be consistent at the end of executing a serial history.

In a distributed database, serializability becomes somewhat involved. Two histories have to be considered at any given time: local histories and global history. For global transactions to be serializable, each local history has to be serializable, and any set of conflicting operations should be in the same relative (if not explicit) order in all of the local histories where they appear together (http://www.cs.ualberta.ca/~database/ddbook/ notes/Transaction/ppframe.htm).

Query Processing

Query Transformations

A query that references global relations has to be transformed into several simpler queries that refer only to fragments. Join strategies are transformations that exploit parallelism.

Transaction Processing

A transaction is a collection of actions that make transformations of system states while at the same time preserving system consistency. Transactions have to satisfy the properties of atomicity, consistency, isolation, durability, and serializabiltiy. A transaction coordinator is responsible for making the final committed or aborted decision. Distributed transactions typically make use of the Two-Phase Commit Protocol, where the transaction coordinator asks all of the participants to prepare for commitment and waits for a reply, sending the final decision to either commit or abort to all of the individual participants.

Concurrency control is accomplished in one of two ways: through a lock-based approach, by a two-phase locking protocol (issues with this approach include deadlock handling and lock management overhead), or through a time stamp-based approach.

There are two types of applications that access a distributed database. The first is the query languages.

Query languages allow manipulation and retrieval of data from a database. The relational model supports simple, powerful query languages. These languages have a strong formal foundation based on logic, while allowing for much optimization and parallelization. Keep in mind that query languages are not programming languages. They are not expected to be able to meet the Turing test for completeness, they are not intended to be used for complex calculations, and they are supposed to be easy to support and provide efficient access to large data sets.

Heterogeneity

Because of the nature of the Grid, and the nature of most companies' data being heterogeneous, accessing and manipulating data within the different databases on different platforms takes on interesting new dimensions.

In the Grid environment, with data housed in DB2, Oracle, MySQL, and SQL Server databases and in flat files, accessing data from different data sources will have to be moderated by something that will format the access request in such a way as to meet the database management software's requirements.

This intermediate layer will have to access the metadata to determine the format and location of the data to be accessed and reformat the request to allow it to access the requested information. This is one of the reasons that accurate metadata is critical to the efficient inner workings of the Grid environment and the Grid database system. Figure 11.5 shows an example of how processing would work in this scenario.

A request enters the system (a job, task, or user request for information) and then enters the translation transformation system, which checks the metadata repository to determine what transformation is necessary. The translation/transformation is done to allow those pieces that go to each type of database to be formatted so that they can be processed. Any information necessary from flat files is retrieved, and the requests are relayed to the individual systems. Once the data processing is complete, the results are sent to the translation system that combines all of the results into a cohesive response to the user and returns that information to the calling program or user process.

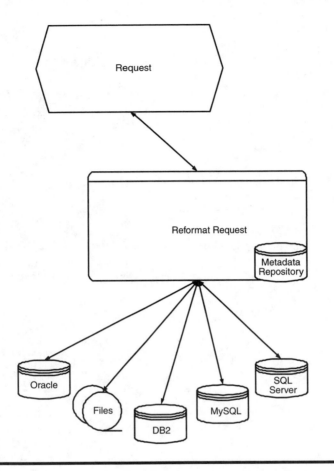

Figure 11.5   Request processing in a heterogeneous environment.

Chapter 12

Conclusion

We have reached the end of our journey. We have journeyed through the history of computing and the history of the Grid. We have defined the components, the users (including the users who are already using the Grid), and the drivers that are involved in driving the decisions that those who have implemented them have made. We have defined databases and addressed not only how data is being dealt with in the current Grids, but ways in which databases can be extended to be used in the Grids in the coming decade.

Will databases evolve as the needs that the users place on them evolve? Naturally. As the needs evolve, databases will evolve, and as the databases evolve, the needs will evolve, it is a vicious cycle.

Many Relational Database Management Systems (RDBMS) today are in a place where they can start to be adopted by and adapted to use in a Grid environment. Oracle has its Real Application Clusters, DB2 its share-nothing architecture, and MySQL its open architecture.

Are any of the databases fully ready to take advantage of, and be taken advantage of by, the Grid and its immense power and flexibility? Of course not. Although many vendors may tout that they are the database for the Grid, it needs to be true that all databases are databases that are to be used in the Grid environment. And the Grid, much like the Internet in the late 1980s, has not been fully defined enough to be able to have anything designed especially for it in the way of databases and data storage. Many existing solutions can be adapted for the Grid, but none can say that they have been designed especially for it.

What will it take for a database to be fully able to be a Grid database? True event-driven processing at the engine level of the database will have to be available before the need for human intervention at some level is eliminated. The database will have to be self-aware and aware of its surroundings before it can be taken completely out of the hands of the administrators to do the distribution and to handle the alterations needed to support the extended distribution.

In the ultimate scenario, in a given organization, there will exist a Grid that is self-aware, notices when a new component joins the Grid, and makes adjustments accordingly. The Grid will read the metadata, determine if the new component is already understood, and make determinations for security, distributability, and accessibility based on what it finds.

This Grid will determine to what extent it needs to replicate or fragment data and adjust accordingly. Whenever the database senses contention, it will make the determination as to where and how to redistribute the data and the processing to take the best advantage of the system and cause the greatest overall performance gains for the Grid and for the users.

It will fluidly make value judgment calls as to who goes where and when the best time for certain jobs to run will be.

Are we there? No. Are we making progress to get us there? Every day. The next five years will be an exciting time.

What can you do now and going forward? Find places in your organizations where the Grid will fit in with both the business drivers and the technology that is in place. Find those places where you have a need for processing power and make use of the emerging technology to ease that need.

You do not have to implement an enterprise Grid solution; you can start at a departmental level or at a project level and find ways to prove the profitability in the Grid decision on small scales. When the return on investment (ROI) is seen at the lowest levels, the push to see even more benefit from the technology will be apparent. Grid is not a total solution for every problem for every company. But it is a solution for many problems for nearly every company. Everywhere that there is a computing bottleneck, everywhere that users are waiting on each other to access resources and data, and everywhere that the window for batch processing is growing narrower and narrower, and the required data that needs to be processed within that window is growing larger and larger, are the places where Grid will benefit you and your organization.

Small organizations and multinational and global organizations alike can benefit from the Grid and its architecture. It is all a matter of finding the place where the utility can be most beneficial.

Index

A

Abacus, historical use, in mechanical computation, 4
Academia, adoption of Grid computing by, 60–62
Access control, 104–107, 159–160
Access Grid, 52–54
Accountability, 112–115
Accounting, 103
Acorn, 25
Advanced Research Projects Agency, 9, 16–19, 22–24, 28
Agramson, Norman, 23
Aiken, Howard, 12
Algebra, relational, 198–200
Allen, Paul, 24
Allow and deny access control, 106–107
ALOHAnet, 23
Altair 8800, 23–24
Alto Aloha System, 24
American Registry for Internet Numbers, 33
America Online, 32
Amplitude jitter, 117
Analog calculator in history of computer development, 10
Analytical engine in history of computer development, 8
Andressen, Marc, 31
Anomalies, 209–210
Apple II, 25
Application, 168–169

Application metadata, 156
Arabic numerals in history of computer development, 4
ARIN. *See* American Registry for Internet Numbers
ARPANet, 9, 16–19, 22–23, 28
Artificial intelligence, challenges of, 160
Attenuation, 116
Attribute data skew, parallel database, 217
Audit, 103–104
Authentication
　basis of identification, 85
　block ciphers, 89
　client, 84
　communication efficiency, 86
　computational efficiency, 85
　in cryptography, 88
　digital signature, 96
　identity confirmation, 84
　impersonation, spoofing, 93
　nature of security, 86–87
　passwords, 87–88
　private key, 88–89
　public key, 91–96
　reciprocity of identification, 85
　secret storage, 87
　server, 84
　stream ciphers, 89–91
　third-party real-time involvement, 86
Authorization, 101–102
Automatic Jacquard loom, 6–8

N

O

P